MURDER AND MAYHEM IN LATE MEDIEVAL ENGLAND

MURDER AND MAYHEM IN LATE MEDIEVAL ENGLAND

Violence in the Thirteenth and Fourteenth Centuries

KATHRYN WARNER

PEN & SWORD
HISTORY

AN IMPRINT OF PEN & SWORD BOOKS LTD
YORKSHIRE – PHILADELPHIA

First published in Great Britain in 2026 by
PEN AND SWORD HISTORY
An imprint of
Pen & Sword Books Ltd
Yorkshire – Philadelphia

Print ISBN 978 1 03610 497 9
ePUB ISBN 978 1 03610 499 3
ePDF ISBN 978 1 03610 501 3

A CIP catalogue record for this book is available from the British Library.

Typeset in Times New Roman 11.5/14 by
SJmagic DESIGN SERVICES, India.
Printed and bound in the UK by CPI Group (UK) Ltd.

The Publisher's authorised representative in the EU for product safety is Authorised Rep Compliance Ltd., Ground Floor, 71 Lower Baggot Street, Dublin D02 P593, Ireland.
www.arccompliance.com

For a complete list of Pen & Sword titles please contact
PEN & SWORD BOOKS LIMITED
George House, Units 12 & 13, Beevor Street, Off Pontefract Road,
Barnsley, South Yorkshire, S71 1HN, England
E-mail: enquiries@pen-and-sword.co.uk
Website: www.pen-and-sword.co.uk

or

PEN AND SWORD BOOKS
1950 Lawrence Rd, Havertown, PA 19083, USA
E-mail: uspen-and-sword@casematepublishers.com
Website: www.penandswordbooks.com

FSC www.fsc.org
MIX
Paper | Supporting responsible forestry
FSC® C013604

Contents

Introduction

It was Monday, 7 December 1321, the day after the feast of St Nicholas and five months into the fifteenth year of the reign of Edward II, one of medieval England's most unsuccessful kings. Edward's chamberlain, favourite, and probably lover, Hugh Despenser the Younger, lord of Glamorgan, had been exiled from England by his and the king's baronial enemies in August that year, and was currently engaged in piracy in the English Channel. Edward was in the middle of preparing for a military campaign in the west of England against the rebel barons who had exiled Hugh, which would end in success for the king and Hugh and in the executions of twenty or so English noblemen and knights in March and April 1322. The Great Famine, which affected most of Northern Europe after years of endless rain and catastrophic harvest failures, was four years past, and the availability of food had hugely improved. The first great pandemic of the Black Death, meanwhile, lay a little over a quarter of a century in the future, while the Hundred Years' War, begun by Edward II's son Edward III when he laid claim to the French throne, would start in 1337. On the Continent in early December 1321, Edward II's brother-in-law Philip V 'the Tall', king of France, was four weeks away from dying at the age of just 30, Jacques Duèse had served as Pope John XXII since August 1316 and was based in Avignon rather than Rome, and the king of Germany, Ludwig von Wittelsbach of Bavaria, was a few months away both from losing his first wife Beatrice of Silesia and from defeating his cousin and enemy Friedrich von Habsburg at the battle of Mühldorf. In Scandinavia, Magnus Eriksson was two years and five months into his forty-four-year reign as king of both Sweden and Norway, and Christoffer II was just under two years into his short and disastrous reign as king of Denmark, which ended in his overthrow by some of the Danish magnates in 1326. The year 1321 also saw the death of King Stefan Milutin of Serbia, the outbreak of a civil war in the Byzantine Empire between Emperor Andronikos II Palaeologus and his grandson, and the death of the great Italian writer Dante Alighieri.

In London, by far England's largest city with about 80,000 to 100,000 residents, the fishmonger Hamo or Hamond Chigwell was serving the second of his eight terms as mayor. Originally called Dene, Hamo took the name of the master fishmonger, Richard Chigwell, to whom he had been apprenticed in the early 1300s. The two city sheriffs were Richard Hakeneye, who worked as a *wollemongere* (wool-seller) and was the father of three sons and five daughters, and Richard Costantyn or Constantyn, who was a draper and married to a woman with the unusual name of Sabyne. London was encircled by walls, as were most English towns in the late Middle Ages; they reached 35 feet high and had seven great gates built into them, which were locked and closely guarded at night. Only one bridge spanned the Thames in the fourteenth-century city, London Bridge, built in the early 1200s, and the river was guarded at night with four boats full of armed men, two on each side of the bridge. At least 200 more men patrolled the city streets during the night, and anyone found wandering around was temporarily imprisoned as a 'nightwalker', as it was forbidden to go outside after curfew.[1] The walls that surrounded London had ditches next to them, which were cleaned by order of Mayor Hamo Chigwell and the city aldermen in early October 1321. This must have been a deeply disagreeable job for the unfortunates who had to do it, as all manner of unpleasant things including dead animals were thrown into the ditches.[2] In the early evening of 19 October 1321, Thomas atte Chirche, who worked for the earl of Arundel, Edmund Fitzalan, was riding too fast along Thames Street and almost knocked down a woman and her baby. Local resident John Harwe shouted to Thomas that he should ride more carefully, whereupon Thomas leapt from his horse in a rage and attacked John with his sword. John staggered back into his house and died of his wounds the following morning. Isabel Pampsworth hanged herself from a beam on an upper floor of her son John's house on 30 November, and on one of the last days of 1321, Elena Scot slipped and fell down the stairs of the house where she lived and worked as a servant to Margaret of Sandwich. She died soon afterwards from a broken neck. The will of Sir Nicholas Wokyndon was proved on 20 July 1321, and in it he left a hundred shillings to maintain 'the new work of *Seint Pool*', i.e. an extension to the east side of Old St Paul's Cathedral which was begun in 1255 and finally completed in 1314.[3]

Near St Paul's and just off Cheapside, the busiest street in medieval London, stood Vedastlane, now called Foster Lane and in the EC2 postal district. In the fourteenth century it was inhabited by goldsmiths and silversmiths, and some of the city's public latrines were located there. One of the goldsmiths of Vedastlane, Henry atte Rowe, had a son, William, who in 1321 was in his teens or at the start of his 20s. In the late afternoon of Monday, 7 December 1321, William atte Rowe availed himself of one of the urinals on Vedastlane that were for public use. He deliberately, perhaps from malicious amusement, directed some of the urine onto the shoe of another young man, unnamed, standing nearby. The man remonstrated with William, who, evidently quick to anger, punched him with his fist. A bystander, Philip Asshendone, then remonstrated with William in turn. The unnamed man punched by William atte Rowe was carrying a *pollax* or poleaxe, presumably because it was a tool of his profession, which fell to the ground when William hit him, and William picked it up and hit Philip Asshendone with it hard across the forehead. He thus inflicted 'a mortal wound an inch long and penetrating to the brain' on Philip, who fell to the ground unconscious. Two onlookers, a saddler named John Waledene and Thomas Welde, who worked for the sheriff Richard Hakeneye, seized hold of William atte Rowe and marched him off to Newgate prison. Philip was 'carried by men unknown, for charity's sake' outside the city walls to the Augustinian priory and hospital of St Mary without Bishopsgate, also known as St Mary Spital. He died there a few weeks later, on 2 January 1322.[4]

England in the late Middle Ages, far from the image it sometimes has as Merrie Olde England, was often a startlingly violent place, with a homicide rate rarely seen in the modern world except in war zones. Many factors made it relatively prone to violence, such as the fact that it was a much more youthful society than the modern UK is, with a large percentage of its population under 20; it suffered from the ever-present fear that harvests would fail, and therefore had huge anxieties around the availability of food and potential hunger, malnutrition and even starvation; it was a profoundly hierarchical society with massive economic and social inequality, the country's wealth and political power were held in the hands of a tiny elite, and social mobility was close to non-existent; life was frequently precarious, with no social welfare other than the charity of strangers or religious houses for those who were too ill or disabled to work, and with numerous diseases that centuries later are curable but then killed many; it was prey to natural disasters such as the Great Famine of the 1310s and the terrifying pandemics of the Black Death beginning in the late 1340s, making life even more precarious and frightening than it had been already; and many of its young men, always the group in any society who are most prone to violence, were trained in warfare from early childhood onwards and had easy access to weapons.

Medieval English people tended to be volatile and easily provoked to violent aggression, as William atte Rowe was in December 1321, unlike their descendants centuries later, who had and have a reputation for being much more phlegmatic. They also tended to be much more openly emotional in public than has generally been the case in the twentieth and twenty-first centuries. To take one example of many, when Peter Grapere of Buckland in Gloucestershire realised in May 1249 that an arrow he had shot in a local wood, with which he intended to kill a wood-pigeon, had in fact struck his friend Ughtred the blacksmith in the head, he 'fell on his face to the ground groaning and crying'.[5] As well as the many people who were violent and belligerent, there were, however, many other medieval English people who did whatever they could to help those in need, such as the unnamed strangers in London who volunteered to carry the unconscious Philip Asshendone over a mile to a place of safety where he would be looked after. Though medieval England was often terrifyingly brutal and full of people with an unnerving tendency to snap, it was in many ways also a kinder place than is sometimes thought.

Justice was often harsh in the Middle Ages, often corrupt, and often unevenly applied. The death penalty was frequently used, as were other punishments which no longer exist, such as cutting off a hand or an ear, locking felons into the pillory or the stocks, and dragging them on the hurdle. This harshness was a function of the kind of society that medieval England was. In a world where newspapers and television did not exist, and where the vast majority were illiterate so had no means of reading about prison sentences or other punishments, to act as a deterrent, justice had to be highly visible and present. The only ways that most people came to know anything at all was either to see it in person, or to hear about it from others. And in a world where most people were desperately poor and owned very little, stealing from them or cheating them or deceiving them into losing or wasting their hard-earned money were, apart from physically harming them, considered the worst things you could do to them. Late medieval England was a place with many laws, rules and regulations, and owing to the frequent scarcity of basic foodstuffs, these were applied with a particular strictness to those who sold food to the public. Dragging bakers who sold bread of insufficient weight to their customers on the hurdle, or locking butchers who sold bad meat into the pillory for an hour or two, was not cruelty for the sake of cruelty; it was intended to protect poor people by warning others that if they did the same thing, they would be punished and subjected to public humiliation and loss of reputation. In the face of the relentless tidal wave of violence and criminality, the justice system, however imperfect it may have been in practice, was at least envisioned as a means of protecting the vulnerable, and victims did at least have recourse to the law. Throughout the Middle Ages, important steps were taken to codify and improve the law, such as the first and second Statutes of Westminster in 1275 and 1285, in Edward I's reign.

Murder and Mayhem will use coroners' rolls, plea rolls, chancery rolls, records of King's Bench and other sources to examine the violence of late medieval England, and to investigate how the authorities dealt with it and how criminals were punished.

Chapter 1

Sheriffs, Keepers of the Peace, and the Posse

Sheriffs

The office of sheriff in England dates from Anglo-Saxon times, and the original Old English word was *scirgerefa*, 'shire reeve'. In the late Middle Ages, sheriffs were responsible for maintaining law and order and for collecting all fines and debts that were due to the king. They were always men in the Middle Ages, excepting only Nicola de la Haye (d. 1230), appointed joint sheriff of Lincolnshire with Philip Mark on 18 October 1216. A landowner in Lincolnshire, Nicola was a staunch supporter and ally of King John, who appointed her as co-sheriff mere hours before his death during the night of 18/19 October 1216.

Medieval London had two sheriffs, who were elected every year on or around 21 September, the feast of St Matthew the Evangelist. Unlike the mayors of London, who were elected every year on or around 28 October (the feast of St Simon and St Jude) and could serve multiple terms of office – Hamo Chigwell was elected nine times and served eight times between the late 1310s and the late 1320s – the city sheriffs only ever served for one year from around 1270 onwards. The importance of London, and its relatively large population, is apparent in the fact that the city always had two sheriffs; the English counties had only one, and in many cases, a sheriff held responsibility for two counties. Shropshire and Staffordshire were usually, albeit not always, doubled up, as were Cambridgeshire and Huntingdonshire, Somerset and Dorset, Nottinghamshire and Derbyshire, Warwickshire and Leicestershire, Buckinghamshire and Bedfordshire, Oxfordshire and Berkshire, Essex and Hertfordshire, Surrey and Sussex, and Norfolk and Suffolk (despite the huge land area covered by the latter two counties). Other counties, e.g. Cornwall, Devon, Kent, Yorkshire, Lincolnshire, Gloucestershire, Herefordshire, Wiltshire and Northamptonshire, almost always formed a single shrievalty. The county of Cumberland in the far northwest of England usually had its own sheriff, but it was sometimes combined with Westmorland and Lancashire. Richard Denton, for example, was appointed sheriff of Cumberland alone in April 1350 and sheriff of Cumberland, Westmorland and Lancashire six months later. In 1354/55, the sheriff of Lancashire was John Cokayn, the sheriff of Westmorland was Hugh Louther, and the sheriff of Cumberland was William Legh.[1]

County sheriffs were chosen by the king, and from Edward III's reign (1327–77) onwards, the appointments were usually made in October or November every year, whereas in earlier reigns, the appointments tended to be made more irregularly. John Seymour, for example, served as sheriff of Northamptonshire from July 1322 until May 1324.[2] In London, it worked very differently: one of the two sheriffs was selected by the mayor and the other by the commonalty, i.e. the two dozen aldermen of the city plus twelve 'good and true' men from each of the two dozen wards. After their annual elections, the mayor and the two sheriffs of London all had to be officially presented to the king in person or to a deputy appointed by him. This ceremony would take place more or less immediately if the king happened to be in London or Westminster at the time, or if not, the next time he visited. On some occasions, the constable of the Tower of London stood in for the king during the ceremonial presentation of the sheriffs. Simon Fraunceys, elected as sheriff by Mayor Hamo Chigwell, and Henry Combemartin, elected as the other sheriff by the commonalty, both on 21 September 1328, were presented to Sir William Zouche, constable of the Tower, on 30 September.[3] A very rare example of a man who served as both sheriff of London and a county sheriff is Richer Refham (*c.* 1260–1328). He was sheriff of London from September 1298 to September 1299, mayor of London from October 1310 to October 1311, and sheriff of Norfolk and Suffolk from October 1314 to May 1316. Richer came originally from Norfolk, probably from Reepham, and was also known as Richer Botoner or 'buttoner', as he worked in the cloth trade.[4]

Edward III spent much of the period from 1338 to 1340 outside England, seeking allies on the Continent against Philip VI of France, whose throne he had recently claimed, thus beginning what we know as the Hundred Years' War. During the king's long absence from England, several new government systems were temporarily put in place, and in September 1338 and again in September 1339, Edward ordered the coroners and knights of each English county to elect their sheriff when they next met at the county court. This experiment did not, however, prove successful. The coroners and knights of just four shrievalties (the joint counties of Somerset and Dorset, Sussex and Surrey, Cambridgeshire and Huntingdonshire, and Essex and Hertfordshire) were the only people who fulfilled the king's orders correctly, and as of 1340 the experiment was not repeated.[5]

Unlike the sheriffs of London, county sheriffs very often served more than one term, and Saer (or Sayer or Saier) Rocheford is a prime example. He was appointed sheriff of Lincolnshire seven times: in November 1343, November 1344, October 1348, October 1349, October 1350, October 1351, and November 1352. His term of office ended in February 1355 when he was finally replaced by Thomas Fulnetby after acting as sheriff continuously for almost six and a half years. The gap between November 1345, when Saer was replaced by John Trehampton, and his reappointment three years later in October 1348 is explained by his joining the retinue of Laurence Hastings, earl of Pembroke (1320–48), and fighting overseas with him. Huge numbers of English noblemen and knights took part in Edward III's wars in France at that time, and the battle of Crécy was fought, and won by the English forces, in August 1346.[6]

Sheriffs were usually knights and important landowners in the county where they held office, and served in their own part of the country, though there were exceptions: in the 1270s and early 1280s, Walter Stirchesley or Strichele was appointed at various times as sheriff of Wiltshire, Nottinghamshire and Derbyshire jointly, Gloucestershire, and Lincolnshire. The village of Stirchley, from where Walter and his family presumably originated, is in Shropshire; he and his wife Alice Hauteyn held the manor of North Leverton in Nottinghamshire; and the couple were given lands in Bourne, Lincolnshire, by Alice's father Hamo Hauteyn. A few years after Walter's death, Alice had her second marriage to William Chaddeworth annulled because he had 'carnally known' her daughter – who was presumably also Walter Stirchesley's daughter – before they wed.[7]

Sir John Coggeshale or Coggeshall (1301–61) and his family provide more typical examples of the career of a medieval sheriff.

John held lands in Essex, including the manors of Duddenhoe End and Codham, and was appointed sheriff of both Essex and Hertfordshire four times between 1334 and 1354.[8] His grandsons Sir William Coggeshale (1358–1426) and William's younger brother Thomas (d. 1422) also served as sheriffs of Essex and Hertfordshire in the 1390s and early 1400s.[9] Sheriffs could be surprisingly youthful, given how much influence they wielded. John Coggeshale was born in or not long before July 1301 and was 33 years old when first selected as sheriff of Essex and Hertfordshire in November 1334. His grandson and ultimate heir William Coggeshale was the same age when he was first appointed to the same position in October 1391; he was born on 20 July 1358 as the eldest son of John's eldest son Henry Coggeshale (1331–75). William's younger brother Thomas (who was only a squire, not a knight like his brother and grandfather) was also appointed sheriff of Essex and Hertfordshire in December 1393, and although Thomas Coggeshale's date of birth was not recorded, he was perhaps about two to five years younger than William and therefore also in his early 30s or so when he served.[10] William Coggeshale married the unusually named Antiocha or Antiochia, daughter of Sir John Hawkwood (d. 1394), a well-known English mercenary in Italy whose second wife Donnina Visconti, Antiocha's stepmother, was an illegitimate daughter of the lord of Milan.

Saer Rocheford's replacement as sheriff of Lincolnshire in February 1355, Sir Thomas Fulnetby, came from West Rasen in the county and was the third husband of Elizabeth Paynell, who was born in March 1317. With her younger sister Margery, born in Yorkshire in September 1319, Elizabeth was the co-heir of the Paynell family, who came originally from the Dorset/Wiltshire area – their father John was born in Dorset in 1296 – but moved to the Yorkshire/Lincolnshire area. Elizabeth Paynell lost her first husband Richard Gascrik on 18 September 1347, married her second husband John Barton very soon afterwards, before 4 November 1347, and married Thomas Fulnetby before 28 August 1349 when she was 32 years old. Whether Thomas was married before Elizabeth is uncertain, and if not, he was perhaps some years her junior, and in his early or mid-30s when he was appointed sheriff. Thomas Fulnetby served as sheriff of Lincolnshire from February 1355 until October 1358, and again from November 1368 until his death on 11 August 1372.[11] As well as acting as sheriffs of Lincolnshire, Saer Rocheford and Thomas Fulnetby were both escheators in the county. Escheators were royal officials who upheld the king's rights as a feudal landlord in their locality, and held inquisitions post mortem when tenants in chief, i.e. the people who held land directly from the king, died. In the thirteenth and early fourteenth centuries, there were only two escheators in England, 'beyond Trent' and 'this side Trent', i.e. north and south of the River Trent. Later, escheators were appointed in every county, and were chosen by the king while he selected the county sheriffs.

Thomas Barentyn was elected as sheriff of Oxfordshire and Berkshire in November 1378, November 1386, January 1392, and November 1394 during Richard II's reign, and was the older brother of Drew (or Drogo) Barentyn, a goldsmith who was mayor of London in 1398/99 and 1408/9. Thomas also served as escheator in the two counties, and inherited the Oxfordshire manor of Chalgrove, 10 miles from Oxford, from his and Drew's father.[12] Their father, Thomas Barentyn the elder, had been appointed sheriff of Oxfordshire and Berkshire in November 1358, and an older Drew Barentyn, the brothers' grandfather or great-grandfather, also held the position for several years beginning in 1322.[13]

Thomas Barentyn the younger first appears on record in July 1378 when he was one of eight men sent to the priory of St Frideswide in Oxford to resolve a dispute between the prior, John Dodeford, and some of his canons, while his younger brother Drew was appointed as one of the two sheriffs of London on 21 September 1393. The brothers' dates of birth were not recorded, but Drew became an apprentice goldsmith in or just before 1364, and would have been about 12 or 13 at the time.[14] This suggests he was born in the early 1350s, and that Thomas was perhaps born in the mid- to late 1340s and would have been 30 or rather more when first elected sheriff in November 1378. Thomas's son and heir Reynold, who was also heir to his childless uncle Drew, was born in February or March 1382. Thomas Barentyn died on 22 June 1400 and Drew on 14 December 1415.[15] One of their grandfather or great-grandfather Drew Barentyn's recent predecessors as sheriff of Oxfordshire and Berkshire was the unusually named Otewel, Otewell or Othelin Purcel, lord of Shareshill in Staffordshire, who also owned land in Tingewick, Buckinghamshire. He served in 1317/18. As was so often the case with men tasked with upholding the law, Otewel had previously broken it: on 1 January 1316, the year before his appointment as sheriff, Otewel and his son Thomas were accused of attacking a property in Tingewick that belonged to the abbot of St Katherine's in Rouen, and abducting two young sisters and heiresses named Cassandra and Juliana who were in the abbot's custody.[16]

Sheriffs were authorised to raise a force of men known as the *posse comitatus* ('county force' or 'power of the county') whenever they needed a large group of armed men to quell a riot or uprising, to find an outlaw or a fugitive, and so on. Like the office of sheriff itself, the concept of the *posse comitatus* dates to Anglo-Saxon times, and in the late Middle Ages all men over the age of 15 had to join it if called upon to do so. When Edward II besieged Leeds Castle in Kent in October 1321, he told the sheriff of Kent to take the *posse*, plus all the knights and footmen of the county, to the castle to aid in the siege, and six years later, the people ruling England during Edward III's minority sent the *posse* of Norfolk and Suffolk to Bury St Edmunds. There was a serious ongoing dispute between the town and its abbey, and some of the townspeople were besieging the abbey and threatening to burn it.[17]

Keepers of the Peace

The parts of England considered to be the most potentially lawless and unruly areas – which was, admittedly, most of them – had several 'keepers of the peace' who were appointed by the king. It was a role established in 1195 during the reign of Richard Lionheart, at almost the same time as the office of coroner (see Chapter 2). The men, and they were always and only men, who served as keepers of the peace were, as was the case with the county sheriffs, some of the important and well-connected landowners of the locality and were usually knights. Their role evolved over time and was fluid, though the sheriff remained the pre-eminent and the highest-ranking law enforcement official in the county, and the keepers of the peace were meant to work with him and ensure that the king's peace was maintained, in an era many centuries before the invention of police forces.

To take just a couple of examples of many, in August 1327 four men were appointed as keepers of the peace in Norfolk and Suffolk.[18] They were Sir Thomas Bardolf (1282–1328), lord of Wormegay in Norfolk; Sir Constantine Mortimer (*c.* 1281–1358/59), lord of Attleborough in Norfolk; Sir Robert Walkfare (d. 1333), lord of Ryburgh in Norfolk; and John Claver, whose identity is not entirely clear but whose appearances in contemporary sources always relate to events in East Anglia. Robert Walkfare had been imprisoned in 1322 for taking part in a baronial rebellion against Edward II, who had appointed him sheriff of Norfolk and Suffolk in 1318, though escaped from captivity in or before 1326.[19] One of the three men appointed as keepers of the peace in Oxfordshire in May 1329 was Sir Richard Damory (*c.* mid-1270s–1330). He was a former guardian of Edward III when the future king was a child, a former sheriff of Oxfordshire and Berkshire, and owned the manors of Headington, Bletchingdon, Bucknell and Woodperry in Oxfordshire.[20]

The three men appointed as keepers of the peace in Dorset in May 1329 were Sir John Maltravers (*c.* 1266–1341), who held eight manors in Dorset including Lytchett Matravers; Sir Robert FitzPayn (*c.* 1285–1354), who held five manors in the county; and Sir John Peverel, who married his wife Isabel in or near Moreton a few miles from Dorchester in June 1305, and had already been appointed as a keeper of the peace in Dorset in July 1315. He was at the start of his 50s in 1329. The appointment of John Maltravers as a keeper of the peace is yet another of the many examples of a man appointed to uphold the law who had broken it; he and a group of his followers attacked an annual fair in the Dorset village of Bere Regis in 1325 and assaulted three of the men holding it.[21]

Another example is Sir Lionel or Leo Bradenham, lord of Langenhoe, 5 miles from Colchester in Essex. He was one of the keepers of the peace in his native Essex in the early 1360s, though Edward III removed him from his position in July 1362. A few years earlier, on Sunday, 8 August 1350, Lionel had taken what was recorded in the chancery rolls as 200 armed men (though this is surely an exaggeration) to Colchester, and 'laid siege on the east side to burn the town and kill the men thereof'. Having entered a suburb of the town, Lionel and the men who formed his private army broke down the doors and smashed the windows of numerous houses, stole food, ale and other items, then broke into a barn belonging to St John's Abbey in Colchester and carried away hay and oats. The assault lasted for much of the day, and the townspeople claimed that Lionel and other knights who were friends of his, John Braham, William Tendryng, and John Gernoun, repeatedly attacked the town and ambushed some of its residents for about three months. Lionel was also charged with removing two 'common thieves' from prison in Colchester Castle while he was its constable: John Bylath and John of Kent. John Bylath promptly committed burglary again, and John of Kent killed his own pregnant wife. Captured by the sheriff of Essex, John of Kent was imprisoned again, but soon escaped.[22]

Chapter 2

Coroners, Deodand, and the Verge

The office of coroner, originally 'crowner', was established in 1194 during Richard Lionheart's reign, the year before the office of keeper of the peace was created. As the website of the Coroners' Society of England and Wales states, originally the office was conceived as 'a form of medieval tax gatherer' and in the Middle Ages, a coroner's duty encompassed 'investigation of almost any aspect of medieval life that had the potential benefit of revenue for the Crown'.[1]

One of a coroner's roles in the Middle Ages was – as it still is many hundreds of years later – to investigate sudden and unexpected deaths. Cases of murder and death by misadventure were reserved to the king and had to be tried before his court. When a human body was found, in cases where it was not obvious whether the death was natural or when it was obvious that the death was not natural, the local coroner was called upon, and his first task was to examine the body. He then summoned a large group of jurors to help him investigate the death. The person who found the dead body, meanwhile, the 'first finder', was obligated to raise the hue and cry immediately, and if he or she did not do so, would come under suspicion by the coroner and his deputies. Any eyewitnesses present plus the four (or occasionally two) neighbours who lived nearest to the incident were almost always attached to appear at the trial.[2]

This being medieval England, coroners and the jurors who aided them were, of course, always men. Each of the English counties had several coroners, usually three to six depending on the size of the population, and larger towns such as Oxford, Northampton, and Lincoln had their own coroners, with anywhere between one and four serving at any time. In the late twelfth and thirteenth centuries, coroners were usually knights – two of the coroners of Berkshire in the early 1240s were Sir Robert Avering and Sir Hugh Pisie, for example – though by the fourteenth, this was no longer the case. Coroners did, however, need to own lands in the county where they were appointed, and county and town coroners were elected to the position in the county court. In London, where things usually worked differently to everywhere else in England, coroners were chosen by the mayor, the two sheriffs, and the two dozen aldermen.

Unlike sheriffs, coroners (whether in counties, in towns, or in London) mostly served until they died, or until illness, physical frailty or another form of incapacity prevented them from properly exercising their office. Occasionally, the king ordered a coroner to be replaced by another man because he deemed him insufficiently qualified. In 1313, Edward II removed John Flory and Ralph Barun, coroners in Somerset and Gloucestershire respectively, from their positions and ordered the sheriffs of the two counties to ensure that other men were elected instead.[3] After the deposition of Richard II in September 1399, Richard's cousin, enemy, and successor, Henry IV (r. 1399–1413), ordered all the English sheriffs to replace the coroners in their counties, 'as by the cession of the late king the power of coroners made in his time is at an end'.[4]

All the coroners of a particular county kept records of the others' cases. A fire in the tiny Kent hamlet of Shyngledewelle or Singlewell south of Gravesend in August 1344 badly damaged the house which belonged to the local coroner, Michael Ifield, and a chest where Michael kept his documents, rolls and memoranda was destroyed. Michael, deeply worried that all his documents had been 'consumed by fire' and that he would not be able to produce them to the royal justices when necessary, petitioned Edward III on the matter. The king assured him that he knew the fire was not Michael's fault – it was started by servants of a knight named Sir Thomas Ovedale while he was staying with a friend in Singlewell – and that the copies of Michael's documents kept by the other coroners of Kent would suffice.[5]

When a coroner proved a death to be natural, nothing was owed to the king, but in cases of misadventure or murder, a fine had to be paid to him, and it was the coroner's job to collect the payment. *Deodand* or 'gift to God' was the name of this fine and was payable when an animate or inanimate object brought about someone's death. Either the object itself was forfeit, or a fine to the value of the object had to be paid.

It was, however, only payable when the object was, or at least could be, in motion or could cause a person to be in motion, such as a flight of steps, a ladder, or a horse. *Deodand* was not payable when a person died in bed. When John atte Wode from Suffolk was killed around Vespers on 11 November 1300 outside Adam Drayton's house on Cheapside in London by a piece of falling timber, the jurors investigating the death asked locals whether anyone had moved or touched the beam. They discovered that although William Branthingge had been inside Adam Drayton's house, shearing cloths, he 'did not move his hand', i.e. did not touch the timber. The jurors decided, however, that as the beam had killed John by falling, and therefore by moving, *deodand* of a penny was payable.[6]

When Henry Curteis died in his friend Luke Havering's home when he fell down some steps two weeks earlier on 28 October 1300, the jurors solemnly noted that 'the right side of the head appeared broken' and stated that Luke's steps were worth 12d as *deodand*. The jurors who investigated the death of Richard Brewere in December 1300 valued the steps of William Cross's house, where Richard fell while drunk, at 2s to be paid as *deodand*, and when 80-year-old Alice Pursere fell down the stairs and died in her home on the last day of 1325, the stairs were valued at 4d. After Isabel Pampesworth hanged herself in her son's home in November 1321, the cord and beam were worth a farthing (¼d) as *deodand*. A carpenter named Hugh St Albans fell from a ladder and 'fatally broke his head' in April 1324, while working on the gate of a house that belonged to Sir Roger Waltham. His colleague Richard Rothyng carried Hugh almost a mile to his (Richard's) house, but Hugh died five days later, and his ladder was valued at 4d. Henry Callere was walking upstairs in his own home in 1340 when he passed away, and his stairs were valued at 18d, a surprisingly large sum.[7] A few decades earlier in 1259, a group of workmen were building a house in London when one of them, Adam Hert, was crushed to death by a falling beam. The *deodand* payable, i.e. the assessed value of the beam, was 18d. The following year, another building accident happened while Peter Gardiner was repairing the roof of his house and fell from the ladder. The ladder was valued at 6d and the board with which he was carrying out repairs also at 6d.[8]

Richard Stoke, a collier (maker of charcoal) who lived in Heighley in Staffordshire, was cutting down a tree early one morning in June

1387. A branch fell on his head and killed him, and he was found a little later by his wife Alice. The local coroner, James Bogay, remarked that 'the branch was of no value' and therefore no *deodand* was due. On the other hand, when Robert Welles was felling trees in the royal park of Brigstock not far from Corby in the early 1320s, the oak branch that fell on him and lethally broke his neck was valued at half a penny. In November 1386, Roger Lillings was crossing a bridge over the River Foss near York on horseback, and the horse stumbled and lost its footing. Roger drowned in the river, and his horse was subsequently valued at 40d (the record does not state whether the horse also drowned).[9]

Both in London and in the English counties, on top of the fine of *deodand*, all the goods of convicted felons were forfeited. They were handed over to the county sheriff or to one of the two city sheriffs, who had to account for their value at the next Assize.[10] The inventories of forfeited goods provide a useful insight into the belongings of medieval people and how very little they – or at least, the criminal class of medieval people – usually owned. John Skut, who stabbed Walter Taillour of Faversham in Kent to death with an *anelaz* (dagger) in January 1325, owned the following: four geese worth 12d, a cock and a hen worth 4d, a 'little pig' worth 12d, timber worth 12d, and a box worth 6d. As he worked in a brewery, 100 flasks of ale and some brewing barley were also found in his possession. Roger Modyngham, a London fishmonger, and Reynold Laurenz, who probably came from Hainault in what is now Belgium, killed Gilbert Getyngtone in September 1323. Roger owned nothing; Reynold had a blanket, a long cloak, and two worn sheets.[11] It is rather startling to see that, like Roger Modyngham, numerous medieval felons were declared to have no possessions at all other than the clothes on their back.

Given the lack of medical knowledge in the Middle Ages, sometimes a coroner and his jurors, or other officials investigating a death, had no way of determining the cause of that death. There are extant cases where they declared that the person 'was suddenly struck by death' or 'fell down and died suddenly' without further explanation. Henry Callere, who 'fell down and died' while walking upstairs in his home in 1340, is a prime example; this was the entire description of his sudden decease. In London in the early 1250s, Alice Lichefeld 'was suffering from some infirmity' when she fell in the street and died, and in 1254 also in London, William of Suffolk was 'suddenly found dead in bed'. A few years earlier in July 1227, Elias Pourtour was 'carrying a load of cheese' when he 'fell dead' in the street, though how exactly the cheese was relevant to his death, and why exactly he fell dead, was not explained.[12] In February 1341 in Sheen west of London, a man named William Byngate was found dead in the River Thames. The local coroner, John atte Crouch, and his jurors admitted that they were 'completely ignorant' as to what could possibly have caused William's death.[13]

Hoggemon Carter of Ramsbury, Wiltshire, found Richard Adynton dead in Oxford in April 1382. Richard was walking in a field on the outskirts of Oxford when 'suddenly he fell, and a tumour burst in his belly, whereof he died at once', according to the local coroner, Thomas Haukyn. Almost a century earlier in 1297, John Attehalle was found with stab wounds in his heart 'even to the belly'.[14] In 1228, Dionise Burford was found 'alive and groaning' in her home in London by her neighbours, and shortly afterwards, she died in their presence. The baffled sheriffs of the city, Stephen Bukerel and Henry Cotham or Cochin, declared that 'nothing was found on her body which could have caused death, save only misadventure'.[15] There was perhaps sometimes a little squeamishness about male investigators examining a female body, though other evidence suggests that late medieval England was not a society where women's bodies had to be hidden away from strange men; it was not the Victorian era. A male surgeon or physician, for example, would examine a woman's *pappes* or breasts if she had pain there.[16] In February 1316, the dowager countess of Gloucester claimed to be pregnant by her late husband – twenty months after the earl of Gloucester's death at the battle of Bannockburn in June 1314. Lawyers told two of the late earl's heirs that they should 'have the belly of the aforesaid countess inspected by knights and discreet matrons (*ad inspiciendum ventrem predicte comitisse per milites et matronas discretas*) to see whether the said countess were pregnant or not; and if so, then when she was expected to give birth'.[17]

A similar case occurred almost exactly a century later, when Drew Barentyn, formerly mayor of London, died in December 1415. His heir was his late brother Thomas's son Reynold, then aged 33, but Drew's widow Christina claimed to be pregnant. The then mayor of

London, two other men and four women were appointed to examine Christina's 'breasts and belly' (*ubera et ventrem*) to ascertain if she was truly pregnant, and if so, when the infant was expected. The seven – Nicholas Wotton the mayor, Robert Chichele, William Crowmere, Elizabeth Curyell, Elizabeth Frauncеys, Rose Louth, and Katherine Frenssh – established that she was not carrying Drew's posthumous child.[18] In both 1316 and 1415, men were permitted to see and touch the bodies and private parts of the dowager countess of Gloucester and the mayor of London's widow. In 1296, a male jury and 'certain women' examined John Wodeureton's widow Margaret to see if she was pregnant, and in July 1304 six women examined another Margaret, widow of 21-year-old Richard Rokele of Norfolk (d. January 1304), in the presence of twelve knights; they 'say positively that she is not pregnant'.[19]

In the late 1290s, one of the coroners of the town of Oxford was Adam Spalding, and his successors were Thomas Lisewys and John Wyth. A case Adam dealt with near the start of his career in 1296 was the murder of a clerk called David Trempedhwy, an odd-looking spelling which probably represents an English scribe's attempt at writing a Welsh name. David was stabbed in the heart just before Christmas 1296 while attempting to enjoy intimate relations with 'a harlot named Christiana of Worcester' in a building on Scolestrete or School Street. Someone was lying in wait for David, though Adam Spalding was unable to determine the identity of the killer or the motive for the attack. He had better luck with the unfortunate death of Maud Crickelade five months later: she made the mistake of trying to intervene between two men having a fight around midnight one Friday in May 1297 and received a lethal blow to the head with an 'ashen staff' that Robert of Acton Burnell (in Shropshire) was aiming at his adversary, William Burnell. Spalding viewed her body on Saturday morning and saw a wound 'two inches long, one inch wide and one inch deep' on the left side of her head, which had killed her almost immediately.[20]

One of the coroners of Northamptonshire in the 1320s was Simon Keylemersche, and one of the cases he dealt with was a woman described as a 'poor beggar' who was found with her throat cut in Long Buckby in May 1321. Despite questioning Alice Derling, who found the woman's body in her and her husband's barn, Simon was unable to discover either her identity or her killer's, except only that the killer was also a beggar who had arrived at the Derlings' property with his victim.[21] Seventy years later at the start of the 1390s, William Percy was the coroner of Scarborough on the Yorkshire coast, and dealt with two cases of death by drowning. One was a sailor, John Lokwode of Hartlepool, who fell from a ship anchored in Scarborough harbour, and the other was Thomas Hall, a member of the garrison of Scarborough Castle, who fell into a fishpond in the castle grounds.[22]

When Henry Curteis died in October 1300 by falling down some steps, the London coroner who noted that 'the right side of the head appeared broken' was using typical medieval language. In March 1305, Philip Port was found dead one Monday afternoon by the city wall in the north of Oxford, and Richard Cantebrigg, who found him, raised the hue and cry. Philip had been badly wounded in the head by a *sparth* (an axe or hatchet) wielded by one John Berdon. The coroners of Oxford had gone to the parliament that was being held by Edward I (r. 1272–1307) at Westminster, and Ralph Hampton and John Fraunceys had been chosen by the mayor and bailiffs of Oxford to act in their absence. They stated that Philip was 'wounded in the front of his head from one ear to another, so that all his brain was scattered outside'. A few months later in June 1306, Richard Lindraper, a cook, was imprisoned on an upper floor of the town gaol of Oxford with other prisoners, and one night rose from his bed to relieve himself. Unfortunately, the floorboards turned out to be unsafe, and Richard fell through them and died instantly. The coroner recorded that 'his skull was utterly broken behind even to the brain'.[23]

In London in February 1324, Gerard Andrew was hit hard on the head with a *balstaf* (cudgel) during a street quarrel, 'so that the skull was broken into the brain'. In October that same year, also in London, William Cok (a cook) was another man hit hard on the head with a *balstaf* wielded by Simon Walssh. William managed to stagger a few yards to a shop 'with his head broken' and died there. Adam Hikesman of Northumberland, aged about 24, was standing outside a stable in March 1368 when a sudden gust of wind loosened a beam and it fell on him, and 'broke his head almost to the brain' (remarkably, Adam survived and was still alive in the 1380s). In and around Bedford in October 1271, two men were attacked, one with an axe wound to the top of the head that 'extended through the skull to the brain, so that the blood and brains flowed forth'.[24]

Within the Verge

In the late Middle Ages, the kings of England were itinerant, and spent the entire year travelling in an endless circuit around the south and midlands of the kingdom (only relatively rarely did they go to the north). The area within a 12-mile radius of where the king happened to be at any given time was known as 'the verge', and the royal household held legal jurisdiction within that area.[25] All local courts ceased until the king left the locality and any court cases were tried before royal officials, while murders or other suspicious or sudden deaths were investigated by the coroner of the king's household rather than by the man who usually acted as coroner in that area. Whenever the king was away from England, he appointed a *custos regni* or 'keeper of the realm', i.e. a regent, and the same rule of the verge applied to the regent and his household.[26] Just before Easter 1347, a serious incident occurred within the verge of Lionel of Antwerp, the second son of Edward III. Although merely a child at the time, born in November 1338, Lionel was the official *custos regni* of England and Wales while his father was in France; the king besieged the port of Calais from early September 1346, shortly after his victory at the battle of Crécy, until it fell to him in early August 1347. The wealthy noblewoman Margery Poynings was abducted from her own home while Lionel and several of his siblings were staying there (see Chapter 12).

Agnes Scardeburgh from Scarborough stole a surcoat (a type of outer garment) and 3 shillings in money in York 'within the verge' of the royal household and was sentenced to be hanged. The execution was postponed because she was pregnant, however, and in April 1333 Edward III pardoned her at the request of his queen, Philippa of Hainault. Sir Roger Syfrewast (or Cifrewast or Syverwast) was killed in Quidhampton, Wiltshire, not long before November 1354, also within Edward III's verge, and the king's household coroners indicted Roger's wife Maud and five men for the murder. In July

1351, Edward III had ordered the sheriff of Berkshire to replace Roger Syfrewast as one of the county coroners, as he was 'insufficiently qualified'.[27] Edward's grandson Richard II (r. 1377–99) pardoned John Yoxhale in April 1388 for stealing a silver dish in Westminster on Sunday, 28 November 1378, within the verge. The dish was worth 26s and 9d, and John had been condemned to death by officials of the royal household.[28]

Chapter 3

The Hue and Cry, and Curfew

Anyone who saw that a crime had been committed or was in the process of being committed had to make a noise to alert anyone in the vicinity, so that the criminal could be pursued, captured, and handed over to local law enforcement officials. The hue and cry was 'raised by horn and voice' or 'by mouth and horn', suggesting that those who discovered a crime had to make a certain kind of noise, either by shouting a particular sequence of words or sounds, or by playing a particular melody on a horn. There were fines both for failing to raise the hue and cry and for failing to respond to it; in other words, anyone who heard a person shouting in the established manner had to down tools immediately and come to his or her aid.[1] In Oxford in *c.* May 1324, a group of men led by Adam Osegodesby and William Topclyve, armed with swords and other weapons, stormed through the streets of the town one night, and killed Henry Bost, a constable who was one of men appointed to 'keep the king's peace by night' in Oxford. Richard Overse, another constable and one of Henry's colleagues, was among those who raised the hue and cry 'throughout the town by mouth and horn'. Numerous residents came out of their houses on hearing the hue and cry, and in the end, two tailors named John Morice and John Senglaunt attacked, wounded, and killed Adam Osegodesby.[2]

In November 1261, Henry III (r. 1216–72) ordered an investigation into the aftermath of a theft at the Abbey of St Mary in Eastry, Kent. A number of locals were suspected of failing to respond to the canons' raising of the hue and cry, and when their identities were discovered, they were ordered to be arrested and 'kept securely' by the sheriff of Kent.[3] Cecily, wife of Henry Sekersteyn, was imprisoned in London in December 1277 for failing to raise the hue and cry when her husband was stabbed to death by their servant Nicholas Wrotham. She was therefore assumed to have 'consented to his death' and to have been an accessory to murder. Sybil de Kerdif ('of Cardiff') was imprisoned in Salisbury in 1279 for failing to raise the hue and cry when one Walter Bray killed Richard de Exonia ('of Exeter') in her presence, and it was therefore assumed that she consented to the murder. Edward I ordered an inquiry on 16 July 1279, and it was found that Sybil 'did not raise hue and cry upon the said felon by reason of her terror and her ignorance of the law'. She was cleared of complicity.[4] The hue also had to be raised when someone found a body. John Fimme of Wolvercote outside Oxford found the body of a man who had been stabbed in the left eye 'in the pasture called *Portmaneyte*' (i.e. Port Meadow near Wolvercote) on 10 April 1307. He raised the hue, and ultimately the dead man was identified as John Herleseye and his killer as Richard Hedlem.[5]

In Stowmarket, Suffolk on 26 December 1355, Thomas Scoulton killed Maud Amundeville. The reason was not given, but they encountered each other in the street and were perhaps old acquaintances or former lovers who began quarrelling or resumed an old quarrel, or perhaps they were merely strangers and one of them picked a fight with the other. Thomas seized a wooden staff (*baculum* in the Latin original) that Maud was carrying and began beating her with it. Maud fell to the ground but managed to raise the hue and cry, and the neighbours who responded to her shouts for aid were Joan Mellere, Richard Prat, William Estone, Roger Badele, and Ralph Wode. Thomas Scoulton took out a knife called a *broche* and stabbed Maud in the head with it before anyone could stop him. She died shortly afterwards in Joan Mellere's arms, and Thomas was arrested by two local 'constables' (*constabularios*), John Neve, and Robert Bextere, and taken to the castle at Eye 13 miles away to be imprisoned.[6]

Sometime between July 1323 and July 1324, a murder took place in Leicester. Robert Kytewild lived just outside Leicester's north gate and allowed a stranger to spend a night in his house. As Robert's house lay just outside one of the gates into Leicester, the stranger had probably missed the curfew at sunset and the gates into the town had been locked, trapping him outside Leicester until they reopened the following morning. Inviting a stranger to stay in your house in these or in similar circumstances was common in medieval England, especially in London, and enabled people to earn a little money by doing so. For an unstated reason, probably because he intended to rob him, Robert Kytewild killed his houseguest while the man was asleep. Rather disturbingly, he then hid the body under his own bed. It was somehow – perhaps because of the smell – discovered by neighbours, who raised the hue and cry, whereupon Robert fled. The murdered stranger's identity remained a mystery.[7] Much later in the fourteenth century, in Wiltshire, John Taillour killed a houseguest with an axe, robbed his body, and buried him in his courtyard, while Stephen Dieghere did much the same thing and tried to hide his victim's body in a pile of straw. Both bodies were eventually found, though in the case of John Taillour's victim, not until a good two months later.[8]

As well as alerting neighbours to a crime, the hue and cry was also used to summon help for a person in trouble. After Isabel Pampesworth hanged herself on an upper floor of her son John's home in London in November 1321, John's servant Christine Iseldone found her and raised the hue and cry. Neighbour William Scot rushed in with a knife and cut Isabel down still alive, but she died shortly afterwards. Just a few weeks later, also in London, Margaret Sandwich found her servant Elena Scot at the bottom of a flight of steps. Margaret and her friend Christine Lovel raised the hue and cry, though to no avail, as Elena had broken her neck in the fall and was already dead. Four of the neighbours who responded were Henry St Osith, Robert Ware, Henry Somersete, and Gilbert Istilworth. Also in London, early one Tuesday morning in July 1322, John Irlaunde (i.e. he came from Ireland, or at least his ancestors did) hanged himself in an upper room of the gateway into a religious house near Aldersgate. He used his own shirt to fashion a noose. Sometime later, he was discovered by a chaplain named Walter Michel and another man, Nicholas Swynbourne. They cut him down and tried to revive him and raised the hue and cry so that other people nearby came too, but it was too late, and John was dead.[9]

On the other hand, intervening to help a person could be risky. Also in July 1322, John Pentyn, a *neylere* (maker of nails), decided to hang himself in the home he rented from Mabel Gisors, sister of a former mayor of London, John Gisors. His wife Clemence raised the hue and cry, and John Chiggewell, a *copresmyth* (coppersmith), was one of the neighbours who rushed into their home to help. He paid for this diligence with his life: John Pentyn hit him over the head with an iron staff, and he died a few days later. Pentyn was forcibly prevented both from killing himself and from escaping, and was imprisoned in Newgate but bailed in April 1323.[10]

Two men, Elias Beverle and John Costard, drowned in 'a certain waste place within the second gate of the Tower' of London in separate incidents on 1 and 15 October 1321. The coroner's report stated that the drawbridge was raised as the king, Edward II, was then staying in the Tower, and that both Elias and John 'accidentally fell into the water', meaning the ditch, while attempting to gain entry to the fortress. Both bodies were discovered by a labourer named Robert Brybour shortly after sunrise on Saturday, 17 October, and after Robert raised the hue and cry, the bodies were taken out of the water and examined by the local coroner.[11] Someone who responded to the hue and cry or someone who dealt with the aftermath of the two drowning incidents must have been able to recognise and identify Elias Beverle and John Costard, even though Elias's body had been in the water for sixteen days. After his identity was clarified, his family, friends and neighbours must have been questioned as to when they had last seen him, to determine the date on which he fell into the water and drowned.

Unfortunately for the stranger murdered by Robert Kytewild in his home near the north gate of Leicester a couple of years later, his body was never identified, unlike Elias's and John's. In a world long before the invention of driving licences, passports, and other forms of written ID with a photo, someone laying eyes on the dead person and recognising him or her was the only way a body could be named. It was highly likely, therefore, that a person who died in a part of England where s/he did not live would never be identified. The stranger killed by Robert Kytewild might have travelled to Leicester from almost anywhere in the country. Without a clue as to which part of England he might have come from, there was not even the possibility to send someone to his native town or village to inquire about a man from there who was missing. The stranger's family and friends would most probably never have found out what happened to him, and they were not alone in this.

At the end of the 1250s in London, a man was 'found dead on the bank of the Thames with his throat cut'. He was never identified, and an 'unknown poor man' who was found dead in East Farndon, a village in Northamptonshire near the Leicestershire border, in the early 1320s was never identified either. He had no wounds on his body and was assumed to have died of the cold.[12] A man whose name was never discovered was found dead in Tiffield, Northamptonshire in 1333. He had been stabbed in the heart with a knife and hit about the head with a *pollax* (poleaxe), and his killer or killers had moved his body from another location, further complicating the matter. In July 1289, Henry Morel left his home in Conington, Cambridgeshire, to travel to Rome on pilgrimage, and never returned. Many years later in 1312, his father William still had no idea what had become of him; whether he had ever left England at all, whether he made it as far as Rome and died in Italy, or died in France or England on his way back to Cambridgeshire.[13] For the families of those who died away from home, the usual fate was years and even decades of silence and uncertainty.

In other cases, the identity of a victim was known, but the identities of his or her attackers were not. In the early 1260s in London, William Berkyngg was badly assaulted in the street, and his neighbours rushed out to help him; they carried him into the home of William Quilter, but he died shortly afterwards. The attackers were never identified.[14] John Lyncoln, son of a London cordwainer (a maker of fine leather shoes) also named John Lyncoln, travelled towards Rochester in Kent early one Friday morning in May 1322, and started talking to an unnamed man journeying in the same direction. As the two men were crossing Blackheath, the traveller pulled John's own *thwitel* (a large knife) from its sheath, stabbed him in the stomach, tied him up, and made off with all John's goods. The unfortunate John lay there for the best part of twenty-four hours until a passing carter found him, untied him and 'for charity's sake' took him on his cart to Greenwich. Here a group of boatmen, also unnamed, 'for the love of God' took John up the river to St Botolph's wharf, where more people carried him into the home of one Agnes St Neot, a friend or relative of John's or perhaps his lover, on Cornhill in the middle of the city. Unhappily, John died of his injury on Monday evening a few days after the incident, and his attacker was never identified or caught.[15] This case reveals that although some people were willing to commit murder for the sake of stealing a few possessions and a few coins, many others – the carter, the boatmen, and the people who carried John a few hundred yards to a place of safety – gladly helped a stranger in dire need. It is a sad irony that John Lyncoln had probably considered it safer to find a travelling companion than to journey alone on the dangerous roads and paths of fourteenth-century England.

Other medieval people proved themselves willing to help those in need, such as the strangers in December 1321 who carried the stricken Philip Asshendone, hit over the head by William atte Rowe, to a religious house where he would be looked after (see Introduction above). In Desborough a few miles from Kettering, Northamptonshire, in the early 1310s, Robert Paylington went out one evening to visit his friend John Hauberge. He slipped on a stone in the street, perhaps because it was dark and wet, and hit his head badly. The people who found him carried into the nearby home of Maud Melchebourne, where Robert lingered for three weeks with his head injury before dying.[16] On 30 December 1325, Ralph of Nottingham, a clerk, was badly wounded in the head after being attacked with a shovel by a fishmonger named Walter Turk near the north end of London Bridge. Ralph was carried into the home of the vintner James Beauflour and his wife Emma, because it was nearby. James and Emma did not summon a physician; they summoned a priest, who gave Ralph the last rites. Ralph died in the Beauflours' home on 7 January 1326. Their house stood close to a popular tavern run by James Beauflour which was called *Drinkewaterestaverne*, as it belonged to Thomas Drinkewatere and was leased by James from 1319 onwards.[17]

Curfew and Disobeying Civic Authority

Medieval English towns enforced a curfew during the hours of darkness. In walled towns, the gates were closed and locked at sunset and opened again at sunrise, in compliance with the Statute of Winchester passed in 1285.[18] During the hours of darkness, the gates and walls were guarded, and watchmen patrolled the streets. Anyone the watchmen found outside in the streets, especially if they were not carrying a light, was deemed a 'nightwalker' and up to no good and was held in custody for the rest of the night, while gatekeepers had the right to keep people out of their town after curfew. In 1300, the nightwatchmen appointed to guard part of the wall and a tower of Newcastle-upon-Tyne, near the convent of the Austin Friars, were Roger Monketon, John Prodow, William Couper, and Robert Carpenter. A few years later in 1311, the two men given the keys to Aldgate in London were Edmund Taylor and Philip May, and at Bishopsgate, the men responsible were Robert Cook and John Little. Even tiny places had men guarding the streets at night: in 1288, Ralph

Forester was one of the watchmen in the small village of Gateforth a few miles from Selby in Yorkshire.[19]

During the night of 27 December 1236, a man called Roger, last name unknown, was found lying in a street in Candlewick Street ward in London, badly beaten and injured so that he could not speak (though apparently was able to gasp out his given name, Roger). Five watchmen found him – they perhaps stumbled over him lying on the ground, given the total darkness of a world without electric light – and carried him into a nearby house, which belonged to one Thomas Pipere. Roger died a few hours later. The watchmen found a group of men armed with swords and other weapons whom they believed to be the perpetrators and tried to arrest them. One of the men, William Large, fled and was therefore suspected of being the murderer, though was not caught.[20] In July 1340, Gerard Armourer, John Lincoln, and John Keu threatened the *bedel* (beadle) of Aldgate ward because he refused to open the gate and let them into London at midnight. Four decades later in April 1382, also in London, William Swalewe, Henry Clemme, and John Medelond were arrested for 'wandering by night … in a suspicious manner', and mainprised (i.e. bailed) under penalty of a massive £20 each. Richard Colman, a weaver, was accused of being a nightwalker in Nottingham in 1467.[21]

In the late Middle Ages, anyone who disobeyed or disrespected authority was dealt with harshly, especially in London, and was likely to find themselves in serious trouble and hauled up in court if they were caught being less than entirely respectful to public officials, even jokingly. Thomas Flete appeared before the mayor of London's court in August 1307 after mocking the mayor, John Blount, and the two dozen city aldermen by neighing like a horse whenever they rode past him.[22] Beatrice Langbourne was caught throwing rubbish into the street by her local alderman, Simon Worstede, in London in 1364. Beatrice reacted to Simon's reprimand by calling him 'a false thief and an old, crooked yokel', and was arrested and placed in the custody of the two city sheriffs. Ralph Atteswych also appeared in court in London in 1376 when he was accused of using 'insulting and opprobrious words' and 'unseemly words' to William Neuport, one of the two sheriffs, though John of Croydon was luckier in December 1370 after using 'opprobrious words' to the mayor, John Bernes, when he encountered him face to face. John Bernes pardoned John of Croydon and ordered him to be released from prison the next day.[23] Physically assaulting a public official was likely to result in execution. In 1340, Thomas Haunsard grabbed Andrew Aubrey, mayor of London, by the throat while the mayor was attempting to placate a group of people involved in an altercation. Haunsard and John Brewere, an associate of his who hit the mayor's sergeant on the head with a stick during the same altercation, were publicly beheaded in the middle of Cheapside four weeks later by the two city sheriffs, William Thorney and Roger Forsham.[24]

Medieval England was a strictly hierarchical society, and those deemed to be on a lower rung of the ladder were bound to obey and show respect to those higher up. Women were of lower rank than their husbands and had to show them obedience, servants were of lower rank than their employers and had to show them obedience, and apprentices likewise to the master craftsmen or tradesmen instructing them. Interestingly, though medieval England was certainly not a place of sexual equality, this held true even when the apprentices were male and their master was female. Roger Gosse of Thame in Oxfordshire moved into London to become an apprentice to William Hatfeld or Hathefeld, a chandler (candle-maker). After William died in or not long before July 1368, his widow Emma began instructing Roger instead, but he became 'rebellious, refused to serve her and was unwilling to be punished by her, as was fitting and proper that he should be'. Roger was therefore imprisoned in Newgate gaol in August 1371.[25] The 1349 Ordinance of Labourers prescribed imprisonment for apprentices or labourers who left their service without an excellent reason. In 1376, the apprentice pie-baker John Boys was imprisoned after running away from and refusing to serve his master, John Pygeon, and every effort was made to locate apprentices who ran away and to make them return to their service. In early 1377, Robert Kendal was fined 'as an example to others' because he had 'grossly abused and slandered' the two masters of the guild of cordwainers in London.[26]

Chapter 4

Misadventure and Accidents

On 8 September 1276, William Hare climbed up the side of a newly built wall in Kenilworth Priory (later St Mary's Abbey) in Warwickshire to dislodge some baby pigeons that had settled in the eaves. He was alone and no one else knew he was there, and disaster struck when he put his foot on a piece of wood that broke. William fell many feet to the ground and was killed instantly. His 'broken' body was discovered the next day by two other men working at the priory, Robert Tene and John Corbyn. Panicking, uncertain what to do for the best and evidently worried that they might somehow be blamed and punished for William's accident, the two carried William's body into a nearby wood and left it there, hoping that it would look as though William had been attacked and killed by robbers. Ralph Melleborn, a local resident passing through the wood afterwards, found the body and raised the hue and cry. The local coroner, William Herdewik, came to examine the body and soon discovered that William Hare had not in fact been killed by robbers. He informed the sheriff of Warwickshire, William Hamelyn, who arrested Robert Tene and John Corbyn as well as Brother Nicholas Bredon, sacristan of the priory, to whom the two men had admitted what they had done. The sheriff William Hamelyn, the coroner William Herdewik, and several local knights held an inquest and determined that William Hare had died by misadventure and was not murdered, so Robert Tene, John Corbyn, and Nicholas Bredon were bailed and released.[1]

Andrew Frank accidentally killed his wife Agnes in June 1319 in Whiteparish, Wiltshire: he threw a knife at the wall of their house, and Agnes unexpectedly came round the corner, and the knife hit her in the leg. An investigation by the sheriff of Wiltshire, Philip de la Beche, and the local coroner, Nicholas Wili, found that she 'died by misadventure', perhaps of gangrene or tetanus or an infection. Andrew had already fled to the local church long before the investigation took place thirteen months after the incident. Apparently unwilling to put his faith in the judicial system – or perhaps because he knew he was lying and had thrown the knife at Agnes on purpose – he disappeared and was not heard of again. A similar case had happened a few decades earlier, in or not long before March 1261, when John Harpetro threw a knife at a cat who was eating a slab of meat in his house. By accident, supposedly, he hit his wife, the unusually named Belechera, in the leg, and she later died. And in Trewhitt, Northumberland in October 1268, Hugh Galun threw a pair of tongs at one of his calves, which was trying to eat some oatcakes that Hugh's servant Margery was baking on a griddle. The tongs bounced off the calf's back and hit Margery hard on the head. She died ten days later, 'by the greatest misadventure', according to an inquiry in March 1269.[2]

Wounds and injuries often resulted in a person's death. In March 1305 in Oxford, Roger Attewyndyate got into an argument with William Compton while clearing out horse manure from a stable. An annoyed William hit Roger on the right hand with a flail or truncheon and broke his index finger in two places. Roger died nine days later in the hospital of St John outside the east gate of Oxford, and when the coroner and his jurors viewed his body, 'his right arm was swollen up to the body'. Robert Anlek of Jersey in the Channel Islands was pardoned by Edward II in August 1324 for the accidental death of Joan Hamond: 'he threw a stone at a dog that was following to bite him, and the stone by accident struck the said Joan and killed her'. In 1261, Christine Swath bit Luke Girdeler on the finger, and 'his whole hand and body swelled up and he died soon afterwards'. She died in Newgate prison. In April 1234 in London, John Neuwelonde bit Laurence Turpyn on the right thumb, and he lost the thumb. Eventually the two men 'made peace' with each other, and John was not punished.[3] Many people who broke an arm or a leg died a few weeks afterwards of gangrene, though many survived as well, generally with a limp if they had broken a leg or ankle.

Being able to swim was relatively rare in the late Middle Ages, and many people drowned, either while washing themselves in a stream or river (which happened often), by falling from a bridge, or by slipping on the riverbank. William Wombe, who worked as a latrine-cleaner, drowned in the Thames around the time of curfew (i.e. late evening) on 2 June 1339, while he was washing himself. The river carried his body as far as the bridge over the River Fleet – which is now culverted over and runs underground – over a mile away, where it was discovered two days later. A sailor from Cliffe in Kent named Thomas Ballard drowned in the River Thames in London during the afternoon of Tuesday, 16 March 1378. He stood on a heap of manure trying to untether a boat which had been moored there, when the heap collapsed and he fell into the river. The tide carried his body to 'the land between the Hospital of St Katherine near the Tower and a watermill called Crashemelle'. Another sailor a century earlier, Richard Rye, made the mistake of leaning out of a boat off the shore of 'Ravenesherod' (later called Ravenspur and now a lost settlement) on the Holderness peninsula in Yorkshire on 17 March 1288. He intended to retrieve an oar which he had dropped, but lost his balance and fell into the water, and drowned. His fellow crewmen, Walter Pixi and Thomas Germethorp, were imprisoned in Grimsby on suspicion of having caused Richard's death, but were pardoned after an investigation and released, though not until 3 February 1290, almost two years later.[4]

In December 1300, 16-year-old Roger Metham had an accident in 'the old hall called Baylolhall', i.e. Balliol College at the University of Oxford, where he was studying. While playing unspecified 'games' with a group of his fellow students, Roger went up a flight of stairs or a ladder to an upper floor. Outside the door of an upstairs room was a small gallery, and Roger fell from it when a plank of wood he was leaning on broke. His friends carried him to his lodgings, but 'because of the anguish of the fall he contracted a fever, and so from that fever he sickened with illness'. Roger died six days later. The following December, John Neushom, a teacher, also died in Oxford when he climbed a willow tree, next to the River Cherwell and near the Magdalen Bridge, to collect twigs for a 'birch to chastise' the boys, his pupils. He fell into the mill-pool at Temple Mill and drowned; his wife, who had gone out to search for him when he failed to come home, found his body.[5]

Henry Fingrye, a wealthy fishmonger who served as one of the two sheriffs of London in 1299/1300, died in July 1318. Four years later in July 1322, his executors decided to distribute alms for Henry's soul on the anniversary of his death and inadvertently caused a tragedy. Very early in the morning before it was properly light, paupers crowded outside the gate of the London convent of Blackfriars (i.e. the Dominican Order) seeking the alms, and when the friars opened the gate, a terrible, deadly crush ensued. The St Paul's annalist states that fifty-five people died, and the coroners' rolls name some of the victims: Beatrix Cole, Joan Peyntures, Alice Norice, Maud the daughter of Robert Carpenter, and twenty-two other women, and Robert Fynel, his sons Simon, Robert and William, and twenty-two other men. This comes to a total of fifty-two.[6]

Arguably the man who suffered the most unique and bizarre death in late medieval England was John, son of Martin Licheffeld (i.e. the family originally came from Lichfield in Staffordshire), who lived in Moulton near Northampton. Sometime in 1352, John was feeding bread to a bear and stroking its head when it swiped him with one of its paws and killed him.[7] How and why John had access to a bear, where it had come from and why it was in a small village in fourteenth-century Northamptonshire was not further explained.

House Fires and Arson

Arson appears to have been a relatively rare crime in the late Middle Ages. Agnes Attehill was accused of 'burning the house' of William Hithe in London in 1276, though ultimately was acquitted, and in or not long before 1323 Geoffrey Steventon burned several houses belonging to John Ashton in Stanwick and Knuston, Northamptonshire. Geoffrey's motives in doing so were not clarified, though it is worth noting that he was a chaplain. Imprisoned in Northampton Castle for the crime, he died there of hunger and thirst.[8] A group of six men with evil intent approached the village of Honeydon near Bedford at twilight on 1 September 1267. They encountered a boy named Philip Gold, who was on his way home after tending to his father Roger's sheep, beat and wounded him badly, and forced him to take them to a nearby house where Ralph of Honeydon lived. Ralph recognised Philip's voice and opened his door, whereupon the six men forced their way in, killed Ralph's mother and a servant, and robbed the place. They repeated this trick at another five houses, using the unwilling Philip Gold to gain entry, and at the last house, William Mott's, they wounded him and left him for dead, then set fire to his house with him still in it. William died the following day. Young Philip eventually managed to escape and raised the hue and cry, and the criminals were pursued, having committed murder, robbery and arson against several of the unfortunate residents of Honeydon.[9]

On other occasions when a house was set on fire deliberately, it was mostly done with the intent that those inside would have to escape from the fire, whereupon they were killed when they emerged outside. On 9 February 1325, for example, John Dunheved of Dunchurch on Dunsmore Heath near Rugby in Warwickshire killed Oliver Dunheved, who was either his younger brother or his cousin; the motive for the attack was not given, though several years earlier, the two men had been jointly accused of raping Edith Grasbrok (see Chapter 7 below for more on the Dunheveds). John pretended that he was about to set the house in Dunchurch where Oliver was staying on fire, then shot him through the heart 'with a bow and a barbed arrow' when Oliver ran outside to escape.[10]

Oliver Dunheved had worked as a tax collector for Sir John Pecche, lord of Hampton in Arden 20 miles from Dunchurch, and not long afterwards, Pecche rode to Dunchurch in the middle of the night with his wife Lady Gorges and about twenty armed men with the intention of killing John Dunheved in revenge for Oliver's murder. John was not at home, but his wife Margery was and stated later that Pecche's men broke down the gates and door of the Dunheveds' house. Still wearing his gauntlets, John Pecche dragged Margery Dunheved out of bed naked and took her into her hall. For reasons which she did not explain, Pecche told his wife and his men to witness that Margery was not pregnant and that John Dunheved had not begotten a child on her, and with that they left, taking some of Margery's goods to a value of 100 shillings with them, or so Margery claimed later, though this seems likely to be an exaggeration. The indignant Margery, when she petitioned the king about the incident, had no sympathy for her husband's murdered kinsman, stating that Oliver Dunheved was merely a 'common thief' who had deserved his unpleasant fate. Before departing, John Pecche's men set fire to a pile of straw outside or in an outhouse for some unexplained reason; perhaps this was an indirect attempt to burn down the Dunheveds' house without being seen to do so, and revenge on John Dunheved for his willingness to burn Oliver alive inside the house where he was staying.[11]

A similar situation to John Dunheved's murder of Oliver occurred sometime in 1241 and involved Roger Sauser and a servant called Inga (this was a very unusual given name in medieval England, and her last name was not recorded). The two left the London home of

Isolde Tateshale, where they presumably worked together, and travelled to Gore in Kent. Here, they set fire to the house of Joce of Gore, and when Joce ran outside to escape from the fire, Roger Sauser killed him with an arrow. Roger fled into sanctuary at a nearby church, and when questioned, claimed that his employer Isolde Tateshale had 'sent him there to defend Inga and burn the house'. Their plan to do so was clearly established before they left London, as they carried the means to start a fire with them in a pot. Roger Sauser subsequently abjured the realm (for more on abjuring, see Chapter 14 below). Inga was captured when she returned to Isolde's home in London, was found guilty of Joce's murder, and burned alive (see also Chapter 10 for this punishment).[12] The motives for killing Joce were not explained, though it sounds as though he was Inga's estranged husband, and perhaps had been violent and abusive towards her.

House fires that started by accident instead of on purpose were incredibly common in the late Middle Ages, an era when most houses were made of wood. Leaving a candle alight during the night led to a considerable number of deaths by smoke inhalation and burning, and the fact that people often slept on straw mattresses helped nighttime fires to burn fiercely and spread quickly and made it extremely difficult for victims to escape. At the end of the thirteenth century, the coroner of Oxford, Adam Spalding, investigated the death of Margery Golde. She and her husband Adam Golde spent the evening of 22 June 1297 in a tavern, where they became 'drunk beyond measure'. After they returned home, Margery attached a lighted candle to the wall above their bed, and as the couple were drunk, they forgot about it and fell asleep. During the night, the candle fell onto their straw mattress, and the unfortunate Margery died of her burns the next day. Adam Golde must also have been in excruciating pain, as his hands and feet were 'burnt to the bones' and he scarcely escaped with his life either. One of the issues raised by the coroner Adam Spalding was whether Adam Golde might have saved his wife's life, but he and the jurors soon discovered that he could not have, and so a verdict of misadventure was recorded, and Adam Golde was held blameless. The fact that Margery survived until the next day and 'had all church rights', i.e. she was shriven by a priest, was also deemed significant in such matters: a victim who was able to confess their sins before death and was therefore conscious and sufficiently compos mentis could have named their attacker, had there been one. Agnes Henxey also died in a house fire in Oxford a few months later, in May 1298. Like the Golde couple, she came home drunk, lit a candle, and fell asleep. Agnes's chamber and the adjoining house were destroyed in the resulting fire, and the unfortunate Agnes was burnt to death. Simon Gerlondere, either a neighbour or perhaps a relative or lover of Agnes, was the first person to find her, and raised the hue and cry.[13]

In September 1276, John Sautreor (whose name means that he was a minstrel who played a stringed instrument called a psaltery) attended 'a certain feast' held in London and became very drunk. He made his way to a house belonging to William and Fynea Cuver, where he, evidently a visitor to London rather than a resident, had hired a bed for the night. John lit a candle to find his way to his bedchamber and to make up his bed but fell asleep with it still alight. He died of his burns a few hours later. William and Fynea, and their son Remund, were questioned on the matter, but it was found that they bore no responsibility for John's unfortunate death.[14] Another horrible fire happened in Oxford during the night of 8/9 August 1298. Alice and John Trivaler were a young couple with a 20-week-old son, Roger, and that night made the mistake of attaching a lighted candle to the wall of their shop, where they worked and slept. The candle fell onto some straw and caught fire immediately. Alice and John fled outside but realised to their horror that they had left their infant son inside the shop. Alice ran back to fetch him but was overcome by the smoke and the 'greatness of the fire'. Tragically, she and her little boy both died.[15]

In the early evening of Thursday, 6 April 1340 in Spondon near Derby, an unnamed woman was drying malt in a furnace prior to making ale with it. An inquisition found that there was a strong east wind that day and that the building where the furnace was located caught fire. The conflagration soon spread and ended up destroying most of the village of Spondon, including the local church. Only four houses were left standing. Henry Penk, described as 'the most important man of the town' in the subsequent inquisition, fled from his house, but was caught by the fire in the middle of the street, and burned to death. There were surely other victims as well.[16] Another great conflagration happened in the village of Little Houghton near Northampton in 1333. John Pavely, who was to become a local landowner after his three older brothers died in the Black Death in 1349, was born there on 2 July 1333, and not long after his birth, 'there was a great fire at Little Houghton, and the whole town was almost burnt, and the said John, lying in a cradle, was carried into a field for fear of the fire'. The bishop of Lincoln, Henry Burghersh (d. 1340), came to the village shortly afterwards to reconsecrate the church, which had been badly damaged by the fire.

The Shropshire village of Stapleton, 8 miles south of Shrewsbury, was yet another place which experienced an awful fire on 8 September 1335 which supposedly destroyed the entire place, though in this case, the supposed destruction seems to be something of an exaggeration.[17] In crowded medieval London, the fear of fire was, understandably, so great that it was prohibited for houses to have roofs made of straw, reeds, rushes or stubble because they were all such a fire hazard. Tiles, shingles, or boards were to be used instead.[18] Regulations for the city spurriers (spur-makers) in August 1345 stated that the men 'blow up their fires so vigorously, that their forges begin all at once to blaze', which endangered both the spurriers themselves and their neighbours, who lived in dread of the sparks that 'issue forth in all directions' from the chimneys in the spurriers' forges. The men were therefore ordered not to work at night, at least.[19]

Other Accidents

In London in the early 1250s, two women named Cecily and her maid Juliana (last names not given) were having an ill-tempered fight in Cecily's home, next to a 'leaden vessel full of hot water'. Both women fell into it and were scalded to death. The vat was worth 4s as *deodand.* A year or two later, also in London, Agnes Barkyng also fell into a vessel of boiling water while working in a house belonging to John and Felice Makerel and was scalded to death.[20]

Medieval houses could be dangerous in their fragility. Sarra Wodeward, for example, died in the 'ruined house' where she lived in Radstone, Northamptonshire in April 1322; the house was 'weak and dilapidated' (*domo debili et ruinosa*), and fell in on her one night. A similar fate befell Agnes Bogwulle in Maiden Bradley, Somerset, and the Haste family in Tisbury, Wiltshire.[21] Adam Plomer died outside his house in Oxford in July 1347. He stood on a 'decayed timber' to mend a gutter, and it broke and pitched him to the ground: 'he fell to the earth on his head, whereby it was broken'.[22] Sometime between July 1313 and July 1314, an earthen wall in Felise Kyng's house in the tiny Northamptonshire village of Haselbech collapsed one night. Agnes Kyng, who was presumably Felise's granddaughter or niece, was crushed to death in her bed. Felise was in the same bed, though escaped with her life. In Bugbrooke, 15 miles from Haselbech, two girls or young women named Juliane Sibford and Margaret Cranok from Coventry were killed one night in 1348 when an earthen exterior wall collapsed on their bed or beds during the night.[23] It is possible that the two were cousins and were staying with their mutual grandmother, Juliane Herry, who owned the house but who was unhurt in the incident.

There is much evidence that medieval people often slept on upper floors, even if it was only a type of mezzanine level that had to be accessed by ladder. Upper floors were often called 'solars', and in January 1326 in London, John Toly fell 30 feet to his death from his solar in the middle of the night after urinating out of the window. He 'crush[ed] his neck and other members'. In February 1340, 11-year-old Juliana Turgeys 'was standing in a window of a solar' at dusk, when she fell out of the window into the street below and was killed.[24] Some houses had stairs, and people often fell down them and died. Joan Cotekyn, while going down the stairs from the solar in the house she rented from Hugh Waltham in London one Saturday evening in August 1324, slipped and fell, and 'fatally crushed her body'. She was found by friends and carried to the house of her father John Cotekyn, but died there early on Tuesday morning; the stairs down which she had slipped were valued at 6d as *deodand*. John Cotekyn outlived his daughter by many years and was one of the jurors who investigated the death of Walter Proudfot also in London in November 1338. They discovered that Walter fell down the stairs in the house that he rented from John Turk, one Monday evening, 'broke his right thigh', and died on the following Thursday.[25]

William Bonefaunt, a skinner, rented a house from William Bokkyng in Candlewick Street (Candelwykstrete) ward in London. Around the time of curfew on Sunday, 31 August 1337, Bonefaunt was drunk, and stood naked at the top of the steps in his home to relieve himself, presumably into a urinal or other receptacle, though this is not stated. He lost his balance and fell down the stairs and died.[26] The drunkenness of Ralph Deblet from Carlisle in Cumberland also caused his death on 1 November 1285. He staggered home that night so drunk that he did not know where he was, went into the wrong house by mistake, walked upstairs into the solar, and fell on top of Thomas Tayllor, who was peacefully asleep in his own bed. Thomas woke up shouting in alarm, whereupon Ralph stumbled down the stairs and tripped over a cartload of wool at the bottom. He 'was wounded in the head even to the brain, whereof he died' (what exactly on the cart of wool inflicted a mortal wound to his head was not specified).[27]

It was extraordinarily common for men in the late Middle Ages to carry a weapon about their person, and this habit sometimes resulted in tragedy. William Stangate was walking along a road called Buleyesdam somewhere in Sussex on 25 May 1267, carrying a crossbow over his shoulder and a poisoned arrow in his belt, when he encountered Desiderata, widow of Robert Champeneys. Desiderata was a good friend of William and the godmother of his child, so they stopped for a chat. Desiderata jokingly asked if William was 'one of the men who were going about the country with crossbows, bows and other weapons, to apprehend robbers and evildoers by the king's order', which was perhaps a reference to the aftermath of a recent baronial rebellion against Henry III and his son, the future Edward I. She pretended to be capturing William as though he was one of the evildoers, and 'crooked her leg' behind his. In doing so, she lost her balance and stumbled into William, and the arrow in his belt pierced her through the heart. She died almost immediately. Henry III pardoned William Stangate for Desiderata's death just a few weeks later.[28]

Two brothers, John and Thomas Aleyn, lived in Walsall in Staffordshire, and on 28 April 1280 attended a feast in the town given by one Thomas Doleberge. They had only one horse between them, and John rode it on their way home with Thomas walking alongside, carrying a bow and five arrows. Eventually, John asked Thomas if he would like to climb up behind him, took his brother's bow and arrows in one hand and pulled him up onto the horse with the other, but the horse's girth had not been sufficiently tightened and it slipped, so that both men tumbled to the ground. One of Thomas's arrows which John was holding pierced John in the armpit, and he died that night. Thomas was pardoned for his brother's death on the grounds of misadventure.[29] In Cogenhoe in Northamptonshire in the late 1270s, Walter Aspale also killed his brother William by misadventure. He was shooting at kites (i.e. birds), but his arrow fell to the ground and hit William in the head.[30] In London, it was a common habit to shoot pigeons and other birds perched on churches or houses with stonebows, a catapult for shooting stones, and arbalests, a kind of crossbow. This was prohibited in 1327 because the missiles wounded passersby and broke windows, though half a century later in 1376, two men shot 'with bolts and arrows' at pigeons perched on houses, 'whereby, but for God's abundant grace, men, women and children might have been killed or seriously wounded'.[31]

Chapter 5

Homicide, Fights, and Frenzy

Medieval people stabbed each other or hit each other over the head during quarrels with tedious regularity. They were cleared of murder if they could prove that they acted in self-defence and had no other option, as they were about to be killed themselves. Weapons often used in the Middle Ages included: *Irysshknyf* (Irish knife), *bidau* or *bydawe* (long, broad knife), *thwitel* or *twytel* (large knife), *misericorde* (long, narrow knife), *baselard* (a dagger or short sword), *balstaf* (cudgel), *anelaz* (dagger), *panade* (poniard, a small dagger), *fauchon* (falchion, a one-handed, single-edged sword), *pol(l)ax* (poleaxe), *sparth* (axe), and *gisarme* (halberd).

The homicide rate in late medieval England was astonishingly high, as much as twenty to fifty times higher than it is in modern times. To avert violence and murder in London, it was proclaimed repeatedly that carrying weapons on the city streets was forbidden, and only city officials, sergeants-at-arms of the king and queen, and great lords and servants 'carrying their lords' swords in their presence' were allowed to do so. In December 1343, a clerk named Hugh Dyngele was imprisoned 'for carrying arms in the streets contrary to proclamation'. Innkeepers in London were ordered to warn their guests who came from outside the city of this prohibition, and innkeeper Adam Grymmesby was committed to prison in July 1372 for failing to warn one of his guests that his knife must be left inside the inn. The unnamed guest was found with the knife, which was confiscated, though he himself was not punished.[1] This prohibition on weapons in England's largest city is somewhat reminiscent of modern-day New York, which has long had some of the strictest gun laws in the U.S.

Oxford, as a university town, was particularly murderous in the Middle Ages, and its homicide rate in the fourteenth century is estimated to have been four to five times higher than in contemporary London or York, which already had sky-high rates. Medieval England was a young society whose mean age was much lower than it is today, with a significant percentage of the population under twenty. As all university students in the Middle Ages were male, medieval Oxford had an unusually high percentage of young men – always the category most prone to violence in any society. Research indicates that its homicide rate was 60 to 75 in 100,000.[2] By contrast, in the twenty-first century roughly 500 to 700 people are murdered every year in England and Wales, which have a combined population of around 60 million, giving an approximately 1 in 100,000 chance that a person will be murdered in any given year.

As an example of how murderous medieval Oxford could be and how gangs of youthful men could egg each other on to greater heights, or rather depths, of violence, a group of men banded together in the town in April 1389 and xenophobically decided to kill any Welsh people they found. The leader was one John Kirkeby, and a chaplain named Thomas Speek also played an important role (as will be noted in Chapter 11 below, medieval chaplains, though men of religion, seemed peculiarly minded to violence, murder and criminality). Kirkeby and Speek gathered a group of like-minded individuals and roamed the streets of Oxford armed with bows and arrows, chanting 'War, war, war, sle [slay], sle, sle the Walshe dogges and her helpes [Welsh dogs and their helpers], and hoso loketh [whoso looks] out of his hous, he shal be dede [dead]'. At least four people in the town were killed and others survived but were badly wounded. Those killed were 'Geoffrey Hawelame of Wales', Edward Sutton, Thomas Rypon, and John Boweman; the three last names all sound as though the men were English. Other Welsh people were forced to agree that they would leave Oxford and were marched to one of the town gates and told to kiss it, and when they did so, their heads were violently smashed into the stone. As well as committing murder and violence, the gang rampaged through the town, breaking into numerous houses and halls and stealing numerous items, including 'books of grammar and dialectic'.[3]

Serial killers are all but impossible to identify as such in late medieval England, though it seems likely that some murderers must have had more than one victim, even if their pattern of behaviour was never spotted or recorded. Plenty of medieval knights, such as the Swynnerton brothers of Staffordshire, did kill more than one victim, but their behaviour and probable motivations do not fit the definition of serial killing.

One curiosity is that two sailors, William Hamptone, an Englishman, and Peter Skomakere of Flanders, drowned in the River Thames in London exactly a week apart, on Sunday, 5 December and Sunday, 12 December 1340. Both men were said to have been drunk and to have gone walking alone along a wharf by the river 'after the hour of curfew', that is, after darkness had fallen.[4] Why two men would separately choose to walk alone on winter evenings in the pitch black of a world long before electric light existed, and when it is likely to have been cold and perhaps wet, is puzzling. Perhaps both sailors were lured onto a wharf away from their crewmates in some way and then pushed into the river by someone who felt the need to kill. As few medieval people knew how to swim, this was an effective way of killing someone without leaving a 'wound or bruise', as the coroner's report on William Hamptone stated.

Many murders in the late Middle Ages occurred during arguments, sometimes while people were drunk, when one party pulled out a weapon and stabbed the other. Perhaps surprisingly, however, alcohol does not appear to have played a huge role in medieval violence and homicide, and scholar Barbara Hanawalt plausibly suggests a more important motive: 'perhaps some of the disputes centred around tensions involved in planting and harvest.' She states that '[t]he location of homicidal disputes provides further evidence of the close relationship with the agricultural calendar.'[5] As medieval England was a place where most people lived hand to mouth and deaths from starvation and diseases related to malnutrition were not uncommon when harvests failed, the availability of food does indeed seem a very likely cause of some murderous arguments in the late Middle Ages.

Drunken quarrels did sometimes, however, result in violence and murder: in Bisbrooke, Rutland in the early 1320s, three friends, Roger Lalleford or Lilford, John (last name unclear), and Robert Whitewell argued one evening in a tavern. Roger took some serious sword wounds to the head from one or both of the others. He survived long enough to be carried almost 30 miles to Cold Ashby in Northamptonshire, presumably where he lived or came from, but died of his wounds five days later. John and Robert both fled, which suggests that both had attacked their friend. A few decades earlier, in Bringhurst, Leicestershire on 11 October 1256, one brother killed another while drunk. Hugh Burton went to his brother Robert's house to borrow a horse from him, at the request of their mother Maud. Robert, who was very drunk and in a foul mood, refused to lend the horse, and hit Hugh over the head with a pitchfork. Hugh, in self-defence, grabbed a spade and threw it at Robert, and hit him on the head. Robert died eight days later.[6] In Canterbury in 1268, a group of twenty-two young men who included several sets of brothers, called 'wilful and quarrelsome youths', spent 'night and day' in their local tavern, and 'played and drank there and quarrelled on the way home'. Lord Edward, the future King Edward I, then the 29-year-old son and heir of Henry III, found some of these men dead in a place outside Canterbury called *Godricheswude* or Godrich's Wood (or at least, some members of Edward's retinue found them) when he was travelling towards Dover. He suspected their friends of committing the murders. Nine years later, in May 1277 between Penrith and Lazonby, Cumberland, William FitzPatrick and his (unnamed) wife were going home one Tuesday afternoon. Having got very drunk at the market in Penrith, they became amorous in what they assumed was a private place. Alexander Chapele, however, breaking stones in a nearby quarry to build his father John's house, heard the wife cry out and assumed she was being raped by a stranger. He ran up to the couple, hit William hard over the head with his shovel, and killed him.[7]

Games, sometimes those played in taverns, could have murderous consequences. One Monday evening just before Christmas 1323, Stephen Lenne, a taverner in London, played at tables for money with Arcus Rikelinge of Brabant (in modern-day Belgium) in a tavern run by William Staneforde. Arcus, losing badly, was 'moved to anger' by Stephen's gloating, and stabbed him in the belly with a knife called a *tranchour* or trencher.[8] In 1344 in the village of Yardley Hastings near Northampton, John Wylk killed his friend John Neubonde in a rage following an argument over a game of *penyprikke* which they were playing at the home of another friend, Roger Eston. *Penyprikke* or *penyperche* was a game where pieces of iron were thrown at a stick which had a penny coin placed on it. The game had led to another unfortunate incident a few decades earlier: in Eaton (later called Eaton Bray) in Bedfordshire on 2 June 1300, Henry Bateman and William Gamelingey were playing *penyperche* in the house of John Mareschal, which doubled as a tavern (medieval taverns often operated out of private houses). They argued so violently over the game that William seized Henry around the throat and grabbed his hair with his other hand as the two men left the tavern. Henry, alarmed, managed to draw his knife. His cousin Reynold Elys, who was sitting in the tavern, rushed to Henry's aid, but in the chaos, received a wound in the right shoulder from Henry's knife, from which he died shortly afterwards.[9]

John Whetley from Chester stabbed John Belringere in the throat with a kind of large knife called a *twytel* or *thwitel* on Thursday, 23 May 1324 as they sat drinking and playing dice together in Roger Haverynge's house in Dowgate ward, London. John Belringere managed to stagger to the door and made his way outside but then fell dead in the street. A neighbour with the unusual name of Richard Chicheboof found him and raised the hue and cry. John Whetley fled to the nearby church of All Hallows at the Hay, admitted his crime to the local coroner shortly afterwards, and agreed to abjure the realm. Unusually, he was allowed to choose his port of departure, and selected Bristol rather than Dover or Southampton. The sheriffs of London, Adam Salisbury and John Oxenford, gave him five days to get there, and told him where to spend each night: High Wycombe, Buckinghamshire; Oxford; Highworth, Wiltshire; and Malmesbury, Wiltshire. Another neighbour, attached to appear as a witness, was Richer Refham (d. 1328), who had served as mayor of London in 1310/11 then returned to his native Norfolk and served as sheriff of Norfolk and Suffolk from October 1314 to May 1316. By the 1320s, Richer was living in London once more, and in August 1326 was again attached as a witness to the death of William Walsshman (i.e. Welshman), a tiler. While tiling a roof, William fell from his ladder to his death.[10]

David of Bristol killed his friend Juliana Cordwaner in the home she shared with her husband Richard in London in 1264. David and Juliana were playing chess with several other friends also present, as well as Richard Cordwaner, in what sounds like a convivial evening. David and Juliana, however, quarrelled over their game of chess, and David, in a rage, stabbed Juliana in the thigh with a sword, and killed her. He fled from justice. In Essex in August 1254, William Wendene and Sir Robert FitzBernard were playing chess and argued over the game. Robert's squire, unnamed, attacked William, and William retaliated by stabbing Robert in the stomach and killing him. He fled into sanctuary in a nearby church but escaped after three days.[11]

Burglars sometimes killed the people whose houses they were robbing. In the Bedfordshire village of Roxton in November 1269, thieves killed two (unnamed) people while robbing their house, then broke into the house of the Cobbler family. John Cobbler, the father, was killed, while his wife Azeline, their daughter Agnes, and their servant Walter were wounded. Alice, the other Cobbler daughter, managed to flee and hide, and after the burglars had gone, found her father's body and raised the hue and cry. Sadly, her mother Azeline later died of her wounds as well, though not before identifying one of her attackers as Richard Neyvile or Neville, a former employee of the prior of Newnham Priory. Thomas Longe from Sandwich in Kent, a skinner by profession, broke into the home of Juliana Prykafeld, a *lavendere* (laundress), next to the hospital of St Katherine (founded in 1147) by the Tower of London. He stole a strong-box containing Juliana's money and jewels to a value of 10 marks (£6.66), which seems a large sum for a woman who worked as a laundress. Juliana was unexpectedly at home, and Thomas attacked her with an *Irysshknyf* or Irish knife, inflicting mortal wounds to her chest and throat. She died immediately, and Thomas fled. According to the jurors investigating Juliana's murder, Thomas was aided by 'a certain Anne, a courtesan' who lived in Juliana's house and who fled with him.[12]

Female Murderers and Criminal Couples

Female murderers in the Middle Ages were rare, and they frequently had a male accomplice. Maud Dunstal, who struck Emma Hendeman on the head with a staff in Brixworth, Northamptonshire, sometime in 1347, and killed her, is an unusual example where a woman killed alone and where her victim was another woman. Maud was captured and taken 7 miles to Northampton Castle, where she was imprisoned.[13]

Sometimes, a couple committed murder together. In the evening of Sunday, 19 September 1322, Lucy Faukes was visiting her friends Richard and Christine Sherman at their home above a shop near the Tower of London, as she had often done before, and intended to spend the night there. Unbeknown to poor Lucy, however, the people she thought of as her friends were deeply envious of her affluence and the excellent quality of the clothes she wore, and deliberately picked a violent quarrel with her to have an excuse to kill her. Richard, with Christine's help and support, took a *balstaf* or cudgel and hit Lucy hard on the top of her head, a blow which 'mortally broke and crushed the whole of her head'. The unfortunate Lucy died immediately, and the covetous and murderous Sherman couple stripped her of her fine clothes and fled into the night. Her body was discovered by one Giles Portour, who raised the hue and cry.[14]

Another murderous London couple was John and Agnes Gaunter, who in the early 1270s beat up a woman named Isabel, the widow of Geoffrey Sachier. Isabel escaped from them and fled home, but during the night John broke into her house and stabbed her to death. The motive for the beating and subsequent killing, if there was one, was not specified. John returned to his own home, where he and Agnes collected all their goods and ran. He was outlawed and Agnes was waived.[15] In the Middle Ages, women could not be outlawed because they were not considered to have legal rights or to be 'in law' in the way that men were, and as they were not in the law, they could not be out of the law either. They could, however, be 'waived' or excluded from the protection of the law, which in practice amounted to the same thing.

In February 1307, a married couple from Leicester named Richard and Isabel Pountfreyt killed a woman, Agnes Toprond, in a lane near the church of St Michael in Leicester, though the motive for the killing was not stated. They both abjured the realm (for which, see Chapter 14 below), Richard from Dover and Isabel from Portsmouth.[16] Juliana Aunsel and John Multon murdered Edmund Brekles, a chaplain and another lover of Juliana, in London in June 1324. John stabbed Edmund in the stomach while he (Edmund) was in bed with Juliana. They both decided to abjure the realm and were sent to Dover. John was ordered to depart London for the port immediately, but Juliana was held back for a month, which was done in a deliberate attempt to prevent the couple from meeting up again. John was given four days to complete the 70-mile walk and Juliana five.[17] Another criminal couple, though not murderous, was Hugh Lattone and Edith, 'his sweetheart' (*amasium suam* in the Latin of the original text). They stole clothes and unspecified 'other things' from Agnes atte Berwe in Essex in 1292.[18] And in the village of Peakirk near Peterborough, a couple named Muriel and William Veyse sought sanctuary in the church of All Saints on 18 May 1309. William confessed to being a thief and a murderer (though his victim was not named), and Muriel admitted to having harboured him after his crimes, a felony in itself. They both abjured the realm, and William was sent to Dover and Muriel to Portsmouth, in what is another example of a murderous couple being deliberately separated by the authorities. The only possessions Muriel had with her were a counterpane, a sheet and a small chest, while William was carrying a few items including a cloak with a separate hood, a bowl 'with a big spoon', and an extra pair of shoes. Muriel, rather interestingly, worked as a blacksmith, an unusual occupation for a woman in fourteenth-century England.[19]

As in all societies and always, male-on-male violence was very common in the English Middle Ages, followed by male-on-female violence. Female-on-female violence was rare but not unheard of. In 1276, Maud Russe of London accused Alice of Kent of inflicting 'wounds and battery' on her, and in the same year Maud of Kent was also accused of 'wounds and battery' by a woman whose name is recorded as 'Alice, daughter of Ralph of New Place'. In the early 1260s near London, Emma Chaloner attacked Alice Attelithe, beating her so severely that Alice died a few days later. No motive for the murderous assault was provided.[20]

A very rare example of two women committing murder together occurred in London in late 1257 or in 1258. Emma Mazon or Mason and a woman referred to as 'Joan daughter of Simon son of Mary' killed Emma's husband, John Mazon, during the night. Emma fled to sanctuary in the church of St Martin Ismongerelane or Ironmonger Lane (the church was later known as St Martin Pomary and was destroyed in the Great Fire of 1666; it stood roughly where Bank Station/Poultry is now) and told the authorities that she wished to abjure the realm. Joan fled, was not caught, and was waived.[21] 'Simon son of Mary' or Simon FitzMary, a sheriff of London who founded the hospital of Bedlam in 1247, in 1241 abducted a boy or young man named William FitzWilliam, who died not long afterwards (see Chapter 12 below). In late 1243 or early 1244, Maud Cocke was killed in her home in London around Vespers, i.e. sunset. Her husband John was then in Reading and was not suspected of any involvement in the murder, and four of their neighbours pointed a finger at a 'certain woman' (*quedam mulier*) who was in the house when Maud was killed. The woman, who was not named, was found, arrested, handed over to the city sheriffs, and imprisoned in Newgate.[22] In September 1275, Abraham and Brunamia Treyer claimed that Maud Stanes went to their house in London and beat up Brunamia, wounding and maiming her. Maud indignantly denied the accusation, and though

Abraham and Brunamia said they could produce witnesses, she was found not guilty. Abraham and Brunamia were committed to gaol for making a false accusation. Their names suggest that they were Jewish, and as this was only a few years before Edward I expelled the entire Jewish population of England in 1290, their religion may explain why a Christian woman was found not guilty of harming Brunamia.[23]

Sometimes women were part of a gang who killed; Sir Thomas Murdak in 1316, for example (see Chapter 10 below), who was killed with the connivance of his wife Juliana Gayton and some of his own servants, including several women. Not long before 24 November 1258, a couple named William and Alice of Clerkenwell were killed in their home at night by John Persone, his sister Katherine Norreyse, her maid Dulcia, Maud Horseye, and Alice Coddred. Supposedly the murders took place 'by procurement of the said Dulcia'. Dulcia and Alice were captured and imprisoned in Newgate. John was outlawed, while Katherine and Maud do not seem to have suffered any consequences.[24] The name Persone means 'parson', suggesting that John and Katherine were the illegitimate children of a parson, and Katherine's last name, Norreyse, means 'nursemaid' or 'wet-nurse', presumably her profession. Sometime between the autumn of 1264 and the summer of 1265, four men and two women beat a man, Thomas Keu, to death in or near London. One man and one woman, Roger Byssop and Cecily Hors, were caught and hanged in Newgate prison before Hugh Despenser, justiciar of England. The others, including Cecily's husband Henry Hors and Maud Lokyere, fled and were outlawed (waived in Maud's case).[25]

Another case involving women happened at almost the same time, also in London. Felice, last name not recorded, worked as a brewster, a female brewer; brewing ale was a job very commonly done by women in late medieval England. She was walking along Wood Street one day when she encountered Lucy, another brewster, standing in the doorway of her employer, Maunsell the Tailor. Lucy accused Felice of deliberately taking trade away from her and dragged her into the house. She and two men, William Mercer and Alan Cheddeworth, set about beating Felice, and horribly, they kept her in the house for three days until she finally died because of their violence. All three subsequently fled and were outlawed or waived. In the summer of 1239, a very unusual murder took place when a woman killed a cleric: Alice, widow of the king's sergeant

William Cheval, killed Peter, chaplain of the church of St Michael. She fled to the church of St Edmund but escaped and was waived.[26]

In August 1239, a Jewish woman named Henna went into the home of a couple named Alvered and Isabel Pyncebrok (or Pincebrecke or Pinchbrek) in London. Alvered was not there at the time, having travelled to the annual fair in Lenne (later called King's Lynn) in Norfolk, though Isabel was at home with her servants Agnes and Maud, and a man called Peter of Shaftesbury. Henna was never seen again, and her husband Jacob brought the three women, Isabel Pyncebrok, Agnes, and Maud, to the attention of the authorities. His wife's whereabouts remained a mystery, though she was presumed to have been killed. The three women were imprisoned in Newgate.[27]

On 20 September 1314, John Baker died in his home in Pilsgate near Stamford in Lincolnshire and was buried in the nearby churchyard on the same day. For some reason, suspicions arose about the cause of his death, and rather remarkably, the local coroner, whose name is recorded as R. de Vere (probably Robert or Richard), ordered John's body to be exhumed so that he could examine it. On doing so, he found a wound on John's head that had been caused by an axe or a hatchet. John's widow Emma and her brother John Reeve, also of Pilsgate, were both arrested, and it transpired that that John Baker had been beating his wife, who asked her brother for help. It was John Reeve who struck the deadly blow, with Emma's approval.[28] John Baker's body was exhumed for investigation relatively soon after burial, though even so, in the context of medieval religious beliefs it seems remarkable that permission was ever given at all.

Mutilations

As well as a frighteningly high homicide rate, appalling physical attacks on a person which involved mutilation of some kind sometimes took place in the late Middle Ages. As will be discussed in Chapter 6 below, Simon Beltoft was one of a gang of people who tore out the eyes and cut out the tongue of their victim John Carewell in 1321. In the village of Bulley, Gloucestershire, in the summer of 1325, Thomas Brokworth was assaulted by two brothers, John and Thomas Faukoner, and unnamed others. They 'broke his arms and legs and tore out his eyes'.[29] In Ravensden near Bedford, 'felons and thieves' came to the house of

John and Maud Rede at twilight on Thursday, 23 April 1271, when the couple and their servants Walter Estwode and Richard Pikhorn were seated at dinner. The thieves tied up the two servants, struck John Rede on the head with an axe and killed him outright, and wounded Maud on the head as well, presumably with the axe. They almost severed her left hand, and deliberately tortured her by lighting a brandreth, an iron grid or frame used to hold pots over a fire, and burning her with it. Maud lay close to death while they burgled her house, though her servant Walter managed to free himself from the rope with which he was tied, and raised the hue and cry. It transpired that the murder of John Rede was carried out by a local miller with the knowledge and advice of Agnes and Maud Pikhorn, presumably the mother and sister or mother and wife of the Redes' servant Richard Pikhorn; Richard was imprisoned. Maud Rede survived her awful ordeal.[30]

A woman named Juliana Gylle and a group of 'thieves unknown' broke into the house of Percival and Agnes Walssh, a very well-off couple, in Hoo in the parish of Hambleden, Buckinghamshire, in December 1390. They stole numerous valuable items from the couple, including a silk gown lined with expensive miniver fur and a pair of rosaries. Percival and Agnes were not at home, but Agnes encountered the thieves the same day and must have realised that they were the people who had stolen from her. Tragically for the unfortunate Agnes, her confrontation with the thieves ended horribly: they 'gouged out her eyes and cut out her tongue'. Juliana Gylle was the only member of the gang who was caught, and was sentenced to death, but it transpired that she was pregnant, and a year later Richard II pardoned her at the request of his queen, Anne of Bohemia.[31]

Fights, Violent Quarrels and Self-Defence

In Haveringdowne, part of the manor of West Wycombe in Buckinghamshire, Henry Verney went to drink at his local tavern on 12 August 1284. Another man present in the tavern, John Penkriche, took offence to Henry for some reason, and started shouting abuse at him. Although Henry protested that he merely wished to drink in peace, John tried to attack him with a sword. Henry immediately left the tavern, but John followed him, and – evidently well-armed, as well as probably very drunk – shot two arrows at him. He then put down his bow and took up his sword again, and Henry, seeing that he was likely to be badly hurt or perhaps killed, saw no other option than to pick up a stick and strike John with it to save his own life. John died soon afterwards, and Henry was arrested and imprisoned for homicide, but was pardoned by the king, Edward I, the following year as he had acted in self-defence and not with malice aforethought.[32]

Almost forty years later, Maud Amyson, widow of William Amyson, was living in the Yorkshire village of Hemingbrough, a few miles from Selby, where she owned a flock of sheep. On 23 March 1323, an escaped criminal named Dionise Ketel, who had fled from justice because of unspecified 'larcenies imputed to her', entered Maud's sheepfold. She killed two ewes and started skinning them, presumably intending to cook and eat the meat. Maud came across Dionise in the sheepfold, and Dionise came at her with the knife with which she was skinning the ewes. Maud fled into her house but was soon cornered, and to save her own life seized an axe and hit Dionise on the head with it, which killed her. As chance would have it, the king, Edward II, had passed just 20 miles from Hemingbrough on his way south mere days earlier, and Maud 'immediately journeyed to the king's court to seek the king's peace'. Fifteen months later in June 1324, following an investigation by the sheriff of Yorkshire, Edward pardoned Maud Amyson for Dionise Ketel's death.[33]

Lambert of Cologne – evidently a German man who lived in England – and a man named Walter, who worked as a squire to a clerk, Master Philip Cancellis, escorted Philip's sister Alice to her home in London in February 1254. As the three passed through the churchyard of St Dunstan in the West, they encountered Henry Merston from Bedfordshire, a clerk of the chancery, and his servant Robert Kyngeston from Staffordshire. The four men began quarrelling over Alice, and Robert Kyngeston, at his master Henry Merston's order, stabbed Lambert just below the right shoulder. Lambert survived the attack for a while but died three days later, whereupon Robert fled. The sheriff of his native Staffordshire was ordered to outlaw him there. Henry Merston, meanwhile, who enjoyed benefit of clergy, was handed over to the bishop of Lincoln to deal with.

Another German man resident in England in the mid-thirteenth century was Konrad of Bruneswyc (Brunswick or Braunschweig), who lived in Northampton. He had a dispute with his servant, Thedric of 'Estland' (which in Middle English meant Estonia or the Baltic States more generally) in his home in December 1248, which resulted in Thedric knocking Konrad to the ground and lying on top of him. Konrad, 'being unable to escape without danger of death', wounded Thedric in the shoulder with a knife that he conveniently had in his hand. Thedric lived for another ten days with the wound, and peculiarly, an investigation by the sheriff of Northamptonshire found that he 'died of drinking half a gallon of wine after dinner on the day of his death' rather than because he had been stabbed in the shoulder. Konrad sought sanctuary in the Northampton convent of the Franciscan friars after Thedric died, though was pardoned by Henry III not long afterwards. And a group of Italians lived in Reading, Berkshire in the late 1270s and early 1280s. On 28 December 1279, Alberto Morone, his brother Guido and their friends Adam of Pavia, Donato of Cremona, and Leonardo of Casalt Motant or Casal Motaut visited the house of another friend, Richard Messager, apparently English, and dined together. Subsequently, the Italians began quarrelling in Italian, and Leonardo drew a knife and wounded three of the others. He ran after Guido, who, seeing that he was in a 'narrow house' from which he could not possibly escape, took out his own knife and stabbed Leonardo in the side. Leonardo died six days later, during which time he 'would neither eat nor drink anything except cold water, which his surgeon forbade him'. The other men were imprisoned firstly by the abbot of Reading, then taken by the sheriff of Berkshire to the Tower of London, though were pardoned by Edward I five months later and released.[34]

In the village of Renhold near Bedford in August 1267, Roger Benfield, Andrew Beufrere, and at least twelve other men broke into the home of the Read family. They struck Simon, the father, with swords on the arms and shoulders, hit his daughter Maud on the leg, and badly wounded his son John with an arrow in his forearm. John managed to find and pick up an axe and hit Roger Benfield on the head with it. Roger fell to the ground and his accomplices fled, whereupon the family raised the hue and cry, and their neighbours pursued the fleeing men. Roger Benfield died the next day, having confessed that the gang had intended to kill the entire family after robbing them. The gang left behind three horses with saddles and bridles, which presumably they had intended to use to carry off their loot, and the sheriff of Bedfordshire took the animals to the county court 'for the use of Lord Edward', Henry III's son and heir, the future King Edward I. The Read family, who had defended themselves against criminals with murderous intent, were not punished.[35]

In London, brawls between different misteries (guilds of craftsmen or tradesmen) were relatively common and sometimes turned violently murderous. In October 1304, eleven tailors and cordwainers were imprisoned after a nighttime affray in Cheapside, and bakers, taverners, millers, and unspecified other misteries had to be ordered not to assault each other with 'swords, bucklers and other arms by night' in February 1320. A dispute in 1325 between the saddlers and the goldsmiths resulted in murder. After curfew on Sunday, 10 November, twelve goldsmiths lay in wait for 'men of the mistery of saddlers in order to beat them'. This resulted in the death of John atte Vyse, saddler, after three goldsmiths beat him up, one stabbed him in the head, one nearly severed his leg with an axe, and yet another hit him repeatedly with a club after John fell to the ground. His friends carried him home, and he somehow lived for four days after the attack.[36]

The saddlers apparently had a talent for quarrelling, as another dispute occurred in 1326/27 between the saddlers on one side, and on the other, the joiners, painters, and lorimers (coppersmiths and ironsmiths who made small metal items). On Thursday, 20 May 1326, some men on each side armed themselves and fought in Cheapside and Cripplegate, so that 'the greater part of the city was in alarm, to the great disgrace and scandal of the whole city' and even the personal intervention of the mayor and sheriffs did not dissuade the men from exchanging 'serious and outrageous blows'. The joiners, painters, and lorimers complained that the saddlers owed them huge debts, but when they tried to collect the money, the saddlers only hurled offensive words at them. Furthermore, they said, the 'great lords of the realm' gave their old saddles to their servants, who sold them back to the saddlers, who deceitfully tried to sell them on as though they were new. Although the king, Edward II, met the mayor, Hamo Chigwell, the sheriffs, Gilbert Mordon and John Coton, and the two dozen aldermen in his chamber in the Tower on 20 June 1326 to try to resolve the issue, it was not until May 1327 that the warring parties met in the Guildhall and came to a 'final peace and accord'.[37]

In August 1340, a massive argument took place between groups of fishmongers and skinners, and the fishmonger Ralph Turk was stabbed to death by several skinners including one called Lyttle Jakke or Little

Jack. The quarrel blew up into something deeply serious when, on the same day as the attack on Ralph, a violent fight between the two misteries resulted in the fishmonger Thomas Haunsard threatening the mayor of London, Andrew Aubrey, with a drawn sword (see also Chapter 3 above).[38]

Killing in a Frenzy and Suicide

People who committed murder during what was called *frensy* in Middle English or *frenesia* in Latin were generally not executed and were treated with a surprising amount of compassion. An inquisition was held to determine whether the person had killed feloniously or in a frenzy, and only if the killing was found to be felonious was the person executed. In the early 1300s, Agnes Birley of Derbyshire killed her daughter Rohese, and was imprisoned in Nottingham. Agnes was released and pardoned in July 1306 after the local justices determined that 'she killed her in a fit of frenzy'. Katherine Ronges of Messing in Essex killed Alice Charles of Maldon in July 1371. The two women were strangers, and when they encountered one another, Katherine killed Alice by throwing 'great tiles and sea-coal' at her head. She was found to be insane and was not punished, and the word 'felonious' was not used to describe her killing of Alice.[39]

In Norfolk sometime in 1270, while Richard Cheddestan and his wife (whose name was not recorded) were coming home from the market, Richard tried to drown himself in a water-filled pit, but his wife pulled him out and saved him, and they went home. Sometime later, his wife had to go out to buy some necessities, leaving Richard at home with their two children. Richard killed them. His wife returned home and cried out with grief at seeing what has happened, and Richard killed her then tried to hang himself. Neighbours, hearing the commotion, rushed in, and though they were too late to save the woman's life, they prevented Richard from taking his own. Richard was imprisoned in Norwich and pleaded not guilty when it came to trial. The jurors found that he committed these awful crimes while in a frenzy, and he remained in prison rather than being executed. Six years later, John Lovetot, the judge at the trial, was charged with finding out whether it was now safe for Richard Cheddestan to be released. John discovered that Richard was currently sensible, but that 'it cannot be said that he is so far restored to sanity as to be set free without danger, especially in the heat of summer'. A century later in Turvey near Bedford, on 24 October 1372, Edmund Mordant or Mordaunt killed his wife, Ellen. An investigation a couple of weeks later found that Edmund 'in his madness slew Ellen his wife' and on the same day, 'being in his madness' still, drowned himself in a nearby pond. The couple had a son, Robert, who, born on 29 October 1355, was not quite 17 at the time. Thankfully, Robert Mordant did not fall victim to his father's murderous insanity and was still alive decades later.[40]

Suicide appears to have been relatively uncommon in late medieval England, perhaps because of religious prohibitions on it, at least in part. William Godeshalve, declared to have been insane (*lunaticus*) killed himself with a knife in the London home of Cecily Clare in late 1237 or 1238. His relationship to Cecily was not specified, though his chattels, worth 2 shillings, were forfeit because he took his own life, and were seized by the sheriffs of London. Alice Warewyk of London also committed suicide when she drowned in the Thames in the evening of 5 February 1339. The jurors learned that she had been *non compos mentis* for half a year, and that she ran out of her home 'in a wild state' to the port of Dowgate a few hundred yards away and threw herself into the river. Thomas Clerck, 'afflicted with frenzy', killed himself with his own knife on 1 September 1282 in Claughton, Lancashire, and sometime in 1346, Agnes, wife of John Smythesson of Middleton in Northamptonshire, went out into their garden one night 'with evil intent', climbed a tree, and hanged herself from it. The rope she used was valued at ½d as *deodand* and the tree at 3d, and it was subsequently cut down. Other Northamptonshire victims who took their own lives were Agnes Martyn of Weston by Welland near the border of Northamptonshire and Leicestershire, who hanged herself in her barn sometime in 1348; Hugh Brochale of Geddington in 1352, who also hanged himself in a barn and was discovered there by his wife Agnes; and Walter Wonge, parson of the church of Hannington, who hanged himself from a beam in 1354. The local communities where these people had lived buried them all *atte landymere*, literally 'at the boundary', i.e. in unconsecrated ground at or close to the border with the next township.[41]

Chapter 6

Family Gangs and Notorious Knights (1)

In the afternoon of Sunday, 19 January 1326, Sir Roger Belers rode from his home in the Leicestershire village of Kirby Bellars towards Leicester, where he had been invited to dine with Henry of Lancaster, the royally born earl of Leicester. Sir Roger was a wealthy and important man in late middle age, a baron and treasurer of the Exchequer, a commissioner of oyer et terminer, and a landowner in six counties. He was married to a much younger wife, Alice, with whom he had two young sons: 7-year-old Roger, the elder son and heir, and Thomas.[1] Once an adherent of Henry of Lancaster's older brother Thomas, who had been beheaded on the orders of their cousin Edward II in March 1322, Sir Roger Belers was now associated with King Edward's detested chamberlain and co-ruler, Hugh Despenser the Younger, lord of Glamorgan, though did his best to hold onto his Lancastrian allegiances as well.

While passing through the village of Rearsby 5 miles into his journey, Sir Roger was surrounded by a large group of men. One of them, Ralph Zouche, son of the lord of Lubbesthorpe 12 miles from Rearsby, drove a knife into his heart and killed him.[2] Edward II, 120 miles away in Norwich, heard of the murder five days later, and appointed three men, all of them former or present associates of the powerful house of Lancaster, to investigate. The investigation took a few weeks, and on 1 March, those responsible for Belers's murder were named. Alongside Ralph Zouche, they included Ralph's brother Roger and their cousins Ivo (whose name is also recorded as Eudo or Eon) and John Zouche, sons of the lord of Harringworth in Northamptonshire 22 miles from Rearsby, and four brothers called Eustace, Robert, Walter, and Richard Folville, the last of whom was parson of the church of Teigh in Leicestershire.

Thomas Folville, another brother, was charged with aiding Eustace to flee from England, though not with complicity in the murder of Roger Belers. The king also ordered the arrest of the eldest Folville brother, John, on 16 February, though it seems to have been determined shortly afterwards that he was not in fact involved.[3]

Some of Roger Belers's killers fled from England to France to evade capture and punishment, and Ivo Zouche, who was about 28 and the father of a 4-year-old son, died in Paris on 27 April 1326.[4] On 25 March 1326, Edward II had given Ivo's father William, Lord Zouche of Harringworth, permission for himself and the men of his household to bear arms, contrary to his general prohibition on carrying weapons, so that Lord Zouche 'may not suffer attack by evildoers who threaten him in many ways'.[5] This suggests that adherents of the murdered Roger Belers were threatening Zouche in revenge for his son's part in Belers's murder. Ivo's cousin Roger Zouche, brother of the man who had knifed Belers to death, was captured and imprisoned in Leicester, though managed to escape and subsequently fled overseas. Edmund Ashby, the newly appointed sheriff of Leicestershire and Warwickshire, was himself arrested and imprisoned for allowing him to do so.[6] Ralph Zouche himself, who had stabbed Belers, was believed on 14 March 1326 to have fled to Wales with some of his associates including his cousin, Ivo Zouche's younger brother John, and the Folville brothers Eustace, Robert, and Walter.[7] Ralph's father Sir Roger Zouche, lord of Lubbesthorpe, was indicted in 1326 for 'assenting to and counselling the death of' Roger Belers, and also fled from justice. He was outlawed, though in October 1329 was appointed sheriff of Leicestershire and Warwickshire for a year and was reappointed in March 1334. The fate of Ralph Zouche himself is unclear.[8]

The murder of Sir Roger Belers in early 1326 was not the first criminal act carried out or aided by the Folville brothers of Leicestershire, though was by far the most notorious they had committed until then and was the one that brought them to national attention. There were seven Folville brothers in total, and they came from the landowning class: the Folville family owned the manor of Ashby Folville in Leicestershire, which lies just 5 miles from Roger Belers's seat at Kirby Bellars and about the same distance from Rearsby, where Belers was murdered. Determining the family's exact pedigree is difficult, not least because so many male members of the family were called either Eustace or John. At any rate, the eldest of the seven Folville brothers was John. He married Mabel, daughter of Geoffrey de la Mare of Northamptonshire, in or before October 1315, and was still alive in the late 1340s. Eustace, whose name often appeared as Stacy or Staci in his own lifetime, was the next eldest, and had a son named John who was born sometime before January 1336.[9] The birth order of the other five Folville brothers, Robert, Walter, Richard, Thomas, and Laurence, is unclear. Richard Folville pursued an ecclesiastical career as a parson, though his six brothers remained in the secular world. Yet another John Folville, who was probably an uncle or cousin of the seven brothers, was parson of Rearsby. This John, his brother Ralph Folville, and his servant William Fisshe were robbed and killed sometime before 10 October 1327 in Hoby, 6 miles from Ashby Folville. A few months later, Robert Folville, one of the seven brothers, complained that he had been assaulted near Ashby Folville, and one of the men he named as his attackers was Ralph Beler or Belers, presumably a relative of the dead Sir Roger Belers.[10] The Folville family swam in a sea of violence, crime, feuding, and murder.

Roger Belers's killing is often assumed to have been connected to national politics, thanks to his association with Hugh Despenser the Younger, the richest and most powerful man in England between 1322 and 1326 and by far the most hated. It might well, however, have been a local vendetta instead, as Belers was growing more powerful in Leicestershire politics in the mid-1320s and had put some people's noses out of joint. Whatever the real motive for the attack, the Zouches, the Folvilles, and their associates had timed it well. A few months later, on 24 September 1326, Edward II's disaffected queen Isabella of France and her allies invaded England from the Continent with an army of mercenaries, intending to bring down the hated Hugh Despenser. Exactly two months after their arrival in England, Despenser was executed in Hereford, and two months after that, in January 1327, Edward II was forced to abdicate his throne to his and Isabella's 14-year-old son Edward III. The dowager queen and her ally Roger Mortimer, lord of Wigmore, made the first earl of March in 1328, were the real rulers of England during the young king's minority. The men who had fled abroad after killing Roger Belers returned to their homeland with the queen and Mortimer, and were pardoned for the murder on 11 February 1327, ten days after the teenage Edward III's coronation.[11]

In October 1330, the month before his eighteenth birthday, Edward III overthrew his mother and Roger Mortimer and began ruling his own kingdom. Making his intentions and his attitudes perfectly clear, on 18 December 1330 the young king ordered the arrest of three brothers named James, Nicholas, and John Coterel – who formed another notorious criminal gang in the north of England – and the Folville brothers Eustace, Robert, Richard, Laurence, and Walter. They were all to be taken to Nottingham Castle and imprisoned there.[12] John, the eldest Folville, who stood somewhat apart from his younger brothers' criminal gang, was not included in the order, and neither was Thomas Folville, perhaps because he was the only one of the six younger brothers who had not played a role in Roger Belers's murder. If the Folvilles were ever imprisoned at all in and after late 1330, however, it was certainly not for long, and their criminal career soon continued. In January 1331, Eustace, Robert, and Walter, as well as their eldest brother John, were accused by Henry, Lord Beaumont, a French-born nobleman who owned large estates in Lincolnshire and Leicestershire, of stealing ten horses, six oxen and forty sheep of his.[13]

Eustace Folville complained in June 1331 that his house in Teigh had been attacked by Sir Robert Coleville, lord of Castle Bytham in Lincolnshire, 10 miles away (William Barkeston, one of the Folvilles' close associates who took part in Belers's murder, came from Castle Bytham). Coleville and a group of his associates broke down Eustace's doors, surrounded his chamber, and assaulted him. This might have been an attempt to follow Edward III's order of the previous December to arrest the Folvilles. William Causton, apparently a neighbour who responded to Eustace's raising of the hue and cry, shot off arrows and killed Edmund Gedding, one of Robert Coleville's associates, then William Helpeston of Pickworth, who had also come with Coleville, killed Causton with his sword.[14]

On 14 January 1332, six years almost to the day after the murder of Roger Belers, the Folvilles carried out perhaps their most audacious and infamous attack: near Waltham on the Wolds, between Melton Mowbray in Leicestershire and Grantham in Lincolnshire, they kidnapped Richard Willoughby, a well-known judge who was a future chief justice of the court of King's Bench. They kept him captive for a while, taking him from place to place so that no one knew where he was, and demanded a ransom of 1,300 marks (£867). The three Coterel brothers James, Nicholas and John, and another knight named Roger Savage, were also involved, as was Geoffrey Maxeye, who was indicted and imprisoned.

Geoffrey was one of only a few of the Folville gang's associates who was ever apprehended and brought to justice. Another associate who took part in Willoughby's abduction was a woman, Alice, referred to as 'late the wife of John Folville of Teigh', who was perhaps the seven brothers' mother. Alice was captured and taken to Stamford, where she was seen in person by King Edward III himself and the sheriff of Lincolnshire, then imprisoned in Lincoln.[15] A few years later in 1340, Richard Willoughby would be arraigned on the grounds that he had 'perverted and sold the laws like oxen or cows' while Edward III was absent from England. It may be that the Folvilles thought they had a genuine grievance against him.[16]

In November 1332, Robert Folville, though not his six brothers, was given a 'general pardon … for all rebellions, felonies and trespasses' by Edward III at the request of the king's twin cousins Edward and William de Bohun, grandsons of Edward I, and the king's friends Sir John Grey of Rotherfield and Sir William Montacute.[17] These four men were all highly influential and very close to the king: William de Bohun and William Montacute would be made earls of Northampton and Salisbury respectively in 1337 (Edward de Bohun drowned in 1334 or would certainly have been ennobled as well), and John Grey was one of the founder members of the Order of the Garter in the late 1340s. Robert Folville went overseas in the service of William de Bohun, now earl of Northampton, in October 1337, and was pardoned again by Edward III, this time for outlawry in Lincolnshire.[18] Eustace 'Stacy' Folville took part in another criminal act in or not long before December 1333 when he and six other men (none of whom were his brothers) abducted a woman named Elizabeth, wife of Henry Hockele, from her home in Wolverton in Warwickshire. The seven men also stole some of Elizabeth and Henry's goods, and at the time that the writ to arrest them was issued on 15 December 1333, they were still holding Elizabeth captive. Either Henry Hockele himself or his father of the same name served as sheriff of Leicestershire and Warwickshire from February 1333 until March 1334.[19]

Edward III ordered the arrest of the parson of Teigh, Richard Folville, on 18 February 1340, and decreed that he was to be imprisoned in the Tower of London. One of the four noblemen given this order was Sir Robert Coleville, lord of Castle Bytham, the man who had attacked Eustace Folville's house in Teigh in 1331.[20] Coleville was to be the Folvilles' nemesis. He was born in the Suffolk village of Bawdsey on 20 October 1304 as the son and heir of Edmund Coleville and Margaret Ufford and lived until January 1363.[21] Robert Coleville was well connected: his cousin Robert Ufford, born in 1298, was a friend of Edward III, who made him earl of Suffolk in 1337.

A letter sent by Pope Clement VI in July 1343 reveals Richard Folville's fate at the hands of Robert Coleville. Clement, admitting that Richard was 'a man guilty of homicide, theft and other crimes', stated that he and his accomplices were pursued to his church by Robert Coleville and barricaded themselves inside. Robert's men surrounded the church, and Richard shot at them with arrows, killing one of Robert's men and wounding others. When Richard Folville ran out of arrows, Robert Coleville had the doors of the church broken down, dragged Richard outside, and summarily beheaded him on the spot. For this action, Pope Clement ordered Robert and his men to go around all the churches in the district, naked except for underclothes, and to be beaten with a rod as penance for laying hands on a churchman.[22] Richard Folville's death marked the end of the family's criminal career, though his brother Eustace, the most notorious member of the gang, lived until 1347.

The brothers Simon and Thomas Beltoft of Nottinghamshire were other thuggish, yet relatively highly born, men active in the first half of the fourteenth century. They were probably relatives of Sir Roger Beltoft of Lincolnshire (d. 1304) and Roger's son and heir William (*c.* 1299/1300–22).[23] An early instance of Simon's violent career dates to September 1313, when he was one of a group of men accused by Thomas Bekyngham of killing his brother John Bekyngham. Simon subsequently launched a counter-accusation that Thomas Bekyngham and Robert Bekyngham, a parson and another of Thomas's brothers, had assaulted and falsely imprisoned him.[24] It was perhaps in connection with this situation that Simon was accused in November 1314 of 'violently assaulting' William Aune, constable of Tickhill Castle and a close ally of the three violent and criminal Coterel brothers, while William was holding court in Wheatley, Nottinghamshire. Simon also 'mocked and threatened' William Aune and drew his sword on him in full court, whereupon William's valet Hugh Carter struck Simon in the throat with his own sword. Edward II ordered Simon Beltoft's arrest in May 1315 on the grounds that he was 'the cause of the contests and debates' between himself and William Aune.[25]

Taking a sword to the throat did not check Simon's career, and in January 1319, he, his brother Thomas and a few others were accused of breaking into the house of William Dodekyn in Pilham, Lincolnshire, and stealing from him.[26] A far more serious and shocking incident occurred in Clayworth, Nottinghamshire, in or not long before August 1321, when John Carewell or Cardewell stated that Simon, Thomas, and several others had 'torn out his eyes, cut out his tongue and inflicted other enormities on him'. This also had something to do with William Aune in some way, as the royal writ to arrest Simon was sent to William, and Simon and his associates were said to be 'lurking' in Tickhill, 10 miles from Clayworth, at the time that Edward II ordered their arrest (the king stated that 'the deed is so horrible'). The two Beltoft brothers were named first in a list of twenty-one people who had carried out the appalling attack, three of whom were women. Simon and Thomas were captured and imprisoned in Tickhill Castle, though more than six years later in November 1327, the unfortunate John Carewell was still pursuing legal action against them and some of their associates.[27]

At some point, Thomas Beltoft escaped from prison in Tickhill, and sometime before November 1327, Simon had obviously escaped or had been released as well, as he was appointed as one of the arrayers (the men who provided soldiers with their armour and equipment) in Nottinghamshire. By October 1328, Simon had been knighted.[28] Soon afterwards, the Beltoft brothers joined the rebellion of the royally born Henry of Lancaster, earl of Lancaster and Leicester, the man with whom Roger Belers had been on his way to dine when he was murdered in January 1326. Lancaster had grown disillusioned with the rule of his niece Isabella of France, Edward II's widow, and her ally Roger Mortimer, the new earl of March, during the minority of Edward II and Isabella's son Edward III. Lancaster took an armed force to Bedford in late 1328, and Simon and Thomas Beltoft were part of it and were therefore ordered to be arrested by the sheriff of Nottinghamshire.[29] They might instead have fled abroad, as some of the earl of Lancaster's other associates certainly did in 1329 and 1330, including the French-born Henry, Lord Beaumont, who was to accuse three of the Folville brothers of stealing some of his livestock in early 1331. After Edward III overthrew Queen Isabella and Roger Mortimer in October 1330 and ordered the arrest of the Folville brothers and the Coterel brothers, he pardoned Lord Beaumont and many other men who had gone overseas because of their opposition to

Isabella and Mortimer and invited them to come home. Simon Beltoft was pardoned for outlawry in Nottinghamshire on 20 December 1330, and the timing suggests that he had recently returned to England with other rebels, perhaps with his brother, with whom he was closely associated for many years. Thomas Beltoft, somewhat improbably, joined the clergy in or before 1330.[30]

In October 1328, Simon Kynardesley (or Kinnersley), who served as sheriff of Lincolnshire from October 1327 until September 1328, accused the two Beltoft brothers and other men, including three whose name was also Beltoft and who were presumably relatives, of breaking into his manor of Clayworth Woodhouse in Nottinghamshire and stealing his horses, oxen and other livestock and fish.[31] And in or not long after December 1330, Simon's widow Margery Kynardesley accused Simon Beltoft of wanting to kill her, and stated that he was falsely claiming to have been exiled with Lord Beaumont, who had recently returned to England. The petition made mention of Simon Beltoft's pardon for outlawry, issued on 20 December 1330.[32] By April 1332, Simon Beltoft was detained in Newgate prison in London for 'maiming and breach of the peace'. Possibly, the maiming referred to his assault on John Carewell eleven years earlier, but it is certainly not impossible he had done something similar to someone else. Simon was still alive and at liberty in July 1335 and thereafter disappears from written record.[33]

Chapter 7

Family Gangs and Notorious Knights (2)

Sir Henry Leybourne (or Leyburn) of Kent was born in *c.* 1276 as a younger son of William, Lord Leybourne (*c.* 1242–1310) and Juliane de Sandwich (*c.* 1245–1328), both of whom held sizeable estates in Kent and Sussex as their inheritance from their families. Henry was knighted in or before December 1298.[1] His older brother Thomas was their parents' heir, and they also had several sisters, one of whom, Agnes (d. September 1324), was the abbess of Malling in Kent.[2] Sir Thomas Leybourne died in May 1307 several years before their father William, leaving his 3-year-old daughter, Juliana, as the family's heir instead.[3] Juliana Leybourne lived until 1367 and was the older half-sister of the earl of Warwick by her mother's second marriage, was the mother of the earl of Pembroke by her own first marriage, and became countess of Huntingdon by her third and last marriage.

Although deprived of the opportunity to inherit his family's extensive estates by the existence of his well-connected young niece, Henry Leybourne did own some lands: on 30 July 1297, he was granted the manor of Byfleet in Surrey by his brother-in-law Geoffrey Lucy, and must have been at least 21 at the time, so cannot have been born later than 30 July 1276. He seems to have given the manor to Piers Gaveston, earl of Cornwall, by June 1308, and after Gaveston's murder four years later in June 1312, Byfleet passed to the king, Edward II.[4] Henry also owned some manors in Kent by right of his wife, Elizabeth Sharstede, whom he married without the required licence from the then king, Edward I, in or not long before November 1297. Elizabeth was the daughter and heir of Simon and Alice Sharstede and lost her father shortly before 3 July 1297. She was said to be 21 years old then, so was almost exactly Henry's age.[5] And Henry's long-lived mother Juliane de Sandwich, dowager Lady Leybourne, gave him two of her manors in Kent in December 1311, though a few years later in March 1318 transferred one of them to John, Lord Hastings, probably on the occasion of his marrying her granddaughter and chief heir, 14-year-old Juliana.[6]

Piers Gaveston, made earl of Cornwall shortly after Edward II's accession to the throne in July 1307, was the king's 'favourite' and probably his lover, and Henry Leybourne was one of the knights in Gaveston's retinue.[7] Like Gaveston himself, Henry was a keen jouster. In November 1302, Edward I ordered his arrest for holding jousts at his manor of Byfleet although the king had forbidden them, and in October 1306, Henry and Piers Gaveston were among the young knights said to have deserted the king on campaign in Scotland to go jousting overseas. Edward I ordered sheriffs across England to arrest all the young knights and confiscate their lands and goods.[8] A jousting tournament was held in Dunstable, Bedfordshire in March or April 1309 as a cover for several noblemen to air their grievances against Edward II and discuss possible solutions. Sir Henry Leybourne was present in the retinue of the king's eldest nephew Gilbert de Clare (b. 1291), earl of Gloucester, who was Piers Gaveston's brother-in-law; Gaveston himself had been exiled from England in June 1308, went to Ireland and returned to England in June 1309. Henry appeared seventy-eighth in the list of Gloucester's enormous retinue of ninety-one knights at the Dunstable tournament.[9]

Not entirely unusually for a fourteenth-century knight, especially one who was a younger son and not an heir, Henry Leybourne turned to a life of crime and lawlessness. In May 1317, he was pardoned for outlawry in Berkshire for non-appearance before the justices of oyer et terminer after breaking into a park in Stratfield Mortimer and stealing deer. The park belonged to Roger Mortimer of Wigmore, an important young nobleman – later the first earl of March and co-ruler of England during Edward III's minority alongside Queen Isabella – who was another of the knights who had deserted the Scottish campaign in 1306 to go jousting overseas. Despite the pardon, however, Henry was still detained in the Tower of London in November 1317 for this 'trespass committed' against Roger.[10] Henry was, in fairness, also sometimes a victim as well as a perpetrator of crime: sometime before November 1315, a Henry Tyremarsh broke into his house in Chatham, Kent, assaulted his servants, then burned his goods as well as the house. Tyremarsh was subsequently imprisoned in the Fleet prison in London.[11]

Henry Leybourne took part in the Contrariant rebellion of 1321/22 against Edward II and his powerful chamberlain and co-ruler Hugh Despenser the Younger, lord of Glamorgan. He perhaps followed in the footsteps of Bartholomew Badlesmere, an important baron of Henry's native Kent whose sister Elizabeth was the predecessor of Henry's sister Agnes Leybourne as abbess of Malling. The two men's association went at least as far back as 1310.[12] Edward II sent Badlesmere, his household steward, to spy on the rebel lords and report their movements to him, but Badlesmere switched sides and joined them. This decision was to result in his grotesque death by drawing, hanging and quartering in April 1322 after the king defeated the Contrariants. Henry Leybourne, meanwhile, fought against the royal army at the battle of Boroughbridge in March 1322, and was captured during the royalist victory. Unlike twenty or so other rebels, he evaded execution, but was imprisoned in Scarborough Castle, Yorkshire. He was still there in December 1325, and in 1326 was transferred to Devizes Castle in Wiltshire. He escaped from Devizes sometime that year, and was pardoned 'for breaking prison' at the start of Edward III's reign in early 1327.[13]

Sometime in 1326, apparently while still imprisoned in Devizes Castle, Henry killed a man named William Cobham. Although he was pardoned in 1327 for escaping from the castle, his lands were declared forfeit on account of the murder, and he was outlawed. He finally received a pardon from the king on 25 November 1330, shortly after Edward III overthrew his mother Queen Isabella and her associate Roger Mortimer of Wigmore, first earl of March (this was the same Roger whose park in Stratfield Mortimer Henry had broken into many years earlier). By then, Henry had joined the retinue of Sir Hugh Audley, later earl of Gloucester, a nephew-in-law and former favourite of Edward II, and the only one who survived the reign.[14] In March 1332, Henry Leybourne was one of five men who broke into the park of Henry of Lancaster, earl of Lancaster and Leicester, near the Hampshire village of Weston Patrick and stole deer, and in June 1334 was one of the men who assaulted the servants of John Mereworth in Wateringbury in Kent and stole John's goods.[15]

Henry was still alive on 18 October 1335 when he was, yet again, pardoned for outlawry: he had burgled the house of Henry Clerynbaude in Elham in Kent – Elham was one of the manors given to him many years earlier by his mother – and stolen 40 shillings. At the same time, he was also pardoned for 'any other felonies and trespasses of which he is indicted', and his pardon was requested by the king's friend Sir William Clinton, later earl of Huntingdon, who was the third husband of Henry's niece Juliana. Henry was dead by 14 April 1337, and evidently had no surviving children from his forty-year marriage to Elizabeth Sharstede (who outlived him), as Juliana was his heir.[16] In his roughly six decades of life, Henry Leybourne managed to be outlawed at least three times, spent at least four years in prison in the 1320s, and was imprisoned in the Tower of London in the 1310s as well.

Henry's contemporary Sir Roger Swynnerton of Staffordshire was born around 1280 or 1282 and succeeded his namesake father (d. 1298) as lord of the village of Swynnerton, north of Stafford and south of Stoke-on-Trent.[17] An early instance of Roger's violent career was his murder of Henry Salt in Stafford sometime between July 1307 and July 1308. An inquisition of 1320 found that Roger murdered Henry because Henry used 'insulting language' towards him, though there is evidence that Henry and another man had previously 'beaten and wounded' Roger in Stafford, so it was perhaps a revenge attack. After he was indicted before the sheriff and coroners of Staffordshire for Henry Salt's murder, Roger Swynnerton forced all the eyewitnesses, including Robert Bythewater and Roger Walton, to pay him large amounts of money and to swear that they would not testify against him in court. He even forced the coroner who had indicted him, Roger Aston, to pay him £100, an enormous sum equivalent to several hundred thousand pounds in modern terms. Another lawless event occurred in or not long before May 1310. Roger Swynnerton and his younger brothers Richard and John, and a group of their followers, broke into Joan Gresley's home in Drakelow, Derbyshire, stole her goods, abducted her, and detained her in the village of Swynnerton for an unstated reason, presumably rape. Joan was the wife of Peter Gresley, who was himself called a 'common malefactor' and had once cut off a man's left hand. Several of Joan and Peter's four or more sons, not entirely unsurprisingly, also committed murder.[18]

In 1320, Roger Swynnerton went overseas in the retinue of Bartholomew Badlesmere, the Kent baron with whom Henry Leybourne was also associated at this time. Roger did, however, remain loyal to the king during the Contrariant rebellion, unlike Henry, and in March 1322 was one of the three men appointed by Edward II to render judgement on Sir Henry Tyes, a Contrariant rebel who was subsequently executed.[19] Roger's namesake eldest son, evidently a chip off the old block, was old enough to commit a murder in July 1324 when he killed a forester named William Wolf in the village of Hopwas near Tamworth. Wolf had tried to arrest a man called Roger Wetewode because he was travelling through the local forest at night – it was against the law to be out and about after curfew – and Roger Swynnerton the younger 'came up suddenly and killed' Wolf. Both he and Wetewode fled. One of the justices who heard this case was Sir Roger Belers, stabbed to death by the Zouches and the Folvilles eighteen months later.[20]

Despite his and his family's brutal careers, Edward II appointed Roger Swynnerton as 'superior keeper of the peace' in Staffordshire and keeper of the town of Stafford in November 1317, and in August 1321 made him constable of the Tower of London. In April 1325, he pardoned him for all murders committed before Christmas 1324.[21] As many others did, even those who had previously shown loyalty to Edward II, Roger switched allegiance to Queen Isabella during the revolution of 1326/27 which brought about Edward's forced abdication. Isabella and Edward's son Edward III trusted Roger as much as his father had done, telling the earl of Surrey in September 1336 that he was sending Roger to him 'on affairs touching the safety of the realm'. In 1328 and 1330, Roger was a knight of the young king's household, and in 1330, his third son and ultimate heir Thomas, then probably in his mid-teens or thereabouts, was named as a squire in the royal household.[22]

Roger Swynnerton's career shows him to be brutal and corrupt, but also, so influential and well connected that he was all but above the law, and in the fourteenth century, it was possible for a man who committed murder to be appointed to serve as a keeper of the peace. Roger died in March 1338 in his late 50s, leaving at least four living sons; his namesake eldest son, the murderer of William Wolf, had predeceased him, and his second, Robert, born in 1312, joined the Church.[23] As well as his sons, Roger had a number of younger brothers, two of whom also took part in the attack on Joan Gresley in 1310, and they were as violent as he. Sir Richard Swynnerton, probably the brother closest in age to Roger, murdered the parson of Penkridge south of Stafford, Henry Persoun, in his own home in July 1315, beat Thomas of Warwick almost to death in the middle of Newcastle-under-Lyme market in 1319 or 1320 for insulting Roger, and cut off the hand of a chaplain called William Whytewyk during a fair in Penkridge in 1322. Richard was described, hardly surprisingly, as a 'common malefactor and beater of men', and was also indicted for preventing Henry Cresswell, the local coroner, from 'performing his office on the body of Henry Persoun', i.e. the murdered parson of Penkridge.[24] John Swynnerton (d. 1340), another brother, abducted Nicholas Picheford in Wolverhampton in 1322 and imprisoned him in Stafford until Picheford paid him £20, while he, John, was serving as sheriff of Staffordshire and Shropshire. John and Nicholas, yet another Swynnerton brother, murdered a man named Robert Esnyngton or Essington in 1314 by shooting a barbed arrow called a *clotherewe*, from a bow made of Spanish yew, into his heart. Robert died soon afterwards in his wife Margaret's arms. Finally, Stephen Swynnerton, parson of Swynnerton and presumably a relative of the brothers, killed Thomas Vernay in Draycote on account of an 'old quarrel' between them.[25] It is instructive to note that just as the eldest Swynnerton brother, Roger, held high office while conducting a murderous, lawless career, so too did John, one of the younger brothers; he was appointed as the sheriff of two counties at the start of 1322.

Sir Henry Cresswell, the Staffordshire coroner whom Richard Swynnerton prevented from examining the parson of Penkridge's body after Richard murdered him, was yet another high-ranking law and order official who employed considerable violence on occasion, and he was, like Richard Swynnerton, described by royal justices as a 'common malefactor and beater of men'. Around Easter 1317, Henry was one of the men accused of killing an Alexander Swynnerton (probably not a relative of the Swynnerton brothers and just someone who lived in the village of Swynnerton), and in May 1320, Sir Richard Swynnerton, the second eldest Swynnerton brother, accused Henry and others of assaulting him and stealing his goods.[26] A few years later, Henry became involved in a longstanding feud concerning the church of St Editha in Church Eaton (for which, see Chapter 8 below). He had a brother called Thomas Cresswell who was also involved in this feud, and, confusingly, Henry's sons were also called Henry and Thomas Cresswell. In or not long before June 1334, these four men killed three others named Richard and William Burton and Roger Sabyn and were outlawed for non-appearance before the justices of oyer et terminer. The four 'became vagabond', and their lands and goods were seized.[27]

Stephen, John, and Thomas Dunheved came from Dunchurch in Warwickshire and were the sons of John Dunheved, who died sometime between May 1305 and April 1308. Their mother, or perhaps stepmother, was named Eustachia, and John, the second son, burned down her grange in Dunchurch sometime before January 1311 and destroyed her corn. John Dunheved and Oliver Dunheved – who was either a cousin of the three brothers or was the fourth and youngest brother – were accused of raping Edith Grasbrok but failed to appear in court, and John was outlawed in Gloucestershire sometime before July 1316.[28] As noted in Chapter 4 above, John murdered his youngest brother or cousin, Oliver, in his native Dunchurch in 1325 and would himself have been killed in retaliation one night a few months later had he been at home with his wife Margery.[29] John's older brother Stephen Dunheved, their father's heir, abjured the realm at an uncertain date before 1322 after committing what must have been a serious felony, though Edward II must have pardoned him and allowed him to come home, as he was active in England in and after 1322. Before Stephen left England, he granted the manor of Dunchurch to Sir John Somery for life, and it reverted to Stephen's next eldest brother John Dunheved after Somery's death in 1322, though Stephen was still alive and had returned to England by then.[30] The third Dunheved brother, Thomas, was a Dominican friar. He was made a papal chaplain in September 1325, which evidently went to his head, as the pope, John XXII, wrote to the prior provincial of the Dominicans in July 1326 asking him to 'keep under obedience and correct' Thomas, who 'considers himself thereby freed from observance of the [Dominican] rule'. The *Lanercost* chronicler called Thomas 'a man of religion, acting irreligiously'.[31]

Both Stephen and Thomas Dunheved were passionate supporters of Edward II after his forced abdication in 1327 and led a group of men who temporarily freed the former king from his incarceration in Berkeley Castle, Gloucestershire. They attacked and sacked the castle sometime in the summer of 1327.[32] The Dunheveds and their men scattered after their attack on Berkeley; Thomas, the friar, was captured not far from their home in Dunchurch, and died in prison in Yorkshire, probably in Pontefract Castle.[33] Stephen made it as far as London, and on 1 July 1327, the mayor and sheriffs of the city were ordered to arrest him. He was sent to Newgate prison, but managed to escape shortly before 7 June 1329, and he was still alive and at liberty in March 1330.[34]

His brother John was still alive in May 1329, when he acknowledged a massive debt of £1,000 to John Pecche, lord of Hampton in Arden, the man who had ridden to Dunchurch in the middle of the night to kill John and apparently to burn down his house several years earlier.[35] Entirely unsurprisingly for a fourteenth-century man who rode to another man's home to kill him in the middle of the night, Sir John Pecche held high office. He was appointed as the keeper of the town and castle of Warwick in November 1321 during the minority of the heir to the earldom of Warwick (Thomas Beauchamp, b. 1314) and was also the constable of Corfe Castle in Dorset and Dover Castle in Kent, and warden of the Cinque Ports, in the 1320s.[36]

Chapter 8

Feuds, Vendettas, Extortion, and Piracy

Medieval English people tended to be volatile and emotional, the famed 'stiff upper lip' being a much later development. Complex family feuds and vendettas were frequently and enthusiastically pursued, such as the grudge between the Swynnerton brothers and the Stafford brothers mentioned in pp. 70–71 below.

On 17 March 1326, the royal justices John Stonor and John Denum sat on a special commission in Tamworth to 'enquire into illicit assemblies, homicides, depredations, burnings and other damages' in Staffordshire. The sheriff of Staffordshire was commanded to summon twenty-four knights or other men from each hundred and borough of the county. The main reason for the justices' commission was a complex feud running since early 1321 between many of the important families of Staffordshire over, of all things, who should be the rector of Church Eaton, a village 6 miles from Stafford. William Ipstones (or Ipstanes or Ibstones) and Thomas Brumpton both claimed the church of St Editha in the village, and both enjoyed much support among the knights and gentry of the county, and their quarrel became extraordinarily complex and violent.

Both Ipstones and Brumpton 'collected a multitude of armed men' in and before August 1325, with the result that around 120 men rode armed around Stafford and Church Eaton that summer and terrified the local populace. William Ipstones managed to gain control of the church building and held it by force against his rival, then he and his allies were ejected by a large armed group of Thomas Brumpton's supporters and Brumpton himself seized the church. One of Thomas Brumpton's main supporters was his kinswoman Isabel, lady of the nearby town of Ingestre. Isabel was questioned by the justices Stonor and Denum in March 1326 on the matter, as were many of Brumpton's other supporters including the knights Roger Trumwyne, Hugh Meignil, and the brothers John, Walter and William Stafford. Sir Thomas Wyther took the side of William Ipstones, his own kinsman, as did Ipstones's brother Sir John Ipstones, John's father-in-law the local coroner and 'beater of men', Sir Henry Cresswell, Henry's brother Thomas Cresswell, and another Ipstones brother or cousin called Philip Ipstones. Several men lost their lives because of the feud, including John Cowley, John Picheford, Roger Hatton, and Robert of Draycote. Henry Cresswell admitted that he had beaten up a Walter Pykstok and extorted 12 marks from Richard Wenlok as a bribe not to beat him up. The Stafford jury taking part in the commission of March 1326 named Cresswell as a 'common malefactor and beater of men', and he was imprisoned. The Ipstones faction besieged Thomas Brumpton's mother Mary in her home at Church Eaton 'with swords, bows and arrows', and the three Ipstones brothers stole two cows, two oxen, fourteen lambs and four brass pots from Brumpton himself. For their part, Thomas Brumpton and about fifteen of his followers broke into William Ipstones's home, stole goods worth £40, and beat his servants.

The royal justices John Stonor and John Denum pointed out in March 1326 that all of this was 'manifestly in contempt of the king and against the king's peace', and the dozens of accused were bailed on condition that they appeared again on 18 July. The two antagonists both failed to appear on that date, and the sheriff of Staffordshire was unable to find them. Proceedings were thus postponed again until Monday, 6 October, but by this time the kingdom was in complete chaos because Edward II's queen, Isabella of France, had recently arrived in the country with an invasion force and the king was in the process of fleeing towards South Wales. The matter had still not been resolved by early 1328, when Pope John XXII ordered the archbishop of Canterbury to remove William Ipstones from the church of Church Eaton and restore Thomas Brumpton. If nothing else, the Church Eaton affair demonstrates that English people of the 1300s could carry out family feuds as enthusiastically as any Sicilian, and the quarrel between the Ipstones and Brumpton families continued into the 1370s, half a century later.[1]

As noted in Chapter 7 above, Sir Richard Swynnerton accused Sir Henry Cresswell, the local coroner, of assaulting him in May 1320. Swynnerton also accused the brothers James, John, and William Stafford of taking part in the same attack. As of the late 1310s, Richard

Swynnerton was feuding with the Stafford brothers, and their father William Stafford was feuding with Richard's older brother Sir Roger. There were at least five Stafford brothers: James, John, William, Walter, and Edmund.[2] Their quarrel with the Swynnertons perhaps concerned lands or influence or perhaps was simply a personal grudge of some kind between neighbouring landowners that was all too typical in the fourteenth century.

Another feud, this one between a prior and a local lord, took place in Lincolnshire in 1312. Sir Robert Coleville of Castle Bytham, nemesis of the Folville brothers – and Richard Folville in particular – was the son of Sir Edmund Coleville, who was born in Castle Bytham on 25 January 1288 and lost his father Roger when he was just a few weeks old. Edmund was only 4 years old when his marriage to Margaret Ufford, sister of the future earl of Suffolk, was arranged in February 1292, and 16 when Margaret gave birth to their son Robert in October 1304. Edmund died shortly before 13 March 1316, aged 28.[3] Sometime not long before 27 July 1312, Edmund Coleville took part in a raid on Sempringham Priory in Lincolnshire alongside Sir Geoffrey Luttrell (1276–1345), who commissioned the *Luttrell Psalter*, now held in the British Library. The Luttrells held the manor of Irnham also in Lincolnshire, just 7 miles from the Colevilles' manor of Castle Bytham, and Sempringham Priory, founded by St Gilbert of Sempringham (d. 1189), was just a few miles from both manors.

On 27 July 1312, Edward II gave a commission of oyer et terminer to three men 'on the information of' Henry Beaumont, a French-born kinsman of the king who was an important landowner in Lincolnshire; he owned Folkingham Castle and the manor of Heckington, among others. John Camelton, prior of Sempringham, had complained that Geoffrey Luttrell, Edmund Coleville, Roger Birthorpe, and his brothers John and Thomas, and four other named men and unnamed others, 'broke his doors and walls' at the priory, stole some of his goods, and assaulted two canons called Thomas Hougate and John Irnham and some of the priory's lay servants. A few weeks later, on 7 September 1312, there is a reference to a retaliatory attack: the prior of Sempringham with Thomas Hougate, John Irnham, and ten other men were said to have raided Roger Birthorpe's home at Birthorpe, a couple of miles from Sempringham. They broke into his park and stole some of his animals, stole some of his goods, and assaulted three of his servants. Roger

Birthorpe presented a petition claiming that he had been involved in a dispute with the prior, John Camelton, and that he and some other local lords had gone in all innocence to the priory to resolve the matter, but the prior broke down his own doors to make it look as though they had done it, and raised the hue and cry against them.[4] The truth of the matter is difficult to ascertain.

Edmund Coleville's wife Margaret Ufford and her brother Robert, made earl of Suffolk in 1337, had another brother, Ralph. Ralph Ufford made an excellent marriage in 1343 to Maud of Lancaster (born *c.* 1312), dowager countess of Ulster, daughter of the earl of Lancaster and Leicester, and a close relative of King Edward III. Their marriage produced one child, Maud Ufford, born in late 1345 or early 1346. She married Thomas de Vere, earl of Oxford, and gave birth to their only child, Robert de Vere, in Earls Colne Priory in Essex on 16 January 1362. Robert was named after his great-uncle and godfather the earl of Suffolk, and his other godfather was Simon Sudbury, then bishop of London and later archbishop of Canterbury, who would be murdered in London during the Peasants' Revolt of 1381. Robert de Vere became the notorious favourite of King Richard II and died in exile in 1392; his mother Maud outlived him by more than twenty years.[5]

Maud de Vere née Ufford, countess of Oxford, must have been on good terms with the prior and convent of Earls Colne, as she gave birth to her son there – the house had been founded by one of her husband's de Vere forebears back in the early 1100s – but many years later in 1400 became embroiled in a feud with the prior. The prior, Henry Colne aka Henry Kebell, claimed that the countess and more than two dozen of her men had him assaulted and imprisoned, and dragged him around many places in Essex 'shamefully clad'. Maud countered that Henry and his own men besieged her in her home in the village of Earls Colne, where they 'threatened her with arson and other evils so that for a long time she dared not leave it'. Further, they stole six of her horses and some livestock and game from her park and beat up some of her servants and 'threw some of them in ditches'. The ultimate cause of the feud between the countess and the prior had something to do with a monk named John Preston, who claimed to be the rightful prior of Earls Colne and whom Countess Maud supported.[6] Like her uncle-in-law Edmund Coleville, Maud de Vere née Ufford was not afraid to become embroiled in a violent dispute with a man of religion.

Neither was another woman of the era, Blanche of Lancaster, who was Maud de Vere née Ufford's aunt. Blanche was born in the early 1300s as the eldest of seven children, six daughters and one son; the third of the six daughters was Maud de Vere née Ufford's mother Maud of Lancaster. Their father Henry of Lancaster, the man with whom Sir Roger Belers was on his way to dine at the time of his murder in January 1326, was a grandson of Henry III, nephew of Edward I, cousin of Edward II and the heir to his executed older brother Thomas, and their mother was Maud Chaworth, an heiress in Wales and the west of England. The only male among the seven Lancaster siblings, also named Henry and born around 1310, was their parents' sole heir. Blanche of Lancaster married Thomas, Lord Wake (b. 1298), an important nobleman and landowner in Cumberland, Yorkshire, and Lincolnshire, in 1316, and they were married for thirty-three years until Thomas died during the first great pandemic of the Black Death in May 1349. They had no children, and Blanche outlived her husband by more than three decades; by the time of her death in July 1380, she was in her mid- or late 70s and had also outlived all six of her younger siblings.[7]

In April 1320, Edward II gave Thomas Wake permission to go overseas on pilgrimage, and Thomas travelled to Santiago de Compostela with two attendants. As it happened, Thomas's parents-in-law Henry of Lancaster and Maud Chaworth were also away from England in 1320, as Henry's younger brother John of Lancaster had died in France and Henry was his heir, and travelled there to claim his lands and pay homage to his nephew the king of France for them.[8] Blanche of Lancaster was left alone in England, and was still only in her teens. Sometime between 6 June and 24 November 1320, she sent a petition to Edward II, her father's cousin, stating that one of her husband's manors – probably Bourne or Market Deeping, though she did not specify – had been attacked and ransacked by 'numerous robbers and murderers' from Spalding in Lincolnshire. They had killed some of her and Thomas Wake's servants and badly wounded and maimed others. Furthermore, the men from Spalding had removed the bodies of those whom they had killed, a most odd and unusual detail to find in a medieval petition. Blanche stated that the reason for this was that the bodies would not be found, and presumably so that the lack of evidence for murder gave the killers plausible deniability. Unfortunately, there are no other references to this attack by a group of men from Spalding, nor to the motive for it, if any.

Even though Blanche was a close relative of both the king of England and the king of France, and though Edward II's powerful chamberlain and favourite Hugh Despenser the Younger was her uncle (her mother Maud Chaworth's younger half-brother), her petition was endorsed to the effect that she had no right to action in the matter. Blanche's rather plaintive remark that 'she remains alone' in the absence of her husband and her parents abroad, and another remark that she and her attendants were too afraid to live on the manor after the murderous assault, had no effect on the two most powerful men in England at the time, despite her close familial relationship to them both.[9]

Many years later in the mid-1350s, Blanche of Lancaster, Lady Wake, became embroiled in an ill-tempered quarrel with Thomas Lisle, who had become a Dominican friar by 1322 and was made bishop of Ely by the pope in 1345.[10] No longer an ignored, abandoned teenager, Blanche was now a middle-aged widow of wealth and influence, and was well connected to the most powerful people in the realm, who decades later were much keener to help her than Edward II and Hugh Despenser had been. There was trouble between the Lancasters and the Lisles as early as July 1350, when the bishop of Ely's brother John Lisle was one of a large group of men accused of burning down some of the Lincolnshire houses of Lady Wake's brother Henry, then earl and later duke of Lancaster. In October 1354, Bishop Thomas, his brother John Lisle, and servants of the bishop burned down four or five of Blanche, Lady Wake's buildings, together with the hay and, horribly, a horse within them. A few months later, Thomas Lisle himself was convicted of robbery and arson and was ordered to pay the enormous sum of £900 to Blanche in compensation. Her servant William Holm was killed in August 1355 as part of the ongoing feud between Blanche Wake and Thomas Lisle and as part of a land dispute between their respective servants.[11]

A parliament was held in Westminster in November 1355, and Blanche, calling herself 'Blanche of Liddel', a manor of her late husband in Cumberland which she held in dower, presented a petition to her kinsman Edward III. Rather dramatically, she declared her fear that Bishop Thomas Lisle might 'vex and harass her all her life'. The king announced that he would take the dispute into his own hands (*jeo prenk la querele en ma main* in the Anglo-Norman original) and told Thomas Lisle not to leave the country. The bishop subsequently fled to the papal court in Avignon, however, apparently fearing what might become of him if he remained in England.[12] Blanche of Lancaster, Lady Wake, used her connections to come out on top in her feud with a high-ranking churchman.

In the same month that Thomas Lisle was consecrated as bishop of Ely by Clement VI, July 1345, the pope wrote a letter about one of the new bishop's servants, Richard Middleton. Richard was a priest of the diocese of Hereford and had formerly been 'in the service of a certain lord', whom Clement did not name. While out walking one day with the lord, Richard and the lord's other servants encountered an enemy of the lord, also unnamed, and the two men's retinues began a violent quarrel. Richard Middleton's former employer the unnamed lord died that same day of wounds sustained during this quarrel, while Richard himself tried unsuccessfully to kill the man who had inflicted the wounds. Pope Clement pardoned Richard for attempted murder on the grounds that 'at the time he was assisting his dying master' and gave him permission to minister in minor orders once more.[13]

Extortion and Deception

The unfortunate inhabitants of Staffordshire in the first few decades of the fourteenth century had much to contend with. As well as the violent, murderous Swynnerton brothers, the misdeeds of the coroner Henry Cresswell and the violent feud between the Ipstones and Brampton factions, they also suffered the presence of a knight called Sir John Somery (b. 1279 or 1280), lord of Dudley. It was he to whom Stephen Dunheved gave the manor of Dunchurch in Warwickshire sometime before 1322 when Stephen abjured the realm. John Somery was accused in 1311 – by the chief justice of the Court of Common Pleas, no less – of 'being more than a king' in the county of Staffordshire, and of having 'acquired such mastery in the county that no one can obtain law or justice' there. Furthermore, 'no one can dwell there unless he buys the protection of the said John'.[14] Somery comes across like a Mafia boss running an extortion racket. Sensitive to criticism, however, he accused the chief justice of the Common Pleas, Sir William Bereford, and a couple of other men who had said the same thing, of defamation.

One of the most infamous extortionists of the Middle Ages was Hugh Despenser the Younger, lord of Glamorgan (*c.* 1288–1326), the chamberlain of Edward II in the late 1310s and 1320s and executed in

November 1326 on the orders of Edward's queen Isabella of France. Hugh used his position as the king's virtual co-ruler to take lands and extort money from anyone he wished to, both men and women, both noble and common, both rich and considerably less rich. One of his victims was, oddly enough, Sir John Somery's brother-in-law and co-heir, Sir John Sutton.

When Somery died in August 1322, he left no children, and his heirs were his two sisters: Margaret, wife of John Sutton, and Joan, widow of the recently deceased Thomas Botetourt (d. July 1322).[15] Hugh Despenser the Younger, with the help of his father and two other men, arrested John Sutton on 11 February 1325. They imprisoned him in chains at Westminster for three weeks until 'through fear of death' and 'through the hardships and duress of the prison and at Hugh's persecution' he assigned eight of the manors he and his wife had inherited from John Somery to Hugh, including the castle and manor of Dudley in Staffordshire. Hugh's steward Sir John Botiller took the fealty of the Suttons' tenants on Hugh's behalf, John Sutton claimed later. He changed his story somewhat over time, stating on another occasion that Hugh had imprisoned him at Westminster on 6 March 1324 and that he wrote letters patent in favour of Hugh on 21 March that year. His release of the eight manors to Hugh Despenser the Younger was witnessed at Westminster on 12 October 1325. It seems odd that Sutton would mix up the date of his imprisonment by more than a year, and his handing over the manors to Hugh took place at least eight months after he was imprisoned, but there is so much evidence supporting his claims that it is impossible to doubt that overall, the story is genuine, if not perhaps in all the details.[16]

John and Maud Botetourt, parents-in-law of John Somery's younger sister and co-heir Joan, were also victims of Hugh Despenser. On Saturday, 14 April 1324, Hugh wrote to John Botetourt reminding him that he had previously sent a man to him to discuss certain unspecified wrongdoings which John had committed and was continuing to commit against Hugh, one of which Hugh declared to be unlawful. Hugh went on to remind John Botetourt that he considered John and his wife Maud's Buckinghamshire manor of Iselhampstead, now called Chenies, to be adequate compensation for the alleged misdemeanours, and that Maud Botetourt, of whose inheritance the manor was, had agreed to him receiving it. Hugh told John that Edward II would 'hang and draw you' if he failed to hand over Iselhampstead to him as Hugh and the king wished. Hugh ordered John to come to Kings Langley in Hertfordshire for a meeting with himself and Edward II 'this Monday morning and absolutely not before' (*iceo Lundy matyn e ne mye auant*), two days later, which was Easter Monday. Iselhampstead lay only 5 miles from Langley, so the command to Botetourt on Saturday not to come before Monday seems deliberately designed to give the baron time to become anxious about the meeting. John Botetourt duly gave the manor of Iselhampstead to Hugh Despenser the Younger on 29 April 1324 and died on 25 November that year.[17]

The Middle English word for a conman or swindler was *faitour* or *faytour*. In 1341, Thomas Beneyt, who claimed to work for the earl of Salisbury, told the mayor of London, Andrew Aubrey, that the earl wished to borrow £40 from him. Andrew, however, noticed that the earl's seal was clumsily placed on the letter which Thomas claimed was from Salisbury, and that he had never seen Thomas before. Thomas, realising that he had been spotted, 'crept away secretly' while the mayor was attending mass, but was found and caught later, despite having changed his clothes to evade detection. He admitted to having forged the letter and to taking an impression of the earl's seal from another letter, and was handed over to the earl of Salisbury, William Montacute, in person to be dealt with.[18]

John Sharryngworth was convicted of being an 'able-bodied vagabond' and a *faitour* who refused to work and pretended to be an invalid and was put on the pillory in July 1355. Richard Lynham of Somerset and John Warde of Yorkshire were condemned to the pillory for an hour on three days, Wednesday, Friday, and Saturday, 'for pretending to have suffered the loss of their tongues by robbers' in October 1382. This was done to support their false claim of being unable to work. Adam Ryebred of Spalding in Lincolnshire also got into trouble in 1381 for 'begging and pretending that he was unfit for work' when in fact he was 'strong and lusty, capable of labour and able to earn his food and clothing'. Adam was threatened with the pillory if he was ever caught begging again, because he was 'defrauding genuine beggars and poor people'.[19] Medieval England, a place where life was relentlessly hard and everyone had to pull together and do what had to be done, refused to tolerate the idle and workshy.

In London in 1327, eight bakers and two *baksters* (female bakers) came up with an ingenious method of stealing their customers' dough. When their neighbours brought their dough to be baked in their professional ovens, the bakers and baksters placed the dough on a table called a *moldingborde* (moulding-board). Unbeknown to their customers, they had all made a small hole in the table and had an accomplice sitting beneath it, who 'bit by bit craftily withdrew some of the dough aforesaid ... falsely, wickedly, and maliciously'. The customers were unlikely to notice, as the amount of dough stolen from each of them was small, but over time, the bakers and baksters built up a sizeable quantity of it. All ten of them were committed to Newgate prison and subsequently locked in the pillory with some of the stolen dough hung around their necks until Vespers (the sunset bell) was rung at St Paul's. This particular con was taken so seriously by the city authorities that they had it proclaimed that anyone else found to have done the same thing in future would be locked in the pillory for an entire day, a remarkably long time given that the usual sentence was an hour or two, and banished from London forever.[20]

In October 1282, Robert Blake, a baker, was found to have sold loaves of bread that did not weigh as much as they should have, and he was dragged on the hurdle; that is, strapped to an assortment of wooden planks that were tied to a horse, and dragged through muck, horse manure, and filth through the streets of London. The procession began and ended at his own home to ensure that his neighbours knew exactly what he had done and why he was being punished and also passed along Cheapside because it was the busiest street in medieval London.[21] Nor was Robert Blake the only baker who suffered the indignity of being dragged on the hurdle. In 1316, Godfrey Rede was found to be selling a penny loaf that was too light and was punished with the hurdle, and at the same time, Richard Lughteburghe (i.e. from Loughborough in Leicestershire) was punished for the same reason. Adam Lyndeseye (originally from the area of Lindsey in Lincolnshire) was found to have baked *pain demaign* – the finest and most expensive type of white bread – that was 'of bad dough within, and good dough without', and was sentenced to the hurdle.[22]

Piracy

As well as his talents as an extortionist, Hugh Despenser the Younger also became a pirate for a while. At a parliament held in London in

August 1321, his baronial enemies forced Edward II to agree to Hugh's and his father's permanent exile from England. Hugh the Elder obligingly went to the Continent; Hugh the Younger became a pirate in the English Channel, or a 'sea-monster ... he was master of the seas, their merchandise and chattel, and no ship got through unharmed', as one contemporary chronicler stated.[23] Edward II's son Edward III paid compensation in July 1336 to a group of Genoese merchants because Hugh 'plundered their ship at the Dunes of Sandwich' and took goods worth more than £20,000 (which in modern terms runs into tens of millions). He admitted that Hugh was 'upon the seas with the late king's ships', thus holding his father Edward II partly accountable for Hugh's piracy.[24]

Perhaps the most notorious pirate active in the waters around England in the Middle Ages was Eustace the Monk. He was a Frenchman of noble origin, born around 1170 in or near Boulogne, and seems at various times to have been a monk, a knight, and a magician. After living in Spain for a while, Eustace became a pirate, privateer, and mercenary in the English Channel and the Dover Strait and served both King John of England (r. 1199–1216) and King Philip II of France (r. 1180–1223). Eustace's career came to an end during the naval battle of Sandwich on 24 August 1217, which was fought between the kingdoms of England and France. His ship was surrounded by English ships, and he was captured and beheaded. Eustace the Monk was so well known in his lifetime and afterwards that a romance was written about him in French later in the thirteenth century.

Another medieval man cast very much in the mould of Eustace the Monk was Carlos de la Cerda, born in *c.* 1326/27, a partly Spanish and partly French nobleman. Carlos's grandfather Alfonso de la Cerda, born in 1270, was a contender for the Spanish kingdoms of Castile and León on the death of his grandfather Alfonso X in 1284, but his late father's younger brother took the throne instead as Sancho IV. Alfonso de la Cerda moved to France, and his children and grandchildren were all born there. His grandson Carlos made an excellent marriage to Marguerite de Blois, a daughter of the duke and duchess of Brittany and a great-niece of Philip VI, king of France (r. 1328–50). In England, meanwhile, Edward III claimed the throne of France from Philip VI in 1337, and defeated French forces at both the naval battle of Sluys in 1340 and the land battle of Crécy in 1346. Edward III was also duke of Aquitaine in southwest France, a territory he inherited from his ancestors, and numerous English ships plied their way between English ports and Bordeaux. In the late 1340s, Carlos de la Cerda made a career out of intercepting some of these ships, stealing their cargo, and throwing their crew overboard to drown. A furious Edward III vowed to put a stop to Carlos's murderous behaviour, and on 10 August 1350 lay in wait off the shore of Winchelsea with his fleet. The subsequent naval battle was colourfully known as The Spaniards on the Sea and ended in Carlos de la Cerda's defeat and the end of his piratical career in the Channel. He did, however, survive the battle, only to be assassinated in France several years later.

Adam Bedeford, who lived in Lincolnshire but presumably came originally from Bedford (or at least his father did), was summarily beheaded as a pirate in 1272 after being found 'in the company of pirates'. Legally this situation proved rather complicated, as Adam was an Englishman and his execution took place on the northern side of the bridge in Berwick-upon-Tweed, which was then on the Scottish side of the border.[25] Relations between England and Scotland at the time were, however, friendlier than they would be later, as the rulers of the two kingdoms, Edward I and Alexander III, were brothers-in-law. In or not long before November 1317, off the coast of Hunstanton (now Old Hunstanton in northern Norfolk), a group of mariners from Zeeland (now a province of the Netherlands), led by a man whose name was recorded by English clerks as William Bald, were said to be 'pirates and sea robbers'. They had attacked a ship from Salthouse and killed its twenty-strong crew including the captain Robert Mowe and attacked another ship from Cley and killed its crew of nineteen, including the captain, Thomas Goscelyn. Henry Burgeys, a mariner from Hunstanton, and his crew captured the pirates at sea, took possession of the items they had stolen from the two ships, and imprisoned the pirates.[26]

Chapter 9

Domestic Violence and Abuse

In London in June 1233, a woman named Maud Marshall was killed by two men visiting her and her husband Gilbert's house; they were Roger Rysingges and his servant Moses (spelt 'Moyses' in the original). Moses hit Maud between the shoulder blades with a hammer then struck her in the face with the hilt of a sword, breaking many of her teeth. She died three days later. It transpired that Gilbert Marshall 'often beat' (*sepius verberavit*) his wife Maud and therefore he was suspected of taking part in the murderous assault on her, though he was ultimately cleared of any involvement as he 'did not beat her on that occasion'. Moses, who had fled, was outlawed, and his master Roger Ryssinges was acquitted of any complicity in Maud's death. Gilbert was briefly imprisoned for falsely accusing Roger of being involved but was not punished for beating his wife repeatedly.[1]

In the Middle Ages it was permitted under English law for men to hit their wives, although women were not expected to tolerate excessive abuse. A victim of domestic violence could apply to the courts for a divorce (or rather, an annulment) *a mensa et thoro*, 'from bed and board', on the grounds of her husband's cruelty or adultery.[2] In 1300, an ecclesiastical court ordered Thomas Louchard of Droitwich in Worcestershire to be whipped for beating his wife with a stick. In York in 1345, Agnes Huntyngdon left her husband, Simon Munkton, a goldsmith. Munkton sought the assistance of the Archbishop of York, William Zouche (d. 1352), who charged Agnes with deserting her husband without just cause. Agnes alleged that she had left Simon because he beat her and she was frightened of him, and furthermore, that she had pre-contracted marriage with John of Bristol and therefore was not Simon's legal wife.[3]

Mabel Smith of London obtained a judicial separation from her husband Robert in 1457 on the grounds that he had 'shamelessly committed adultery' with numerous women and 'was treating her so cruelly that she could no longer cohabit with him without danger of her person', and Anne Cope of the diocese of Lincoln was granted a separation from her husband John in 1475, because he cheated on her with many women and 'behaved to her with such violence that it was not safe for her to live with him'. Cristina Sewale of London also obtained a judicial separation from her husband John Archer in 1457 because he 'has so inhumanly beaten and wounded her beyond her deserts, even when she was pregnant, that he caused her to bring forth two stillborn children, and still treats her so cruelly that she is in fear of her life'. Although it was far less common, men could also be granted an annulment if their wives were cruel and abusive or adulterous. John Marston petitioned the dean of London in 1400, stating that his wife Alice had committed adultery and he dared not live with her because she 'has, he knows not why, several times sought his death'.[4]

In London in June 1231, Edward Bray supposedly assaulted Alice Wilton and broke her arm in two places; she later died. Her sister appealed Edward for the death then also died, and he purged himself of any responsibility for Alice's death by the 'thirty-sixth hand oath'.[5] Those accused of committing a crime were sometimes permitted to 'purge themselves with the seventh hand', which meant that they swore an oath that they were not guilty of the crime, and subsequently six other men swore that they spoke the truth. The thirty-sixth hand oath, where a person swore six times and had it confirmed by six different men each time, and the fiftieth hand, with forty-nine oath-helpers, also existed (and see Chapter 10 below for an example).[6]

Miscarriages and Murder

Deliberately bringing about miscarriage or premature labour by assaulting a woman was a felony punishable by death in medieval England. The foetus was deemed to have acquired a soul at the time of 'quickening' around the fourth month (i.e. when a woman first feels the foetus stirring), and killing it after this stage, though not before, was deemed homicide. In the mid-thirteenth century, Henry Bracton composed a work in Latin called *On the Laws and Customs of England* and stated, 'If one strikes a pregnant woman or gives her poison in order to procure an abortion, if the foetus is already formed or quickened, especially if it is quickened, he commits homicide.' An anonymous treatise called *Fleta*, dating from around 1290, confirms that a person was guilty of homicide if he struck a woman or gave her poison, thereby 'not allowing conception' or causing an abortion (*faciat abortivum*). This also applied to a pregnant woman who deliberately drank something to destroy the 'quickened child' she carried.[7]

In London in November 1255, Robert Cordwainer beat up Sarra, the pregnant wife of Henry Tailor, so badly that she gave birth to a daughter soon afterwards. Although it is not specifically stated, Sarra and her infant must both have died, as Robert fled and was outlawed. On 23 December 1273, Robert Taillehaste broke into the home of Robert and Isabel Gras on Wood Street in London. Robert and Isabel were entertaining friends, John and Isabel Benteley, and the two Isabels were both pregnant. Taillehaste supposedly beat up the two women so that they both gave birth shortly afterwards to stillborn boys, though eventually he was acquitted of any wrongdoing. Edward William of Wainfleet raped Ada Milner in Hollym, Yorkshire in June 1348, and three days later she gave birth to a dead son. He was indicted before the bailiff of Holderness. One evening in March 1301, John Sherman and Augustine Curzon broke into a house in Smithfield near London, but the residents, Adam and Alice Cobel, were at home. On discovering the couple there, Sherman and Curzon beat up Adam very badly, and Alice tried to prevent them but was herself badly beaten. She gave birth to a premature child shortly afterwards who did not live, and herself died a few weeks later.[8]

Stephen Tulbuche was said to have beaten Alice of St Albans so badly in March 1234 that she miscarried. However, a court decided that although Stephen did beat up Alice, this was not the cause of her miscarriage, and Alice was imprisoned for making a false allegation. On 26 August 1237 in London, three men 'beat a pregnant woman named Maud' so that she gave birth prematurely to a boy. The men were John Petiprestre, Richard the Deacon, and 'Thomas, brother of the parson of St Giles'. They fled and were outlawed. A few months later, on 4 June 1238, Sarra Portour was, so she claimed, badly beaten in her own home in London by two women: Maud Buk and her unusually named daughter Stanota. Almost three months later, on 29 August 1238, Sarra gave birth to a son prematurely, who lived long enough to be baptised but died at only three days old. Sarra claimed that this was a result of the beating she had endured while pregnant. Maud and Stanota denied the beating altogether, and furthermore, denied that Sarra had even borne a child prematurely. Their testimony was believed, and Sarra was imprisoned for making a false allegation.[9] Maud and Stanota Buk were not the only women accused of assaulting another woman so that she miscarried. In another example of a woman being murderously violent, the peculiarly named Agnes Houdydoudy beat and kicked Lucy Barstaple to the ground near the Tower of London in late June 1326. Lucy gave birth prematurely three weeks later and herself died a month after the attack.[10] And in Peterborough in 1368, Agnes of Chesterfield had a bad argument with Agnes Spicer, and punched her in the stomach. This brought about a stillbirth, though Agnes Spicer survived.[11]

Those who killed a pregnant woman after the 'quickening' of the foetus technically should have faced the death penalty, but juries often seemed reluctant to convict. William Ammory broke into the London home of a 'poor woman', Emma Whitewell, who was pregnant, on Ash Wednesday in 1355. He assaulted her 'so violently and in so horrible a manner' that she gave birth prematurely to a stillborn infant and was bedridden for seven weeks. A jury, however, acquitted Ammory of wrongdoing. Ten years later also in London, in September 1365, John Fraunceys pulled a knife on Joan Lord and beat her. Joan miscarried the child she was carrying, but a jury found that although John had indeed assaulted Joan and threatened her with a knife, he had not caused her miscarriage. John was set free, though had to pay a fine of half a mark (80d) for wielding the knife.[12]

Child Murders and Child Abuse

Child murders were thankfully very rare in the late Middle Ages. Children did, however, die in accidents fairly frequently, most often by drowning in ponds, wells, or streams, or by succumbing to a fire in their home, or by being scalded by boiling liquid in their home, or by drowning in a large container of liquid. In Bedfordshire in 1363, for example, 6-month-old Joan Ross died when a pot of boiling water on her parents' hearth overturned, and in Cowley, Gloucestershire, in September 1396, a 3-year-old boy named Robert Fox drowned in a large pan of milk. In 1267 almost a century before Joan Ross's death, also in Bedfordshire, two little sisters called Muriel and Blanche, aged 6 and 3, died in a house fire while their parents were out working in the fields – apparently they had been left alone to fend for themselves – and in the mid-1310s in Ashton, Cambridgeshire, 2-year-old Margaret, daughter of Robert and Emma Strake, died in 'a fire started by chickens' in the Strakes' house.

In March 1332, 5-year-old William Furse was running through a garden in Althorp, Northamptonshire, when a stone wall collapsed on him and killed him. In 1377/78, two 1-year-old baby boys, John Maltman and Thomas Squyer, died in fires in their homes in Welford and Yardley Hastings, Northamptonshire. Both boys were said to be lying in their cradle at the time. Sometime between July 1319 and July 1320, 3-year-old John Aleyn of Clopton a few miles southwest of Peterborough drowned in a well in his parents' garden one evening. The unfortunate little boy had gone out of the house by himself to pick some flowers growing near the well. Nine-year-old Mary, daughter of Agnes of Billingsgate in London, drowned in the Thames on a Sunday evening in April 1340 while standing on a wharf to fill an earthenware pot with river water (the reference in the coroner's report to Mary as the daughter of her mother, rather than of her father, indicates that she was illegitimate). And in the early 1320s, 10-year-old Thomas Coupere and 9-year-old Gilbert Sampson were playing together while looking after livestock in the fields outside Thrapston when Thomas fell and hit his head. He died a few days later.[13]

These are all typical examples of lethal accidents involving children in the late Middle Ages, and children and adults alike drowned in rivers or streams while washing themselves on a regular basis. Another, thankfully relatively uncommon, cause of death occurred when very young children lying in their cradles were attacked by pigs. In Oxford in May 1392, 6-month-old Agnes Perone was killed by a sow which, horribly, began eating her head while she was still alive. The sow belonged to, of all people, the abbess of Godstow Abbey near Oxford. In Westminster a century earlier, on a March evening in 1290, a sow 'entered the house of Geoffrey Paneterye while Lucy the wife of Geoffrey was looking for milk for her son Simon, dragged the child forth from his cradle and killed him'. In May 1322 in London, a 1-month-old baby named Joan was bitten by a sow as she lay in her cradle in her father's shop, and she died a day and a half later. And in Higham Ferrers, Northamptonshire in 1353, 2-year-old Isabel, daughter of Agnes Sawere, was bitten by a small pig and died.[14]

There were also numerous diseases which carried off young children, and the infant mortality rate was horrifically high. Despite that, there were clearly considerable anxieties around the deaths of children, and an interest in determining whether they had died naturally or not. In London, the deaths of 1-day-old Dionise Snowe at sunrise on 15 June 1339, 7-day-old Joan Parlepott on 17 May 1340, and 9-day-old John Russell on 19 July 1340, were investigated by the local coroner. In all three cases, there was a suspicion that the infant 'lay dead of a death other than her/his rightful death', though in all three cases, they were found to be natural.[15] Given how incredibly often infants died during or soon after birth, there must have been something about the demise of these three tiny children that led to suspicions of murder or abuse, and caused their deaths to be investigated. The death of a boy called Richard Norman (whose age was not recorded) in London in October 1252 also triggered an investigation. Richard was found drowned in a pit at the bottom of his father William's garden on Aldersgate Street, and because it could not at first be ascertained 'whether he died by misadventure or felony', twelve men from the ward were closely questioned on the matter. Unfortunately, the outcome appears not to have been recorded, or the record has not survived.[16]

Another example of an investigation into a child's death is that of 9-year-old John Staunford in the village of Padbury near Buckingham on 29 September 1321, which occurred while he was being looked after and educated by his uncle, William Offynton, the vicar of Padbury. The boy's death raised sufficient concern that nearly three years later in May 1324, Edward II ordered the sheriff of Buckinghamshire and Bedfordshire, Sir Ingelram Berenger, to investigate it. Berenger found that John Staunford 'fell ill, but his uncle did not notice this at first and continued to teach him'. John's condition worsened, so William took him home to his mother Margery – presumably the vicar's own sister – elsewhere in Padbury, where the boy died soon afterwards. He was buried in Padbury church, a wake was held for him, and masses were sung for his soul. In 1324, his uncle William Offynton was cleared of any wrongdoing, and John was declared to have died naturally.[17] It is interesting to note that two years and eight months after young John Staunford's death, there was still sufficient anxiety surrounding the circumstances of his demise that it came to the ears of the king himself, and despite the length of time that had passed, an investigation was ordered.

Medieval executions, an image made in the sixteenth century. (Public domain)

Above left: The pillory in the seventeenth century. (Public domain)

Above right: The stocks. (Public domain)

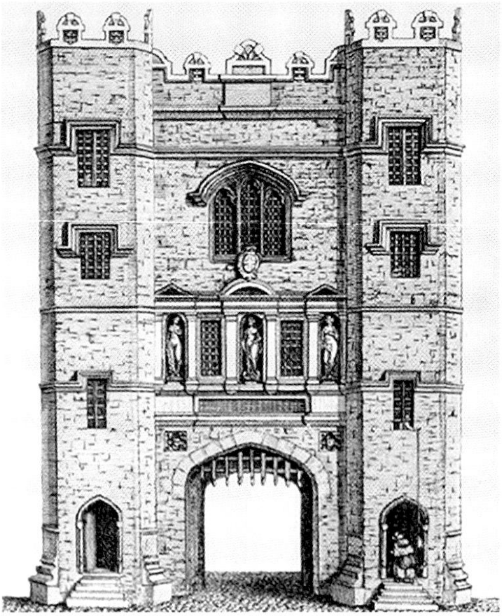

Above left: An image of Newgate prison in London before it was rebuilt in the eighteenth century. (Public domain)

Above right: Ludgate prison in London; an image made around the middle of the seventeenth century. (Public domain)

An image made in the late nineteenth century depicting the area around Ludgate prison centuries earlier. (Public domain)

Above: An eighteenth-century illustration of a cucking stool, later called a ducking stool, which punished people, usually women, convicted of being scolds. (Public domain)

Right: St Vedast Church, Foster Lane, London. William atte Rowe, son of a local goldsmith, attacked Philip Asshendone near here with a poleaxe on 7 December 1321, and Philip died of his wounds four weeks later. (Lonpicman, Wikimedia Commons)

Above: Holy Trinity Church, Teigh, Leicestershire. In its original form (it was rebuilt in the 1700s), it was the location of Sir Robert Coleville's attack on Richard Folville, parson of Teigh and a member of the notorious Folville gang of brothers, in 1340. (John Salmon, Wikimedia Commons)

Left: Tickhill Castle near Doncaster in South Yorkshire, where the brothers Simon and Thomas Beltoft, two of the many criminal knights of the era, were imprisoned in the 1320s after attacking and mutilating a clerk, John Carewell. (penske666 on Flickr)

All Saints Church, Leicester, a Grade 1 listed building that stands close to the former North Gate of the city. Between July 1323 and July 1324, Robert Kytewild, who lived nearby, murdered an unnamed stranger who was staying in his house and shoved the body under his own bed. The man was never identified. (Kris1973, Wikimedia Commons)

Pleshey Castle in Essex, where the adolescent Henry Frowyk was held captive from July to October 1308 and forced to marry Margaret Pountz, daughter and sister of two of his abductors. (Richard Nevell, Flickr)

Bolingbroke Castle in Lincolnshire. It belonged to Alice de Lacy, countess of Lincoln, who was abducted from there in late 1335 or early 1336 by the young knight Sir Hugh Frene. He took her 30 miles away to Somerton Castle and forced her into marriage. (Author's Collection)

Cockermouth Castle, Cumbria (formerly in Cumberland), where Simon Fot and Michael Alde were imprisoned at the start of the 1300s. Both men escaped and were pursued, caught, and summarily beheaded. (Richard Nevell, Wikimedia Commons)

Sutton Bank in Yorkshire, between Thirsk and Helmsley and 25 miles north of York, part of the area called Blackhow Moor in the Middle Ages. Forcing captured felons to decapitate their associates was the custom of the moor, according to an inquisition of 1282. (Author's Collection)

The Church of St Mary in Swynnerton, Staffordshire, a village which in the fourteenth century belonged to the violent and criminal Swynnerton family. (Brian Deegan, Geograph)

Sempringham Priory in Lincolnshire, attacked by the local lords Sir Geoffrey Luttrell, Sir Edmund Coleville and Sir Roger Birthorp in or not long before July 1312 as part of a local feud between themselves and the prior. (Author's Collection)

The keep of York Castle, known as Clifford's Tower, a prison in the Middle Ages. (Author's Collection)

Dunchurch, a village near Rugby in Warwickshire, where John Dunheved killed Oliver Dunheved, his brother or cousin, on 9 February 1325. Oliver's employer Sir John Pecche rode to Dunchurch a few weeks later intending to kill John Dunheved in revenge. (G-13114, Wikimedia Commons)

The extant medieval gatehouse of St Mary's Abbey in Kenilworth, Warwickshire, formerly Kenilworth Priory. William Hare died in September 1276 when he fell from a newly built wall at the priory. The two men who found him panicked and carried his body into a nearby wood. (Snowmanradio, Wikimedia Commons)

In late 1231, the body of a girl thought to be about 8 years old was found in the churchyard of St Mary Somerset in London. Bizarrely, she was believed to have been 'thrown there by some prostitute' (*proiecta ibidem ab aliqua meretrice*). The unfortunate child's identity and the truth of what had happened to her were never discovered.[18] Also in London a few years later in late 1252 or 1253, a woman called Alice Mercer beat a boy called John to death. She immediately fled and was waived.[19] Geoffrey Cook killed a little girl of 20 weeks old in London in 1238. She was the daughter of John Lorimer, though her own name and that of her mother were not recorded. The motive and circumstances of the killing were not recorded either. Geoffrey's wife Isabel was suspected of complicity and was waived; Geoffrey was outlawed in absentia, found, arrested, and imprisoned.[20]

A few decades later in October 1266, in the village of Wilden near Bedford, 'unknown evildoers' broke into Jordan Hull's house while he was away. His wife Agnes and their 8-year-old daughter Emma were, however, at home (it is not clear whether the break-in happened at night or in the daytime). The thieves attacked and wounded Agnes and, horribly, killed her young child. Agnes herself also died of her wounds eight days later. The identities of the thieves and murderers, who seem to have stripped the Hull house bare of goods after their brutal assault on Agnes and Emma, were never discovered.[21]

In Wittering near Peterborough, sometime in the fifteenth year of Edward II's reign (July 1321 to July 1322), 6-year-old William Johnet was out in the fields, looking after sheep. Two men, names unknown, who had apparently burgled a house nearby, hit him hard on the head with a wooden staff, perhaps because they were in the process of trying to flee with their stolen items and young William took them by surprise. Hugh Miller, presumably the local miller, found William and carried him into his house, but he died soon afterwards. In the same year, just 4 miles away in Easton on the Hill, two sisters, 7-year-old Juliana and 3-year-old Joan, daughters of Roger and Emma Pyncheboch, were left at home while their parents went to Stamford, 3 miles away. Another sister, Beatrice, was also there, and was perhaps considered old enough to look after the two little girls. A man named Richard Plante broke into the house to burgle it and killed both Juliana and Joan: he attacked Juliana about the head with a hatchet, while Joan had her throat cut with a knife. If Juliana survived this appalling assault, she did not live long and was already dead when her older sister Beatrice found her and their youngest sister Joan.[22]

A heartrending case of a child's death occurred in London on 24 May 1339. John Stolere, just 7 years old, a pauper and a beggar, sat on Cheapside around sunrise, relieving himself. A cart carrying a large container of water and pulled by two horses, driven by 12-year-old Ralph Mymmes, came past, and a wheel crushed little John. He died immediately, and the horrified Ralph fled, leaving the cart and horses behind. Ralph's subsequent fate is uncertain. Another accidental killing occurred around sunset on 30 April 1324, when 5-year-old John Burgh went into the house of his neighbours, Richard and Emma Latthere, in Farringdon Without ward in London. The little boy playfully picked up a parcel of Emma's wool and placed it under his cap, whereupon an annoyed Emma smacked him under the left ear. John's mother Isabel heard him weeping and raised the hue and cry and carried her son into the home of another neighbour, Walter Hengham, but it was too late, and John died around curfew that evening. Emma Latthere fled before her neighbours responding to the hue and cry could capture her but later gave herself up and was imprisoned in Newgate.[23]

One rare example of a murderous child is a boy named John Shaffeld, who sneaked into a brewhouse in London one evening in August 1339. The brewhouse belonged to Walter Seynmore, and the brewer who worked for him was William Kempstone. William saw John steal a hood from a female customer and gave chase. He caught up with him in Secollane, now called Old Seacoal Lane and in the EC4 postal district, and the boy stabbed him in the belly with a broad knife called a *bydawe*. William managed to stagger back to the brewhouse and explain what had happened but died the following day. John Shaffeld was never found or caught. In a wood close to Eastrington in Yorkshire, a few miles southeast of York, in or not long before April 1285, two boys called Henry Neweland and John Reeve, with a group of other boys, were playing some kind of game where the aim was to hit a target with a stick. Both boys were under 9 years old. Henry accidentally hit John on the head with his stick and killed him. Despite his youth, he was imprisoned in York until an investigation determined what had happened, whereupon he was released. A similar case occurred on 17 April 1278, Easter Sunday, in the Cambridgeshire village of Over. Two young cousins, Henry Oure and William Oure, were shooting at marks with bows and pellets, and Henry hit William in the head with a pellet as William went to see who had come closest to the marks. He died three days later. The king, Edward I, pardoned Henry Oure for the death, though not until April 1286.[24]

It is very difficult to identify cases of child abuse in late medieval England, as children's ages were only rarely recorded. One case, however, dating to *c*. 1320, appears in a petition now in the National Archives. Robert Reppes of Norfolk placed his 10-year-old daughter Eleyne 'with a recluse in Doncaster', but while she was there, the child was abducted by Sir Matthew Bassyngburne, his kinsman Sir Humphrey Bassyngburne, Hugh Bray, John Clopton, and other men, who broke into the house of the unnamed recluse. Matthew Bassyngburne imprisoned the child in his home and abused her for half a year. Eleyne's father stated that what had been done to his daughter was *encontre son gre e sa volunte*, which either means 'against her social rank and her will' or, more probably, 'against his social rank and his will', meaning her father's. The word used for 'abducted' was *raverunt*, and for what Bassyngburne had done to Eleyne, Robert Reppes used the word *tucha* or 'touched', obviously meant in a sexual sense.[25] Matthew Bassyngburne (or Bassingbourn) came from Badlingham, a hamlet a few miles to the northeast of Cambridge, and was sheriff of Cambridgeshire and Huntingdonshire from November 1318 to October 1319 and from April 1327 to August 1328. He was also appointed as one of the three keepers of the peace in Cambridgeshire by Edward II in 1319 and again by the government of the underage Edward III in 1329, and as a commissioner of oyer et terminer on several occasions in 1327/28.[26] Matthew's kinsman Humphrey Bassyngburne, who aided him in the abduction of Eleyne Reppes, was sheriff of Northamptonshire in 1321/22. Humphrey's granddaughter and heir Margaret Bassyngburne married Walter Coleville, son and heir of the Folville gang's nemesis Robert Coleville of Castle Bytham, in or before January 1349 when she was 14 and he was 8.[27]

A particularly horrible case of incest and brutal rape was recorded in July 1346. Roger, son of Sir John Hales, was 'indicted of having ravished and deflowered Alice his own daughter, whereof she died'. Edward III pardoned Hales for the rape, and for another, lesser crime, that of assaulting a couple and their young son after breaking into their house. Just two weeks earlier, Hales had been pardoned for raping another girl or woman, Alice Layton or Laxton. His brutal rape of his own daughter

Alice Hales was so appalling that a royal clerk believed, thankfully erroneously, that it had killed her. In fact, she lived into adulthood and married, though appears not to have had children, which was perhaps a consequence of her awful ordeal. Alice's age is not known, but her grandfather Sir John Hales was born in *c*. 1306/8 and was still barely 40 years old in 1346, so his son Roger, Alice's father, must have been a young adult and she must have been a young child.[28]

Another case of child abduction and rape is the ordeal of Elizabeth Luttrell in 1309. Elizabeth's age is, like Alice's, not specifically recorded, but her father Sir Geoffrey Luttrell, a landowner in Lincolnshire who commissioned the famous *Luttrell Psalter*, was born in 1276 and was 33 years old in 1309. Elizabeth's brother Sir Andrew Luttrell, their father's heir, was born in 1313 and lived until 1390, and she had another three brothers as well, who were all younger than Andrew.[29] Elizabeth was a good bit older than her siblings, though must still have been a young child when she first appears on record as the fiancée of Walter Gloucestre on 1 June 1309. Walter was born in late 1293 or early 1294, and held the manor of Heydour in Lincolnshire, about 10 miles from the Luttrells' manor of Irnham in the same county. Elizabeth was old enough to give birth in 1315, and her son was older than some of her brothers.[30]

In the early summer of 1309, Elizabeth Luttrell was already living with her fiancé's family, the Gloucestres. She and Amice Gloucestre, who was probably her future sister-in-law, were in Launde a few miles east of Leicester when the unfortunate Elizabeth was seized and abducted by John Ellerker, a clerk. He subsequently raped her. At some point, Elizabeth was restored to her future in-laws, but her father-in-law, Walter Gloucestre the elder (d. 1311), was so furious with Ellerker that John Langton, bishop of Chichester and chancellor of England (d. 1337), was compelled to intervene. John Ellerker, the abductor and rapist, swore on the gospels on 1 July 1309 that he would 'not claim the said Elizabeth as his wife in court Christian, or ravish or abduct her [again], or cause her to be ravished or abducted'. He would have to pay a fine of £1,000 to Walter Gloucestre the father if he ever did so. A few weeks later, on 5 August, Edward II pardoned Elleker 'for the rape and abduction of Elizabeth, daughter of Geoffrey Luterel'.[31] Ellerker's swearing of an oath that he would not kidnap her again suggests that he was obsessed with her and that she was still believed to be in danger from him.

Elizabeth Gloucestre née Luttrell gave birth to her son, yet another Walter Gloucestre, in or not long before July 1315, and was widowed in February 1323. She is mentioned on record in March 1324, and may possibly be the woman named as 'my daughter Isabella, nun of the house of St Gilbert of Sempringham' (i.e. Sempringham Priory in Lincolnshire) in her father Geoffrey Luttrell's will of April 1345; the names 'Elizabeth' and 'Isabella' were often interchangeable in this era.[32] One hopes that whatever Elizabeth's fate, she found some measure of happiness in life after her brutal early experience at the hands of John Ellerker.

Chapter 10

Murdering Your Spouse (1)

Elizabeth Daubeney was born in the Gloucestershire village of Cromhall, 15 miles from Bristol in the direction of Gloucester, on 11 November 1354. She was the daughter and ultimate heir of Elias and Agnes Daubeney, and was named after Elizabeth Ryver, one of her two godmothers. Her father Elias was 39 years old when she was born, himself born on 29 September 1315 in his maternal grandfather and godfather Elias Godele's manor of West Parley not far from the Dorset/Hampshire border; the identity of Elizabeth's mother Agnes is unknown, as are the dates of Agnes's birth and death. Elizabeth had an older brother, Richard Daubeney, who married a girl called Joan in or not long before October 1359, but the young couple died mere days apart in September 1361, almost certainly victims of the second great pandemic of the Black Death which struck England in 1361/62. As the sole remaining Daubeney child, Elizabeth inherited the manors of Hinton Daubney in Hampshire and Cromhall in Gloucestershire, her birthplace, as well as part of the manor of Kingsholm also in Gloucestershire.[1] In a sadly all-too-common example of the abduction and ravishment of a landowning woman in the Middle Ages, in or not long before September 1334 twenty years before Elizabeth was born, her paternal grandmother Cecily Daubeney née Godele was abducted by and married to her second husband, William atte Merssh. This abduction occurred a few months after Cecily's first husband John Daubeney, Elias's father and Elizabeth's grandfather, died at the end of 1333 or beginning of 1334.[2]

By June 1369, Elizabeth Daubeney was married to Sir Gilbert Giffard, to whom she had been betrothed since 1364, and on 3 July 1369 she proved in the Gloucestershire village of Wotton-under-Edge, 5 miles from her birthplace, that she was now 14 years old.[3] Married women came of age at 14 in the fourteenth century (and at 16 if not married), so Elizabeth and Gilbert were now allowed to take possession of the moiety of the manor of Kingsholm which Elizabeth had inherited from her late brother Richard. In and after 1370, Gilbert Giffard was commissioned to raise armed forces for Edward III's wars overseas, and in March 1373 joined Edward's own retinue at wages of £50 a year. He had almost certainly served previously in the retinue of the king's kinsman Humphrey de Bohun, earl of Hereford, Essex, and Northampton (b. March 1342, d. January 1373), as the earl gave him the manor of Ascott-under-Wychwood in Oxfordshire to hold for life.[4]

Gilbert Giffard was still in England on 26 June 1373, though had received letters of protection the day before to serve in France in a military capacity. He was in Edward III's own presence on or shortly before 25 June, when he begged the king to grant a pardon to John Dolent, one of Gilbert's retainers, 'for being a common robber'.[5] Gilbert died outside England, presumably in France, on either 10 October or 1 December 1373. He and Elizabeth, who was 19 or almost when she was widowed, had no children; on 31 January 1374, Gilbert's heir was named as 'John Giffard, his kinsman, of full age' (John was presumably Gilbert's uncle or cousin). In widowhood and during her second marriage, Elizabeth née Daubeney continued to use her first husband's family name, and a boy or young man rather confusingly named in 1393 as 'John, son of Elizabeth Giffard' was her second husband's child rather than Gilbert's.[6] By 1373, the year of his death, Gilbert had run up debts of a massive £160 – in modern values this amounts to hundreds of thousands – with a Wiltshire merchant named Thomas Hungerford, and Elizabeth was responsible for this sum after Gilbert died. The debt remained unpaid in October 1380.[7]

Elizabeth married her second husband, Andrew Wauton (or Walton), sometime before 28 June 1383, and her father Elias Daubeney died on 6 February 1384 in his late sixties. By 6 July that year, Elizabeth and Andrew had at least one child together. On that date, 'by reason of issue between them begotten', Andrew performed homage and fealty to the king, Edward III's grandson and successor Richard II, for the manor of Hinton Daubney in Hampshire which Elizabeth inherited after Elias's death.[8] It is likely that this child was the 'John, son of Elizabeth Giffard' who appears on record a few years later. Andrew Wauton was of lower rank than Gilbert Giffard had been, and unlike Gilbert was an esquire, not a knight. It was perhaps for this reason that Elizabeth kept the name of her higher-ranking first husband, though Andrew did have some measure of wealth and influence: in July 1380, he was named as one of the executors of Sir Roger Beauchamp, who had died a few months earlier, and in February 1382, a William Paumes made Andrew a recognisance of £100. In December 1385, Andrew was named first in a list of nine men appointed to collect a tax in Hampshire.[9]

The joint history of the Daubeney and Wauton families went back decades before Elizabeth and Andrew's marriage, and earlier in the fourteenth century, the Wautons had been lords of Cromhall in Gloucestershire, later Elizabeth's birthplace. In February 1311, William Wauton was granted a royal licence to 'crenellate his chamber within his dwelling house of Crumhale', i.e. Cromhall. Nearly forty years later in July 1350, Sir William Wauton of Essex (presumably the son or grandson of the man of this name in 1311) acknowledged a debt of £100 to Elizabeth's parents Elias and Agnes Daubeney. The three arranged that William's brother Thomas Wauton would release the manor of Cromhall to Elias and Agnes for two years in exchange for some lands in Wiltshire. In October 1352, Thomas Wauton released Cromhall to them perpetually, and Elizabeth Daubeney was born in the village two years later.[10]

The family tree of the Wautons is unclear, though in 1325 there is a mention of a William Wauton – perhaps the same man who crenellated Cromhall in 1311 – his brother John, and William's sons John and Andrew Wauton.[11] Clearly this Andrew cannot be the same man who married Elizabeth Giffard née Daubeney nearly sixty years later, but 'Andrew' was evidently a Wauton family name. Elizabeth's husband Andrew might have been a relative of yet another William Wauton, a knight of Essex who was active in the 1370s and 1380s, and perhaps Andrew was a son or grandson or nephew of the Thomas Wauton who gave the manor of Cromhall to Elizabeth's parents in the early 1350s.[12] Andrew was summoned to accompany Henry Despenser, bishop of Norwich, on a military campaign to Flanders in April 1383, and this seems to be the earliest reference to his military career. This implies that he might have been a few years younger than his wife Elizabeth, who was 28 in April 1383. Andrew also received letters of protection on 13 March 1387 to go on a naval campaign with Richard, earl of Arundel, and an archer named Henry Wauton, perhaps another relative, was summoned as well.[13]

For what happened next, we have two main sources: a record of the court of King's Bench, and a chronicle written at Westminster. On 24 February 1388, Richard II ordered two of his justices to carry out a 'delivery of the king's gaol of Winchester Castle' in Hampshire. Three people were imprisoned there: a chaplain named Robert Blake, a servant named John Ball, and Elizabeth Giffard née Daubeney. Blake and Ball had served Elizabeth's husband Andrew Wauton, who was now dead. The justices' record states that on Monday, 24 June 1387, Robert Blake and John Ball lay in wait for Andrew at Hinton Daubney and 'slew him feloniously and treasonably' after waiting for about two weeks for him to return there. Elizabeth was indicted for giving 'consent and aid to the slaying of the said Andrew, her husband'. The Westminster chronicle adds the details, though without naming any of the people, that a noblewoman was involved in a nefarious liaison with 'a certain priest' while her husband was overseas. On Andrew Wauton's return to England and to Hinton Daubney in particular – evidently from the earl of Arundel's naval campaign of 1387 – the Westminster chronicle's narrative states that he was killed in bed by the besotted 'priest' Robert Blake (though he was in fact a chaplain, not a priest) at Elizabeth's urging. Shortly afterwards, Elizabeth and Robert were arrested at dawn, lying together in the same bed where Andrew had been murdered. John Ball's culpability is not clear in this reading of the case, though the King's Bench record states that he and Robert Blake had intended to drown Andrew by throwing him into a well. Their motives for doing so are unclear.

John Ball was drawn and hanged for the murder of Andrew Wauton, while Robert Blake claimed benefit of clergy, and, according to the chronicle, died in prison. Elizabeth Giffard née Daubeney pleaded not guilty to consenting to and aiding the murder of her husband but was convicted by a jury. She was therefore sentenced to be burned alive, the horrifying – though, mercifully, rare – punishment for women who killed their husbands. Elizabeth claimed to be pregnant, and a 'jury of matrons' examined her and found that this was indeed the case. As always happened when a woman sentenced to death was pregnant, execution was postponed, though not for very long; if the Westminster chronicle is to be believed, Elizabeth was burned alive at Bermondsey on 17 April 1388.[14] Assuming this date is correct or at least approximately correct, she was 33 years old.

Another piece of evidence for the events of 1387/88 is an entry on the Fine Roll of November 1395, which states that Elizabeth 'was convicted of the death of Andrew Wauton, sometime her husband, and was burned by virtue of the said conviction'. Her manors of Hinton Daubney and Cromhall fell forfeit to the king owing to her crime, though they passed to her rightful heirs in 1395 several years after the death of her son John – who was presumably also Andrew Wauton's son – who would eventually have inherited them when he came of age at 21. The heirs were Elizabeth's aunt Cecily Sage, who was Elias Daubeney's only surviving sister and must have been of advanced age in the mid-1390s (Cecily's father John Daubeney was born in 1292 and her brother Elias in 1315), and Elizabeth's cousins Eve Cadel, John Swonhongre and Nicholas Mattesdon Droys, the children or grandchildren of Elias's three other sisters Maud, Christine and Isabel. The child whom Elizabeth was carrying when she was granted a temporary stay of execution in 1388 must have died before March 1393, when her son John's inquisition post mortem took place. He died on 5 August 1392, age unknown, though he must still have been a child.[15]

<u>The Daubeneys</u>
John Daubeney (b. 1 August 1292, d. shortly before 7 January 1334) m. Cecily Godele (d. 3 October 1345), daughter of Elias Godele (alive October 1336) and Christine
/
Cecily Sage née Daubeney (alive November 1395)
Maud (grandmother of Nicholas Mattesdon Droys)
Christine (mother of Eve Cadel, d. 1413)
Isabel (grandmother of John Swonhongre)
Elias Daubeney (September 1315–February 1384) m. Agnes, last name unknown (alive October 1359)
/
Richard Daubeney (d. September 1361) m. Joan, last name unknown (d. September 1361)
Elizabeth Daubeney (November 1354–April 1388) m. (1) Gilbert Giffard (d. 1373); m. (2) Andrew Wauton (d. 1387)
/
John (Wauton?) (d. 5 August 1392)
At least one other Wauton child, d. young

It is of course not at all implausible that a married woman might have had an affair with another man while her husband was away, though perhaps more surprisingly, it is also not at all implausible that a chaplain might have been Elizabeth's lover. Numerous chaplains of the fourteenth and fifteenth centuries, though they were men of religion and should have practised celibacy, did have intimate relations with women (and men). In November 1387, mere months after Andrew Wauton's murder, Margaret Morys of Loddon in Norfolk discovered that she was pregnant by the local chaplain, Thomas Holm, and 'for shame took her goods on the following day and left the town'. In 1328, John Cales, a chaplain of Jersey in the Channel Islands, admitted to having fathered eight illegitimate children, and in the early 1400s, a London chaplain named William Langford had a sexual relationship with Margaret Dod with the consent of her husband William Dod.[16] There are numerous other examples, and some chaplains were also prone to shocking violence. In Yelvertoft, Northamptonshire, in November 1311, the local chaplain, William Wellington, sent his clerk to a neighbour's house to ask him for a candle. John Cobbler, the neighbour, requested payment of a penny before handing over the candle, and when the clerk told William of this, William marched round to John's house in a rage and struck him hard on the head with a stick as soon as he opened the door, so that 'his brains flowed forth and he died forthwith'.[17]

In the same year, Richard Heryng, a chaplain in London, was accused of being a 'bruiser', and six years earlier in 1305 had wounded a man in the head and arm with a sword so badly that he was confined to bed for several months. In September 1388, the year of Elizabeth Daubeney's execution, the chaplain of Charlbury in Oxfordshire, William Lorimer, killed one Ralph Hosier by stabbing him in the head with a blade. And a century earlier in 1287, Hugh Weston, the chaplain of Acton Scott near Church Stretton in Shropshire, was extremely drunk on Christmas Day and quarrelled with a group of people who were standing outside a tavern around sunset and singing to celebrate Christmas. One of the singers was a man whose name was rather peculiarly recorded as John Quercubus, which means 'oak tree' in Latin. Hugh Weston the chaplain was jealous of John because he 'had the love of certain women … whom Hugh much affected' and because he sang well and attacked John about the head with his sword. John raised his hands to defend himself and two fingers of his left hand were almost severed by the drunken, angry chaplain.[18] As is the case with chaplains who had illicit relationships with women and men, there are many other examples of medieval chaplains attacking people, killing them, or otherwise committing serious violence.

The joint history of the Daubeney and Wauton families concerning the Gloucestershire village of Cromhall might lead one to wonder whether the account of Elizabeth taking a lover is false and that the real issue between Andrew and herself had something to do with the ownership of land. As Elizabeth's husband, however, Andrew was the rightful owner of the manors she had inherited as long as she lived, and was, by the custom called 'the courtesy of England', entitled to hold them all for the rest of his own life even if she died before him as long as they had a child together, as they did. It is unfortunately impossible to know for sure what created such discord between the couple that Elizabeth apparently instigated, connived at, or even participated in her husband's murder. The chronicler's story of Elizabeth's affair with a chaplain who was so in love with her that he killed her husband because she asked him to may have a kernel of truth in it, though medieval chronicles sometimes come across as the tabloid newspapers of their day, and the salacious tale might be an invention or at least an exaggeration. As Paul Strohm has noted, the Middle Ages tended to assume that female murderers must have had male accomplices and to hold the two jointly responsible, either because this was indeed the case, or because women were not deemed capable of committing murder alone.[19] Another example is Juliana Aunsel, who in 1324 was involved in the murder of Edmund Brekles, a chaplain who was her lover. Her accomplice John Multon was the one who killed Edmund: he stabbed him in the stomach as he (Edmund) lay in bed with Juliana. Juliana Aunsel and John Multon lived in the same house and were perhaps also lovers, and they both abjured the realm after confessing to Edmund's murder (see also Chapter 5 above).[20]

At a parliament held at Westminster in January and February 1352, Edward III and his government passed the Statute of Treasons, which formally codified what had been informally the case for many years: a woman who killed her husband had committed petty treason. This was also the case when a servant killed his master, or 'when any secular man or man of religion kills his prelate to whom he owes fidelity and obedience'. The wording in the original Anglo-Norman is *une femme qe tue son baron*, 'a woman who kills her baron'.[21] The word 'baron' for 'husband' is typical of the late Middle Ages, and was used by and for people of the lower ranks of society as well as those of baronial rank.[22] Noblewomen referred to their husband as their *seigneur* or lord, whereas noblemen called their wife *ma compaigne*, 'my consort', and the difference in language points to the different legal status between wives and husbands. Women who killed their husbands were severely punished, often by the one of the cruellest executions imaginable, being burned alive. Men who killed their wives, by contrast, were not always punished at all.

Sir Ralph and Alice Wake were landowners in Somerset, Dorset, and Hampshire in the late 1200s. Little is known about them, except that Ralph's parents were named Andrew and Joan and he had sisters named Gonore and Joan. From his parents, Ralph inherited the Somerset manors of Dowlish Wake and Compton Martin and the Dorset manor of Bishop's Caundle, then often called Caundelwake, among other lands.[23] Ralph and the parson of the village of Cricket St Thomas were accused of attacking Richard Loveny, tenant of the king's manor of Queen Camel (18 miles from Ralph's manor of Dowlish Wake) in September 1289. At this time, Ralph was said to be a member of the chancellor of England's household. Other than making a gift of land to Shaftesbury Abbey in Dorset and the occasional mention in the chancery rolls when he acknowledged a debt or was given permission to go overseas, Ralph is difficult to find on record, and his wife Alice even more so; her identity is unclear.[24] Ralph died not long before 6 February 1299, and on 13 February there is a reference to 'the heir of Ralph Wake' in the inquisition post mortem of Alan Plucknett, who married Ralph's sister Joan Wake and died in December 1298. The heir to Alan's lands was his and Joan's 22-year-old son Alan Plucknett the younger, Ralph Wake's nephew. Ralph's own heir was his and Alice's son John Wake, whose age is unrecorded but who was old enough to become a grandfather in July 1327 when his eldest daughter Isabel gave birth to her son Thomas Keynes. John lived until 1348, the year when the Black Death first reached England.[25]

After John Wake's death, half a century after his father's, his inquisition post mortem was held, and the jurors found that his heirs were his two living daughters, Isabel Keynes and Elizabeth Michel, and his 9-year-old grandson John Tyrell, son of his late third daughter, Margery. At the inquisition taken at John Wake's manor of Compton Martin in Somerset in late March 1348, the jurors stated that his mother Alice had forfeited the manor 'by feloniously plotting the death' of Ralph Wake, her husband and John's father. According to the inquisition, Alice was punished by being burned alive. The only other certain reference to this event is an entry on the Close Roll in March 1309, ten years after Ralph's death. This states that a priest named Philip Waspray had been 'indicted for the poisoning of Ralph Wake, knight', but had purged his innocence before the bishop of Salisbury and was therefore being restored to his lands and goods.

Philip Waspray and presumably Alice Wake were indicted before the justices of oyer et terminer in Somerset and Dorset, and one of them was Sir William Martin (*c.* 1257–1324). Martin was the chief lord of Compton Martin and occupied the manor for seven years after Alice's conviction, until he was ousted by Ralph and Alice's son John Wake.[26] Although William Martin certainly did act as a justice of oyer et terminer in Somerset and Dorset at the end of the 1200s and start of the 1300s, there is no surviving record of the indictment of Alice Wake and Philip Waspray for the poisoning of Alice's husband, nor of an order to William Martin or anyone else to investigate Ralph Wake's death.[27] Frustratingly, the only two references to Alice Wake's conviction and punishment for killing her husband do not appear until ten years and just under fifty years later, and it is therefore impossible to know for sure what happened. It is, however, interesting to note that in the cases of both Alice Wake and Elizabeth Daubeney almost a century later, a man of religion was believed to be involved in the murder of their respective husbands.

Philip Gayton died at Grove Park in Budbrooke parish near Warwick on Tuesday, 20 January 1316, and his brother and heir Theobald died in the same place just five days later. The brothers' deaths occurred at the height of the Great Famine of 1315 to 1317, when a sizeable percentage of the population of England and elsewhere in Northern Europe died of starvation and diseases exacerbated by malnutrition. Although Philip and Theobald Gayton were members of the wealthy, landowning elite who would have found it much easier than everyone else to avoid dying of hunger, epidemics of diseases such as typhus swept through the country at this time and attacked the weakened populace, and perhaps they were among the victims. The Gayton brothers were both childless but had two sisters, who were, in accordance with English inheritance law of the late Middle Ages, their joint and equal heirs; primogeniture did not apply to women, who inherited equal shares of an estate in the absence of male heirs.

The elder Gayton sister was Juliana, who, according to the brothers' inquisitions post mortem, was 26 years old in 1316. She was married to Thomas Murdak, lord of Edgcote in Northamptonshire and Stourton Castle in Kinver Forest, Staffordshire, who was said to be 28. The younger Gayton sister was Scholastica, whose unusual name sometimes appears on record as Escolate or Escholace, who was apparently 24 and was the widow of Godfrey Mewes or Meaux of Yorkshire. The ages given for Juliana Gayton and her husband Thomas Murdak cannot be correct, however, as their first son John Murdak was said to have been born around 24 August 1298 and to be 18 years old in the summer of 1316. He was certainly of age, i.e. at least 21, by 1323, and was knighted by 1324. Dates of birth for both Thomas Murdak and his wife Juliana Gayton in the 1270s or early 1280s seem more plausible than the late 1280s or early 1290s.[28] As well as losing both her brothers just days apart in early 1316, Scholastica Mewes née Gayton had lost her husband five years earlier, not long after she had given birth. She bore their son John Mewes on 8 September 1310 and was widowed mere months later when Godfrey Mewes died shortly before 3 February 1311.[29]

Juliana's husband Thomas Murdak died only three months after his two Gayton brothers-in-law, probably on 12 April 1316. The widowed Juliana appears to have married a second husband, John Vaux or Vaus, just three days later.[30] Edward II had appointed Vaux as keeper of the manor of Stourton and of Kinver Forest in late 1310, though replaced him on 29 May 1316, a few weeks after Thomas Murdak's death.[31] Sensationally, in the summer of 1320 King Edward ordered the arrest of John Vaux 'and Juliana his wife' on the grounds that they had murdered Thomas Murdak. A number of other people, men and women, were also named as being involved in the murder, including John Vaux's brother Elias Vaux, Adam Someter aka Adam Palfreyman, who looked after some of John Vaux's horses, Alice Chaumberer, Juliana Murdak's chamberlain Roger, Thomas Murdak's chamberlain Robert, Murdak's chaplain and steward Robert Prudhomme, Murdak's esquire William FitzRichard, Maud Hastang, William Bodeskisham, Adam Boffard, Thomas Taillou, John Vaux's cook William Shene, Mabel Blayworth, 'Mabel the wife of Hugh Clerk', and 'John, son of Juliana, the chaplain'.

Presumably John the chaplain was the son of another woman named Juliana, rather than Thomas Murdak and Juliana Gayton's son John Murdak.[32]

On Friday, 30 September 1317, a man named Robert Yolretoft aka Robert Rugel or Ruggele of Yelvertoft in Northamptonshire – where the local chaplain had murdered his neighbour after an argument over a candle less than six years earlier (see a few paragraphs above) – spoke to Hamo Vieleston, one of the coroners of the county of Northamptonshire. Robert Rugel 'acknowledged himself to have aided and abetted the death of Thomas Murdak, who had been feloniously killed' in Stourton Castle on the Monday of Easter week, i.e. on 12 April, in 1316. He turned king's evidence and accused Juliana Gayton and John Vaux, and numerous others, of the murder. Rugel related how, after Thomas Murdak had gone to bed, William Bodeskisham tried to incapacitate him with a blow to the head from a staff. Thomas awoke and tried to rise, but his chaplain and steward Robert Prudhomme stabbed him with a *bydawe* (a long, broad knife) up to the hilt, then Juliana Murdak's chamberlain Roger stabbed him in the stomach, just above the navel, with another knife. His body was 'cut in two in the middle', the head was cut off, and then the two halves of his body were again cut in half. Thomas Murdak's remains were then taken nearly 60 miles from Stourton Castle and dumped at his manor of Edgcote, though exactly who undertook this grisly journey was never specified. Presumably the aim of moving his body was to keep the murder hidden for as long as possible, to conceal the identities of those responsible, and to conceal the true location of the murder.

The way Thomas Murdak's killers murdered him and treated his body afterwards is somewhat reminiscent of the penalty that was inflicted on men convicted of treason (who were disembowelled and had other internal organs removed while they were still alive and were finally killed by being beheaded. After death, their body was cut into quarters and put on public display in five different places, one location for the head and four for each quarter of the body). What is also noteworthy here is that several of the accused were women – though their role in the murder was not clarified – and that several of Thomas Murdak's killers were his own servants, including his chamberlain and his chaplain. As noted above, a few decades later in 1352, the government of Edward II's son Edward III clarified that servants who killed their masters committed petty treason. Interestingly, the manner of Thomas's murder and the treatment of his body seems to indicate that his killers might have believed that he himself had committed treason in some way, though the true motives are murky, and Edward II, who was about halfway through his reign at the time of Murdak's murder, was deeply unpopular throughout the reign and ended up being forced to abdicate his throne to his teenage son Edward III in early 1327. The start of the year 1316 saw Juliana Murdak and her sister Scholastica Mewes become wealthier than they had perhaps ever expected when their two brothers died mere days apart, and this may have been a motive in some way for Juliana committing murder just three months later, though the involvement of so many of Thomas Murdak's servants in his death strongly implies that he was a dreadful and perhaps abusive lord. Perhaps, given the timing of his murder during the Great Famine, a period of starvation, hunger, and suffering throughout England, Murdak failed to ensure sufficient availability of food to his own people, and their desperation drove them to extreme measures. Juliana's role in the murder was not specified, and she evidently did not strike one of the killing blows, though presumably was an accessory to it.

Juliana appeared in court on 23 June 1320, more than four years after her husband's murder and two years and nine months after Robert Rugel accused her of involvement. She was subsequently imprisoned in London until her trial before the King's Bench was due to take place but was said to be 'so ill and weak' that the trial was postponed for a few months. She was finally tried by a jury of twelve knights of Staffordshire on 23 January 1321 ('the Friday after the Octaves of St Hilary, 14 Edward II') and was found guilty; the word *comburenda*, 'to be burned', was written in the margin of the trial document.

It is beyond all doubt that Juliana Murdak or Vaux, née Gayton, was convicted of her husband Thomas Murdak's murder and executed in 1321, though whether she was in fact burned alive as per her conviction is uncertain. In July 1322 and again in July 1325, it was stated on the Close Roll that she was 'hanged for felony', and there are two other references in the *Inquisitions Miscellaneous*, both dating to 1324, which also state that she was hanged. A royal writ of October 1321 ordering another inquisition post mortem on her brother Theobald Gayton, however, states both that Juliana 'suffered capital punishment' and that she was burned alive on 20 May 1321, and an inquisition of April 1322 also refers to her being 'burned for felony'.[33] Her second husband John Vaux fared considerably better. He was indicted for Thomas Murdak's murder sometime before April 1319 and was imprisoned in the Tower of London, but was acquitted of the murder in October 1325, freed, and restored to his lands and goods.[34] The fate of his brother and alleged co-conspirator Elias Vaux appears not to be recorded. As for Juliana's family, her elder son John Murdak died before 1342, though her younger son Thomas lived longer and was eventually knighted. Her younger sister Scholastica Mewes, the only survivor of the four Gayton siblings after 1321, died in late 1353 when her son and heir John Mewes was 43 years old.[35]

The punishment of burning was such a dreadful one that there was, perhaps, a reluctance to convict women unless their guilt was beyond all possible doubt. Other women who were accused of killing their husbands were found innocent and set free, as happened in the case of Hugh and Maud Mortimer. Hugh, lord of Richard's Castle in Herefordshire, was born in late 1274 as the son and heir of Robert Mortimer (b. *c.* 1252) and Joyce la Zouche.[36] Sometime before late 1290, in his teens, Hugh married a woman called Maud. Her identity is uncertain, but evidently she was related to Edward I's first queen Leonor of Castile: Leonor's son Edward of Caernarfon, prince of Wales, referred to Maud as his kinswoman.[37] Hugh and Maud's first daughter, Joan Mortimer, was born on 24 November 1291 at Caerphilly Castle in Glamorgan when Hugh was 17 or almost, and their second, Margaret, was born on *c.* 14 September 1295. Caerphilly Castle belonged to Edward I and Leonor of Castile's son-in-law Gilbert 'the Red' de Clare, earl of Gloucester, which tends to confirm that Maud Mortimer did indeed have close blood ties to the royal family, especially as King Edward and Queen Leonor's eldest granddaughter Eleanor de Clare was also born in Caerphilly Castle a year after Joan Mortimer. Two extant letters from Edward of Caernarfon sent in 1305 state that his late mother Leonor, who died on 28 November 1290, had arranged Hugh and Maud's marriage 'in this country', phrasing which also strongly suggests that Maud was not English (Queen Leonor was Spanish, daughter of King Fernando III of Castile-León, and had a French mother, Jeanne of Ponthieu).[38] In June 1300, Hugh Mortimer took part in Edward I's siege of Caerlaverock Castle in Scotland, and a herald called him 'Hugh Mortimer, who well knew how to make himself beloved'.[39] His wife Maud was seemingly much less enamoured of him.

Hugh died on 20 July 1304 at not yet 30 years old, and was buried in Worcester on 15 August, the feast of the Assumption. His daughters Joan and Margaret, who were 12 and 8 at the time of his death, were his joint heirs, and on 10 October 1304, his widow Maud was granted possession of six manors in Shropshire, Worcestershire, Northamptonshire, and Essex which she had held jointly with Hugh.[40] Not long afterwards, however, Maud was indicted in Hereford on suspicion of poisoning her husband, and in August 1305 she was again indicted for killing another man called Hugh Kyngeshemede or Kingsmede. Her damsel (i.e. female attendant) Sybil was also accused of taking part in Kingsmede's murder, and William Billebury or Blebury, Maud's chamberlain, was accused of complicity in both men's deaths. One of the justices of oyer et terminer in Herefordshire and Worcestershire who dealt with Hugh Mortimer's alleged murder was William Martin, the same man who presided over the Ralph and Alice Wake case at about the same time.[41]

Thankfully for Maud Mortimer, she had a highly influential kinsman who took a strong interest in the matter: Edward of Caernarfon, prince of Wales, heir to the English throne (he was to succeed his father as King Edward II in July 1307). In the summer of 1305, the prince despatched numerous letters to royal officials regarding Maud's supposed murder of her husband. One letter which Edward sent to his sister Elizabeth, countess of Hereford, on 10 August 1305 indicates how keen he was to help 'our dear cousin' Maud, 'for the sake of our dear lady and mother, whom God absolve', i.e. the late Queen Leonor. At this time, the prince was banished from the court of his and Elizabeth's elderly father the king after they had a terrible quarrel, and he asked Elizabeth to do whatever she could to expedite Maud Mortimer's hearing, as he had heard it would not take place until the end of September 1305 and that this was too long for Maud and her two co-accused (the damsel Sybil and William Blebury) to wait. Edward of Caernarfon also asked his stepmother Marguerite of France, Edward I's second wife, to intervene with the king on Maud's behalf. This was a sensible intervention on the prince's part, as Queen Marguerite also had a vested interest in the matter: on 13 April 1305, the king had given her the rights to Maud Mortimer's second marriage, meaning that Marguerite would be able to arrange another marriage for Maud and would receive the fine Maud would have to pay if she wed someone without the queen's permission. The queen was also given custody of the lands that would ultimately pass to Hugh and Maud Mortimer's two daughters when they came of age.[42]

A few days after the prince's letter to his sister Elizabeth, on 16 August 1305, three men were given a commission of oyer et terminer to investigate the murder of Hugh Kingsmede at the request of Hugh's brothers Walter, Adam, and Simon Kingsmede. Maud Mortimer, her damsel Sybil and her chamberlain William Blebury were jointly accused of this murder. In December 1306, William Blebury was pardoned for failing to appear before the justices regarding the murder of Hugh Mortimer on condition that he surrendered to gaol immediately, so he had evidently fled rather than face justice. Maud herself was pardoned on 16 September 1305 'for a felony she is said to have committed in poisoning her husband', and was restored to all her lands and goods, which had been confiscated by the king.[43] Whether she was guilty of poisoning her husband and taking part in the death of Hugh Kingsmede is impossible to determine for certain. In the end, Maud never married again and died shortly before 15 February 1308; one of the two executors of her will was William Blebury.[44]

Curiously, another case of husband-murder involving a woman named Maud happened at almost the same time, and Edward of Caernarfon, prince of Wales, took an interest in this case too. Maud Belhus (or Bellhouse) was imprisoned in the Tower of London sometime before April 1304 for murdering her husband Thomas. Thomas Belhus was born in *c.* 1272 as the son and heir of Richard and Sarra Belhus, from whom he inherited the Norfolk manors of Bodney and Bilney, and when he married Maud in *c.* 1294, his father Richard gave them another manor, Barkestone in Leicestershire. An older Thomas Belhus, married to a woman named Floria and appointed sheriff of Huntingdonshire and Cambridgeshire in 1281, was perhaps Thomas's grandfather or uncle.

Richard Belhus died in December 1300, though he and Sarra held their two Norfolk manors jointly and they did not immediately pass to their son Thomas, then about 28 years old. Sarra did not long outlive her husband, however, and was dead by early February 1302 when Thomas did fealty to Edward I for Bodney and Bilney.[45] The identity of Thomas's wife Maud herself is unfortunately not clear. She and Thomas had a son whom they named Richard after Thomas's father, and who was about 6 years old when his father was killed: Richard Belhus the son proved his age and swore fealty to Edward II for his lands shortly before 1 December 1318 and must therefore have been born not too long before 1 December 1297, and he was knighted before November 1320.[46]

What happened to Thomas Belhus is also unclear, except that he was killed at nighttime in his manor of Bodney, perhaps in 1303 or early 1304. His widow Maud was indicted in Norfolk for the murder and was imprisoned in the Tower of London. On 20 April 1304, Edward I pardoned her at the request of his son and heir the prince of Wales, although she was evidently still being held in the Tower on 27 December 1305 when the king ordered her release. Thomas's murder was still being investigated in 1305, with unspecified 'malefactors' now being deemed responsible.[47] Maud was granted her widow's dower, a third of her late husband's estate, on 17 October 1304, and still held the entirety of the manor of Barkestone in Leicestershire, as it had been granted to her and Thomas jointly by her father-in-law about ten years earlier.[48] After late 1305, it is difficult to find any more references to Thomas Belhus's murder on record, and it is impossible to determine who was responsible and why – not to mention how – he was killed. It is also unclear precisely why Maud Belhus was ever thought to have killed her husband, though she seems genuinely to have proved her innocence.

Geoffrey Askeby, who came from the village of Ashby in Suffolk, married Maud Ubbeston sometime before the fifty-first year of Henry III's reign, which ran from 28 October 1266 to 27 October 1267. They had a son named Philip and a daughter named Emma. Geoffrey was killed in Ipswich between 8 September 1271 and 16 November 1272, and in May 1273, William Benges was accused of the murder and was mainprised (bailed) when twelve men guaranteed that he would appear before court. A few years later in November 1283, however, Geoffrey's wife Maud was pardoned for Geoffrey's death, 'as it appears by inquisition made by the sheriff and coroners of Suffolk that she is not guilty'. She was released from prison. Why Maud was ever charged with her husband's murder in the first place, and what happened to William Benges, is unclear.[49]

The unusually named Jollan Durham, whose name also appears on record as Jolland Duremen or Durame or Duresme, lived in a house called *Suthalle* or 'south hall' in Great Dunmow, Essex in the 1250s and 1260s. He was married to Cecily, and they had a son also called Jollan, born in *c.* April 1259. In 1270, Jollan the father's nephew Bartholomew claimed that sometime during the forty-eighth year of Henry III's reign, i.e. between 28 October 1263 and 27 October 1264, Cecily Durham gave her husband a 'poisoned drink' to kill him. The date given is correct: the royal writ to hold Jollan's inquisition post mortem was issued on 11 December 1263, and he must have died shortly before. Cecily denied the allegation, and as Bartholomew did not appear to prosecute his appeal, he was ordered to be arrested.

Cecily was told to purge herself 'thirty-six-handed' at a folkmoot, which took place in February 1276 in the churchyard of St Paul's in London (see also Chapter 9 for the 'thirty-sixth hand oath'). In front of the justices, Cecily swore that she did not give her husband Jollan a poisoned drink nor 'did anything by which he was nearer to death or further from life'. Six men swore that her oath was a true one; she repeated the oath and another six men swore that it was true; and so on, six times, until thirty-six men confirmed her oath. She was therefore cleared of any complicity in Jollan's death. The false accusation of killing her husband was not, however, the only difficult thing with which Cecily had to contend after Jollan's death: on 15 September 1264, her 5-year-old son Jollan the younger was abducted from her home by Walter Frowyk, who also stole from her a gold brooch worth 40 shillings, a silk girdle worth 20 shillings, eighteen silver spoons worth a shilling each, six gold rings worth 20 shillings, and a horse worth 40 shillings. And strangely, in *c.* 1272 a man called Eustace Laufare (who came from either Little Laver, High Laver, or Magdalen Laver about 15 miles from Great Dunmow) fell from a pear tree in her garden and died.[50]

Chapter 11

Murdering Your Spouse (2)

A horrifying case of a man murdering his wife happened in Essex in the early spring of 1371. John Dryvere (or Driver) came from Little Baddow near Chelmsford and appears on record as 'the son of Emma Badewe'; when medieval men are named as the son of their mother, not the son of their father, it means that they were of illegitimate birth. John took his wife Agnes to a field called Westfield near Little Coggeshall in Essex, beat her around the head and neck, and threw her into the well in the field, believing her to be dead. The attack happened on Palm Sunday, which fell on 30 March in 1371, and Agnes was not found until Good Friday, 4 April. Horribly, it transpired that she was still alive; her husband's assault had in fact not killed her, and the unfortunate woman had lain at the bottom of the well for five days with only her head and neck above the water. A local resident, John Growel, found her, and immediately ran to fetch his nearest neighbours, Edmund Fullere, Walter Trewe, John Sterre, and Richard Heyward. Between them, the five men managed to lift Agnes out of the well, and carried her into the house of Margery Russh, another neighbour. Agnes lingered in Margery's home for another six days and died on Thursday, 10 April 1371. Thomas Peacock, bailiff of the local hundred, was informed of the matter, and he in turn informed John Gestyngthorp, the local coroner. Gestyngthorp came to Coggeshall the day after Agnes's death, Friday 11 April, and John Growel showed him where he had found Agnes. Gestyngthorp examined her body and listened to the evidence of the men who had found her. With the aid of twelve jurors, he determined that 'John Dryvere feloniously killed [*felonice interfecit*] the aforesaid Agnes'. Dryvere fled and never faced trial, and what happened to him is uncertain, though it is apparent that the coroner and jurors thought that what he had done to Agnes was unconscionable.[1]

On 20 April 1242, Easter Sunday, John Loundoneston of London attacked his wife Alice with a sword, and she died of her wounds five days later. Six other people, four men and two women, lived in the same household, and as none of them nor John himself raised the hue and cry after John struck his wife with a weapon, the six were imprisoned. John himself fled after Alice died, having lived at home for the five days between the attack and her death, and was outlawed. In or not long before 1266, in or not far from London, Roger Tuler killed his wife, whose name is recorded in Latin as 'Elicia', in their home. He immediately fled, was caught and imprisoned in Newgate, but then escaped (the number of times people in the Middle Ages escaped from prison is truly astonishing).[2] In Oxford in the early autumn of 1391, William Burlond killed his wife Agnes: one Saturday, he stabbed her in the head with a knife 'even to the brain'. He buried her body in their cesspit, but apparently unskilfully, as she was found two days later by a neighbour. William fled to the church of St Giles and remained there for two days, then decided to abjure the realm and was assigned the port of Southampton as his place of departure.[3]

Walter Bedell from Renhold near Bedford killed his wife Isabel on Sunday, 29 March 1271, a murder which occurred a century almost exactly to the day before John Dryvere threw his wife Agnes into a well, and which has some similarities with that case. Walter stabbed Isabel over the left ear in a meadow called Longemede ('long meadow'), and threw her body into a nearby stream, the Ravensbrook, where it was discovered the following morning by Isabel's own mother, Maud. Walter and Isabel had evidently been living apart, as the coroner's record of her murder states that Walter went to Isabel's house in Ravensden, 2½ miles from Renhold, and asked her to come to the local grange with him so that he could give her a bushel of wheat. On their way there, he killed her. Walter evidently fled from justice, and his only possession of any value was a lamb, worth 12d, which he kept at Wilden, 4 miles from Renhold, and which was forfeited.[4] Another killing of a married woman took place in London on Sunday, 20 December 1339. Robert of Portsmouth hit his wife Alice on the neck with a type of stick or staff called a *wombedstaf* (the meaning of this Middle English word is not entirely clear), and she fell downstairs and broke her neck, and died. During the local coroner's investigation, it transpired that Robert's son Robert the younger, Alice's stepson, also hit her, but with his hand, which was not the cause of her death. Robert the father fled, and Robert the son was imprisoned in Newgate.[5]

Alice of Norfolk was one of the most highly born women in England in the first half of the fourteenth century. Born in 1323 or 1324, she was the younger daughter and co-heir of Thomas of Brotherton (1300–38), earl of Norfolk and Earl Marshal of England, a son of Edward I and a much younger half-brother of Edward II. Thomas of Brotherton's mother, Queen Marguerite, was a daughter of Philip III of France (r. 1270–85) and a younger half-sister of Philip IV (r. 1285–1314). On her mother's side, however, Alice's ancestry was far less impressive. Her royal father, shortly after a match to a daughter of the king of Aragon in Spain planned by Edward II fell through in 1321, instead married Alice Hales, daughter of a coroner of Norfolk, Sir Roger Hales. This was, by the standards of the time, a misalliance that must have been a love-match or lust-match and must have baffled Thomas's contemporaries. Still, via her father, Alice of Norfolk was a granddaughter and niece of kings of England, and a great-granddaughter and great-niece of kings of France. Her younger brother, Edward of Norfolk, died as a child in the early or mid-1330s, and she and her older sister Margaret, Lady Segrave (most probably born in 1322), were joint heirs to her father's earldom and lands when Thomas of Brotherton died at age 38 in August 1338.[6]

Women, even highly born women, were vulnerable in fourteenth-century England without a male protector. For all the two Norfolk sisters' high birth, the death of their father Thomas of Brotherton left them with no close male relatives who were powerful and influential and who might be expected to take a keen interest in their welfare. Their uncle Edward II, Thomas's older half-brother, was deposed in early 1327 when they were small children, and Thomas's only full brother, Edmund, earl of Kent, was executed in March 1330. Their younger brother died as a child, and their mother's kin were mere Norfolk gentry with little if any influence beyond their county. Nor could they expect any support from their grandmother Queen Marguerite's native France. Marguerite died in 1318 before the sisters were born, her half-brother Philip IV died in 1314, and Philip's three sons were all dead by the late 1320s. The older Norfolk sister Margaret's husband, John, Lord Segrave (b. 1315), was of much lower rank than his wife, and was far from being one of the premier noblemen of the kingdom. The sisters' nearest male relative and would-be protector was, therefore, their cousin Edward III

(b. 1312), son and successor of Edward II, but the king showed little interest in or concern for his many female first cousins except for Joan of Kent, who married his eldest son the prince of Wales in 1361 and was the mother of his grandson and successor, Richard II.

Alice of Norfolk was betrothed in early 1333 to William Montacute (or Montagu), son and heir of William Montacute the elder, who would be made earl of Salisbury by his friend Edward III in 1337.[7] Born in June 1328, the younger William was some years Alice's junior, and just 4 years old when his marriage to her was arranged. For some reason, however, the marriage did not go ahead, and in or before 1338, Alice married her fiancé's uncle Sir Edward Montacute instead. Edward was one of the ten children – four sons and six daughters – of Sir William Montacute (d. 1319) and Elizabeth Montfort (d. 1354). His date of birth is not known, though he was the youngest of the four Montacute brothers, and the second brother, William, earl of Salisbury, was born in 1301. The third brother, Simon, was born in 1303 or 1304 and was elected bishop of Worcester in late 1333. Edward might have been born any time between *c.* 1305 and *c.* 1315, and where he was placed in the birth order among his six sisters is unclear, though he was certainly many years older than Alice of Norfolk, perhaps more than fifteen years older. Edward was old enough to accompany his father Sir William to Gascony in southwest France, where Alice's uncle King Edward II appointed William as steward in late 1318 less than a year before William's death, and a boat called the *Peronele* which Edward Montacute had formerly owned in Gascony is mentioned in Edward II's accounts in May 1324, perhaps around the time that Montacute's future wife Alice of Norfolk was born.[8]

Alice and Edward Montacute had one son, named Edward after his father, and four daughters: Audrey, whose name also appears on record as 'Etheldreda', Elizabeth, Maud, and Joan. The fact that none of the daughters was named after Alice herself or after her sister Margaret is unusual by fourteenth-century standards. Audrey and Edward were the eldest of the five Montacute children, and had both been born by 13 March 1342, when their parents and their uncle the earl of Salisbury negotiated their future marriages (which ultimately did not take place) to Lord Mowbray's children John and Blanche. They were both alive in June 1349, but dead by 1359.[9] The second Montacute daughter, Elizabeth, married Walter Ufford but died in the autumn of 1361, aged about 17, leaving no children; the third daughter, Maud, became a nun at Barking Abbey in Essex, and was its abbess from 1377 to 1393; and Joan, the youngest child, was born on 2 February 1349, married William Ufford (b. 1338), future earl of Suffolk, in or before July 1360, and was already known to be pregnant a few days after her fourteenth birthday in February 1363.[10]

One of the places that Alice of Norfolk inherited from her father Thomas was the castle and town of Bungay in Suffolk, where she gave birth to her fifth child Joan Montacute in February 1349.[11] On Sunday, 19 June 1351, the following happened there:

> Item, that the said Sir Edward [Montacute], William Dunch, and Thomas, parson of the church of Kelsale, with force and arms feloniously beat Alice, daughter of Thomas of Brotherton, cousin of our lord the king, and wife of the said Sir Edward, at Bungay … of which assault the said Alice fell ill unto death and she died within the year and the day.[12]

This appallingly violent assault by her husband, one of his retainers, and a man of religion left Alice badly injured, perhaps unconscious, and close to death. Five months later, on 16 November 1351, she was called 'late the wife of' Edward Montacute, and her cousin the king sent two of her daughters – probably the youngest two, Maud and Joan, then aged 4 and 2 – to live in the custody of their paternal grandmother Elizabeth Montfort, the long-lived widow of Sir William Montacute (d. 1319).[13] Alice of Norfolk was clearly believed to be dead by mid-November 1351, and a royal writ dated 14 November ordered her lands to be taken into the hands of her cousin Edward III because of her death. This order, however, was cancelled and a memorandum was added underneath to the effect that 'it is testified that Alice is alive'. A royal order to the sheriff of Norfolk dated 15 January 1352 to pay some money owing to Alice's stepmother Mary (Thomas of Brotherton's second wife and widow) refers to the 'assent' to the payment by Alice's sister Margaret and Alice herself, and their husbands John Segrave and Edward Montacute.[14] It is most unlikely that Alice, probably in a coma or unconscious, was able to give assent to anything, but the order does not refer to her as being dead. She did not have much longer to live, however: the order to take her lands into the king's hands was repeated on 30 January 1352, and was not cancelled on this occasion, so apparently Alice truly was dead by then. On 10 February, the escheator in Norfolk and Suffolk was ordered 'not to intermeddle with the lands' which Edward Montacute 'holds by reason of the death of Alice his wife', and on 15 February 1352, there is a reference to 'Alice wife of Edward Montacute, deceased'.[15] It would seem, therefore, that Alice lingered for a few months after the violent attack on her by her husband, William Dunch, and Thomas the parson of Kelsale on 19 June 1351. On 14 and 16 November 1351, royal clerks heard that she was dead, which she apparently was not, and she did not die until a couple of months later. She had perhaps lapsed into a coma, and her husband and attendants wrongly believed her to be dead and informed the authorities, then realised later that she was still breathing. The indictment against Edward Montacute talks about *force et armes*, i.e. he and the other two men did not merely beat Alice with their fists, they launched a full-out assault on her with weapons. Alice of Norfolk, from the evidence above, would seem to have passed away sometime between 15 and 30 January 1352, about seven months after this brutal assault. She was about 27 or 28 years old when she died. The motive for her husband's attack on her was not clarified, nor is it clear why the parson of a village a few miles from Bungay took part in it. One of Alice's murderers, William Dunch, was pardoned for his role in her death by her cousin Edward III on 4 June 1361 because of his 'good service done in the war of France'.[16]

Edward Montacute married a second wife, Joan, whose identity is uncertain. With her, he had three more children, who were named Audrey, Elizabeth, and Edward like his three eldest children with Alice of Norfolk. Montacute died on 14 July 1361, and his and Joan's little son Edward, who was mere months old, died on 4 October the same year. Their daughter Elizabeth, alive in January 1361, also died before November that year, and Montacute's second wife Joan might have perished as well as there is no record of her being granted her widow's dower. Their 2-year-old daughter Audrey survived and was still alive in 1382.[17] It seems likely that they were all victims of the second pandemic of the Black Death that wreaked havoc in England in 1361/62. Edward Montacute and Alice of Norfolk's third child and second daughter, 17-year-old Elizabeth (the elder), was yet another member of the family who died in 1361, and by early 1363 their youngest child Joan was married and pregnant, despite her youth. Joan Ufford née Montacute died sometime before June 1376, only in her 20s, and Alice of Norfolk's fourth child Maud, abbess of Barking, was the only one of her children who did not die relatively young.[18] As Alice's widower and as the father of her children, Edward Montacute had the right to hold all the lands of her inheritance for the rest of his own life, by a custom called the 'courtesy of England'. On 15 February 1352, just weeks after Alice finally slipped away from life, Edward III gave Montacute the marriage rights of his and Alice's daughters, which would normally belong to the king. This was done, Edward declared, 'as a special grace'.[19] The king's apparent indifference to his cousin's brutal death stands in stark contrast to his willingness to help another kinswoman, Blanche of Lancaster, Lady Wake, in her dispute with Thomas Lisle, bishop of Ely, three years later in 1355 (see Chapter 8 above). Edward III never punished Edward Montacute for his murderous assault on his royal wife, though his decision to send two of Montacute's young daughters to live with Montacute's mother perhaps reveals, however, the king's unease about leaving two small girls in the custody of their father.

Chapter 12

Abduction and Ravishment (1)

To be a married woman in the late Middle Ages brought the risk that your husband might hurt and even kill you and not suffer any punishment for doing so. Being an unmarried woman with property in the late Middle Ages also brought risks, and it is astonishing how many of them were abducted from their own homes and forced into marriage. In the Latin and French vocabulary in which many medieval documents were written, their ordeal was generally described with the Latin words *rapuit* or *raptus*, or the medieval French word *ravir*. These words can mean to ravish or to rape, but can also mean to seize, abduct, or take by force.

Margery Poynings was the daughter of Sir Michael (I) Poynings of Sussex, who was killed at the battle of Bannockburn on 24 June 1314, and she had brothers named Thomas and Michael (II). Margery's date of birth is not known, though her brother Thomas Poynings, their father's eldest son and heir, was old enough to be knighted in May 1306 (and is therefore unlikely to have been born after *c*. 1290), and his son Michael (III), heir of the Poynings family, was born in 1317.[1] Margery was probably a few years Thomas's junior and born in the late 1290s or early 1300s. She married her first husband, Sir Edmund Bacon of Ewelme in Oxfordshire, before September 1326.[2] Margery and Edmund had one child, a daughter called Margery Bacon, who was born in *c*. 1334, married William Molyns in or before October 1352, and lived until June 1399. Margery Poynings was left a widow with a very young child when Edmund Bacon died in March 1336. She married her second husband, Sir Nicholas de la Beche of Aldworth, a landowner in Berkshire, Wiltshire, Oxfordshire, and Sussex, and constable of the Tower of London, in or before August 1337.[3] Nicholas died on 3 February 1345, probably aged around 50 or thereabouts. He had no surviving children, and his heirs were his late brother John's daughters Joan, Isabel, and Alice, all 'of full age', i.e. they were over 16.[4]

Just before Easter 1347, a little over two years after she lost her second husband Nicholas, Margery Poynings was living at Beaumys Castle not far from Reading in Berkshire, one of the many properties she held in dower from her two marriages.[5] She was a well-off widow with lands in no fewer than ten counties – by English law of the era, she was entitled to hold a third of her late husbands' estates for the rest of her life – and decided to embark on a third round of matrimony. Her choice of husband was Sir Gerard Lisle (*c.* 1304/5–60), another landowning nobleman and the widower of the earl of Arundel's sister Eleanor, with whom he had a teenaged son, Warin Lisle. The wedding ceremony was due to take place on or shortly after Good Friday, which in 1347 fell on 30 March. Present at Beaumys for the wedding were Margery's brother Michael (II) Poynings and Edward III's second eldest son, 8-year-old Lionel, the official keeper of the realm during the current absence from England of the king himself and his eldest son the prince of Wales. The 'rest of the king's children' were also said to be there, which would mean Lionel's older sisters Isabella (b. 1332) and Joan (b. 1334), his younger brothers John (b. 1340) and Edmund (b. 1341), and perhaps his very young sisters Mary (b. October 1344) and Margaret (b. July 1346).

A knight of Lancashire named Sir John Dalton, however, had other plans, and decided to attack Beaumys and abduct Margery before she married Gerard Lisle so that he could marry her himself and enjoy her wealth. With a large force of knights and other armed men, in the early hours of Good Friday before dawn and when it was still dark, John attacked Beaumys and successfully abducted Margery from her home. Her brother Michael (II) Poynings was killed while trying to defend her. Thomas Clerk, a member of Margery's household, and unnamed others were also killed, while Margery's chaplain Robert Hunte, who was already ill, apparently died of fright and shock. The bridegroom Gerard Lisle himself is not mentioned as being present during the incident and had presumably not yet arrived at the castle for the wedding. The day after the attack happened, he was ordered to find and arrest the perpetrators and was given special licence for himself and his retinue to be armed while doing so, as he 'fears bodily harm ... from the said evildoers, who are plotting to do him all the evil they can'. John Dalton's many named accomplices who either aided in the attack directly or helped to plan it included his parents Sir Robert and Mary Dalton, his cousin, also called Robert Dalton, Robert's mother Sarra Bailoff, Sir Robert Holland, Sir Edmund Mancestre (i.e. Manchester), Sir Thomas Ardern, Sir William Trussell, Sir Thomas Charnels, and Sir Matthew Haydok. It seems possible that some of Margery's servants or friends had also aided John Dalton; the fact that he abducted her with the aim of marrying her mere hours or days before she would have wedded Gerald Lisle, after she had lived as a widow for more than two years, suggests inside knowledge.

The day after the assault, John Dalton was ordered to bring Margery safe and unharmed before the royal council in Westminster as soon as possible. Dalton and his gang had already, however, taken Margery on a long journey to the north of England. In the Lancashire village of Upholland between Skelmersdale and Wigan, about 210 miles from Beaumys, Margery was forced to marry Dalton either on Saturday, 7 April or Monday, 9 April, just over a week after her abduction. The manor of Upholland belonged to Maud Holland née Zouche (*c.* 1290–1349), widowed mother of John Dalton's accomplice Sir Robert Holland. Maud later claimed to have had no knowledge of the matter and was probably telling the truth as neither she nor anyone else lived on the manor. John Dalton, his kidnap victim and new wife Margery, and some of his adherents stayed at Upholland until John Cokayn, the sheriff of Lancashire, and a royal sergeant-at-arms called Roger Archer came there looking for them. Cokayn was ordered on 10 May 1347 to search for and arrest the men and have them sent to the Tower of London; someone had evidently learned of their presence in Lancashire and perhaps in Upholland more specifically. After their near-discovery, John Dalton and the others 'withdrew by night to the north'. John's father Robert Dalton was found, arrested, and imprisoned in the Tower by the end of July 1347, though other evidence states that he went to see Edward III in person in the port of Calais (which the king was currently besieging) and gave himself up to him. John himself and the rest of his gang were still at large on 4 October 1347.[6] The fact that this attack took place in the castle where the royal children were staying was deemed an outrage and a scandal, not least by the furious king. As for what Margery herself thought, this was not recorded, though her inquisition post mortem states that although she did not consent to the abduction, she did consent to marry John Dalton and did so of her own free will.

Given that he broke into her home and that he or one of his men killed her brother, this seems unlikely.

Margery died in early October 1349, just two and a half years later, so John Dalton did not have long to enjoy her lands and wealth – and Edward III had, at any rate, given her lands to her nephew Michael (III) Poynings as punishment for marrying without his licence. Her heir was her 15-year-old daughter Margery Bacon, later Molyns. Edward III pardoned Dalton on 4 May 1350 for abducting Margery Poynings and for his 'felonies and trespasses' committed in the presence of the royal children, on the grounds that Dalton 'has humbly submitted himself to the king's grace'. The king also spoke of Dalton's 'good service', meaning his good military service. A few weeks later, Edward granted Dalton an income of £50 a year in order 'that he may the better maintain himself' in the royal retinue.[7] John Dalton died in September 1369, leaving a 6-year-old son and heir, also John, born in February 1363, and a younger son, Robert, from his subsequent marriage to a woman named Ellen.[8] The year 1369 saw the third great pandemic of the Black Death in England, and Dalton was perhaps a victim, though there is no way to know for sure.

John's father Sir Robert Dalton died in June 1353, and John was then said to be 'aged 30 years and more'.[9] The 'and more' might encompass a fair few years, but it may be that John Dalton was considerably younger than Margery Poynings, who was in her mid-40s or thereabouts in 1347. His father Robert was still young enough to fight at the battle of Crécy, as did John himself, both men in the king's own retinue, in August 1346.[10] John's abduction of Margery is reminiscent of another abduction of a noblewoman which had taken place just a handful of years earlier, when Alice de Lacy was abducted by and forcibly married to Hugh Frene, also her third husband, and many years her junior. Alice, countess of Lincoln in her own right, was born on or around Christmas Day 1281, and in the autumn of 1294 married Edward I's nephew Thomas of Lancaster, later earl of Lancaster and Leicester, who was about four years her senior.[11] Although Alice was pregnant in 1307 or 1308, and although Thomas fathered at least two illegitimate sons, the couple had no surviving children.[12] This perhaps contributed to their marital difficulties, and Alice left Thomas in 1317 to live alone. Thomas was beheaded for treason by his cousin Edward II five years later in March 1322.

Not long before 10 November 1324, Alice de Lacy married her second husband, Sir Eble Lestrange of Knockyn.[13] Eble was a younger son and therefore not an heir and was of much lower rank than Alice. He did not, however, call himself 'earl of Lincoln' as he had the right to do as her husband, and there is little doubt that their marriage was both a genuine love-match and a happy one. Sir Eble died on 8 September 1335, and his heir was his nephew Roger Lestrange, who was in his 30s. Alice was now almost 54 years old, and decided to take a vow of chastity, as widows often did when they had no wish to marry again.[14] Within months of her beloved husband's death, however, and despite her vow, sometime in late 1335 or in the first few weeks of 1336, Alice was abducted from her own home of Bolingbroke Castle in Lincolnshire. The culprit was an obscure knight called Sir Hugh Frene (or Freyne or Frayn), and as was with the case with John Dalton eleven years later, he was aided by a large group of armed men. Frene and his gang took Alice the 30 miles to Somerton Castle, which also lay in Lincolnshire and belonged to King Edward III personally, and married her there against her will.

Hugh Frene must have been much younger than Countess Alice, as he was knighted in early 1327, which implies that he was born after 1300. His identity is uncertain, though he was probably a relative of John Frene, lord of Moccas in Herefordshire. Fourteen-year-old Edward III, or rather the people ruling his kingdom during his minority, granted a favour 'at the request of Hugh Frene' in August 1327, so he clearly had access to the royal court and enjoyed no small measure of influence.[15] Hugh was appointed custodian of Cardigan Castle, South Wales, in December 1330, and two years later was made its constable for life. He appears to have had connections to Ireland, as a royal servant called Elias Asseburn included him in a list of men to be prayed for daily in the chapel of St Laud in Dublin in 1332, and a Fulk Freyn, presumably a relative, was 'lord of the castle of Faytheli' in Ireland in 1334.[16]

Edward III heard of Alice's abduction on or before 20 February 1336, on which date he ordered three men to arrest Frene and his victim as well, and to take Alice's lands into his own hands.[17] Peculiarly, this order states that Alice de Lacy and Hugh Frene had both escaped from Somerton Castle, 'the king having ordered them to be kept separately' there. Alice described her ordeal in a subsequent petition to Edward III, and it makes uncomfortable reading. Although she did not explicitly describe it as such, there is no doubt that what happened to her was kidnap and rape, and after Alice escaped from Somerton and Edward III ordered her to be arrested, Hugh Frene took her to the Tower of London. She remained there 'in such confinement that none of her friends or well-wishers could go near her or talk to her', only Frene's adherents and members of his retinue. She appears to have still been incarcerated in the Tower against her will at the time she dictated her petition, as she asked Edward III to remedy her situation as quickly as possible so that she might again be 'at liberty among her friends'. The constable of the Tower at the time, appointed in October 1335, was none other than Nicholas de la Beche, later the second husband of Margery Poynings, whose first husband Edmund Bacon died in March 1336 while Alice de Lacy was going through her ordeal.[18] Why Nicholas did nothing to aid Alice, one of the greatest noblewomen in the country, is unclear, and even the king himself stayed at the Tower a few times in March and April 1336 at about the time that Alice must have been there.[19]

Alice's petition to Edward III makes it all too painfully apparent how frightened, distressed, and angry she was about the matter and about her close confinement in the Tower. She pointed out twice in her petition that what had happened to her was 'against her status' and against her vow of chastity. Other than the temporary imprisonment at Somerton Castle, Edward III did not punish Hugh Frene in any way, and to add insult to injury, Pope Benedict XII ordered the bishop of Lincoln to 'warn and compel' Alice 'by spiritual penalties' to keep the vow of chastity she had taken, as though she was responsible for having failed to do so. Benedict claimed that Alice had 'consented to live with [Frene] in matrimony until his death', but as she had absolutely no way to stop being married to Frene after he kidnapped her and forced her to go through a wedding ceremony with him, her alleged consent was meaningless. Perhaps the only meagre consolation for Alice was that Hugh Frene was sent on campaign to Scotland not too long after their wedding and died there in December 1336 or January 1337, only a few months after his abduction and rape of her; they cannot have lived together very long, and Frene gained very little benefit from his abduction of her.[20] What must have made Alice's nightmare even worse was her knowledge that Frene had kidnapped her in her own home thanks to the 'betrayal', as she called it, of her own half-brother John de Lacy and some of her servants.[21] A born survivor, however, Alice de Lacy, countess of Lincoln, lived until October 1348 when she was almost sixty-seven.[22]

Alice de Lacy's grandmother was also subjected to abduction and forced marriage. Maud Clifford was the daughter and heir of Walter Clifford (d. 1263) and Marared ferch Llywelyn, and married William Longespee, earl of Salisbury (d. 1256/57), with whom she had one child, Margaret, countess of Salisbury and Lincoln, Alice de Lacy's mother. On 1 October 1270, fourteen years after she was widowed, Maud Clifford was forcibly taken from her manor of Canford in Dorset by John, Lord Giffard of Brimpsfield, and a 'great multitude of armed men'. The abduction came to Henry III's ears four days later on 5 October, and he demonstrated concern for Maud's well-being and ordered Giffard to appear before him and explain himself on pain of forfeiting all his lands. Giffard duly appeared and claimed that he did not abduct Maud against her will, but the statement that on 10 March 1271 she was 'so inflicted by infirmity that she cannot come before the king at present' is surely revealing.[23] Katherine, the eldest of John Giffard and Maud Clifford's three daughters, appears to have been born in 1272, and one might speculate that Maud became pregnant as a result of rape and therefore concluded that she had little choice but to marry her abductor and rapist.[24]

Chapter 13

Abduction and Ravishment (2)

In the late Middle Ages, it was also reasonably common for boys or young men under the age of 21 to be abducted with the aim of marrying them off, usually to a member of the abductor's family. Men came of age at 21 and thereafter owned the rights to their own marriages; this was not the case for women, who could be and often were abducted and forcibly married at any age. Alice de Lacy was 54 when it happened to her in late 1335 or early 1336, and by contrast, the great heiress Margaret Audley was probably only 13 or 14 when she was abducted by and forcibly married to Sir Ralph Stafford at almost the same time, in *c.* February 1336. The Second Statute of Westminster in 1285 set the punishment for abducting a child (whether male or female) whose marriage belonged to someone else at two years' imprisonment, if the person restored the child still unmarried or paid what the marriage was worth. Otherwise, the punishment was either life imprisonment or abjuration of the realm, i.e. permanent exile from England.[1]

At the start of the 1240s, William FitzWilliam was in the custody of Christine Spicer, widow of Joce Spicer, after losing his parents. While Christine and William were worshipping in the church of All Hallows in Bread Street ward in London around 9 a.m. on Saturday, 4 May 1241, Simon FitzMary and Robert Herbintun came into the church 'by force' and dragged William out. They kept him imprisoned in various places for over seven months until the unfortunate youngster died on 13 December 1241. Simon and Robert admitted having William in their custody, but denied taking him by force, and claimed that he died a natural death. A couple of years later, Simon FitzMary complained that a group of eight men and one woman broke out into his house and assaulted him, and a couple of months later in October 1243, they came back. On this occasion, they threw him out of his house and stole some of his charters and documents, so this was perhaps a retaliatory move in some way for his actions against William FitzWilliam. On the other hand, Simon withdrew his appeal and was taken into custody for making a false claim, so seemingly invented or at least grossly exaggerated the whole scenario.[2] Ironically, Simon FitzMary served as sheriff of London in 1233/34 and again in 1246/47, and in 1247 founded the hospital of St Mary of Bethlehem, better known as Bedlam. His forceful abduction of young William FitzWilliam is one of the many medieval examples where even those men appointed to uphold the law sometimes broke it violently. Simon's motive for the abduction is nowhere explained, but it almost certainly had something to do with arranging William's marriage to one of Simon's relatives and thereby keeping the boy's inheritance within Simon's family.

John Chaucer, father of the great poet Geoffrey Chaucer, was born in London probably in 1312. His mother was Mary, widow of John Heyron or Heron, with whom she had a son, John's older half-brother Thomas Heyron. His father was Robert Chaucer, who had moved to London from Ipswich in the late 1200s or early 1300s and died in 1315 when John was about 3 years old. The boy was raised by his mother and her third husband, Richard Chaucer (who was most probably not a relative of her second husband but worked in the same profession).

John's paternal family remained in Ipswich, and his father's sister Agnes Chaucer married Walter Westhale and had a daughter, Joan Westhale. After she was widowed, Agnes married a second husband, Geoffrey Stace, sometime before 1324. That year, Agnes and Geoffrey Stace cooked up a harebrained scheme to marry her nephew John Chaucer to his cousin, Agnes's daughter Joan Westhale, and to that end abducted him from his mother and stepfather's home in London. Their aim was to keep property in Ipswich within the family, though how exactly their plan would have worked is another matter; marrying one's first cousin was all but unknown in fourteenth-century England, and it seems unlikely that the pope would have granted a dispensation for consanguinity, as would have been required. The royal writs ordering the arrest and imprisonment of Agnes and her husband call their abduction of Agnes's nephew a 'ravishing'.[3] In the end, John Chaucer married Agnes Copton, and in *c.* 1342/43 they became the parents of Geoffrey Chaucer.

In or not long before July 1315, a boy or young man named Thomas Frauanceys, eldest son and heir of the late Alan Fraunceys, was abducted from his mother Joan's custody in Beckingham, Nottinghamshire. Those responsible were two brothers who confusingly were both called John Darcy, and several other men: William Gorham, Richard Alkebarowe, Robert Laun, who was a chaplain, and William Weyburn or Wybourne, who was the parson of Saundby just over a mile from Beckingham. A few months earlier, William Weyburn the parson was accused of assaulting the brothers Simon and Thomas Beltoft (see Chapter 6 above), and in September 1315, Joan Fraunceys stated that Simon Beltoft had broken into her house and stolen her goods.[4] The outcome of Thomas Fraunceys' abduction is unknown.

Reynold Frowyk, a goldsmith of London, died in or shortly before October 1300. He was the son of Henry Frowyk, who served as one of the sheriffs of London in 1274/75 and died in 1286, and Isabella, who died in 1300 at almost the same time as her son. Reynold came from a large family and had five brothers and five sisters. He married a woman called Agnes, and they had a son whom they named Henry after Reynold's late father. Henry Frowyk the younger was born in 1294 or 1295, and was officially placed in his mother Agnes's custody in November 1300, not long after he lost his father (as children in the Middle Ages were considered to 'belong' to their father rather than to their mother, it was not always a given that their mother would be named as their official guardian if their father was dead). By the summer of 1308, Agnes and Henry were living in the Hertfordshire village of Furneux Pelham, about 35 miles from London.[5]

Henry was either 14 years old or not yet 13 years old – his age was fiercely debated by the justices of the King's Bench – when he was abducted from his and his mother's home in Furneux Pelham on 6 July 1308. The four men responsible were Sir Thomas Leukenore or Lewknor, John Felsted or Falstede, and William Pountz or Poyns and his son Richard. They took Henry to the earl of Hereford's castle of Pleshey in Essex and kept him there for nearly three months until 2 October 1308, and he was married off at Pleshey to Margaret Pountz, daughter of William and sister of Richard. Agnes Frowyk submitted a petition to Edward II stating that the marriage had been carried out against her will as Henry's mother and guardian and against Henry's own will and also took the case before the court of King's Bench.

One of the conditions of Agnes's being granted custody of her own son in November 1300 was that she would 'not let him be disparaged or marry without the consent of the mayor and aldermen' of London. In the records of the King's Bench, Agnes called what had been done to her son *ravissement*, 'ravishment'. She was eventually awarded damages of 200 marks (£133).[6]

The earl of Hereford, at whose castle the unauthorised wedding took place, was Humphrey de Bohun, who was in his early 30s in 1308 and married to Edward II's sister Elizabeth of Rhuddlan. William Pountz was appointed as one of two tax-collectors in Middlesex in December 1306 (by Edward I) and again in November 1307 (by Edward II), so held a position of some responsibility.[7] Sir Thomas Leukenore was born in *c*. 1270/71 as the son and heir of Sir Roger Leukenore (d. 1295), had a son named Roger born in *c*. 1304, and was knighted in May 1306.[8] He owned the manor of South Mimms, then in Middlesex and now in Hertfordshire, and it was held from the earl of Hereford. This is surely the reason why Leukenore and his accomplices took Henry Frowyk to Pleshey, one of the many properties that belonged to the earl, his overlord. John Felsted, the fourth accomplice to Henry's abduction, was the parson of Hadley, now in the London borough of Barnet, less than 4 miles from South Mimms. The Frowyk family also had strong links to South Mimms: Henry Frowyk's father Reynold and paternal grandparents had owned property there.[9] Henry's son Thomas (d. 1375) and grandson Henry Frowyk the younger (d. 1386), and Henry the grandson's maternal grandfather John Durham (d. 1369) were all buried in the churchyard of St Giles in South Mimms.

Henry Frowyk himself, the boy abducted and forcibly married in 1308, and his son Thomas witnessed a grant alongside Sir Thomas Leukenore's son and heir Sir Roger Leukenore in South Mimms in June 1349, during the Black Death, and in 1342 Henry was specifically named as 'Henry Frowyk of South Mimms'.[10] Henry outlived his son Thomas and did not die until April or May 1377, when he was over 80 years old. His will does not mention Margaret Pountz, the girl or young woman to whom he had been married without his consent so many decades earlier, and though she had surely already died, it is perhaps telling that he did not ask to be buried next to her, nor ask for masses to be sung for her soul.[11] As for Thomas Leukenore, Edward II appointed him as one of the keepers of the peace in Sussex with Andrew Peverel in July 1315.[12] It would hardly be the first time that a man charged with upholding the law broke it.

Henry Frowyk, sheriff and alderman of London (d. 1286)
m. Isabella (d. 1300)
/
Reynold Frowyk (d. 1300) m. Agnes (alive 1310)
/
Henry Frowyk (1294/95–1377) m. Margaret Pountz,
daughter of William Pountz
/
Thomas Frowyk (d. 1375) m. Maud Durham, daughter of
John Durham (d. 1369)
/
Henry Frowyk (d. 1386) m. Alice Cornwall
/
Descendants

In the First Statute of Westminster of 1275, early in Edward I's reign, the punishment for rape was set at two years' imprisonment and a fine, and the statute referred to the crime as 'ravishment or taking by force'. This was, however, a deliberately low sentence because the law on rape was undergoing a major change, and another statute that was passed ten years later imposed the death penalty as the maximum sentence. For the first time in English history, women were allowed to prosecute their attackers, and the new law did not distinguish between married women and virgin women, which also represented a major step forward.[13] In London in October 1226, a few decades before this statute was passed, Emma, daughter of Walter of Coggeshall in Essex, appealed Gregory, son of master Gregory the Physician, of violently raping and deflowering (*rapuit et defloravit*) her, and Richard, son of Thomas the Imagemaker of aiding and abetting him. Richard was acquitted of complicity, but Gregory was taken into custody. Thirteen years later also in London, Lettice, daughter of Roese of Wimbledon, accused a vintner named Richard Norton of 'raping and deflowering' her, though he was acquitted.[14] Sometime before May 1276, the year after the Statute of Westminster, Isabella Chaddeston appealed Richard Staunford for rape, and he was outlawed, though was subsequently pardoned by the king. In September 1290 in Devon, Maud Shepstere accused Richard Pultimore of rape, and Edward I ordered a commission of oyer er terminer, to 'hear and determine' what had happened.[15]

The concept of consent evolved during the Middle Ages, and became well understood: in September 1328, someone acting on Edward III's behalf – Edward was then not yet 16 years old – sent three men to search for Joan Breton, and to determine 'whether it was against her will that she was ravished, abducted or detained' in Clipstone, Nottinghamshire. If they found that what had happened to Joan was without her consent, the three were 'to cause her to be safely and decently kept'.[16] It was, however, often difficult to secure a conviction for rape, and even when this happened, men were frequently pardoned not too long afterwards. Sometime before January 1350, the unfortunate Elianore Merton was raped by three men, Nicholas Bolton, John Lavenham, and John Waltham. The rapists sent three separate petitions to Edward III, all written by different scribes, but with such similar wording that it is apparent that the three men worked together to devise them. They all asked to be pardoned for their crime, which was called *ravissement* in the medieval French in which the petitions were written, on the grounds that they had done excellent service for the king during his military campaign in France in 1346/47. They all cited the Magna Carta, and two of them, Lavenham and Bolton, also declared that the king should have regard for the soul of his late father Edward II and issue them a pardon. Their efforts paid off: in January 1350, Edward III duly pardoned the three and released them from prison 'in consideration of [their] good service' during his siege of Calais in 1347.[17]

In Wiggenhall, Norfolk, Margaret Kerevyll stated in October 1349 that she had been abducted and 'ravished' by eight people, one of whom, surprisingly, was a woman: Katherine, widow of John Wygenhale. Margaret Kerevyll stated that the eight had come armed to her home, seized her, and imprisoned her in Katherine's house. Margaret's brothers and friends themselves went to Katherine's house and freed her. However, the 'evildoers' continued to plot 'day and night to ravish her again', Margaret said, and to kill her brothers in revenge. In fairness to the Norfolk authorities, 1349 was the year of the first great epidemic of the Black Death, which killed at least a third of the population, so they had much else on their minds, and it is entirely possible that local law enforcement officials were among the dead.[18]

Richard Loges, who owned the manors of Great Wyrley and Rodbaston in Staffordshire and was probably born in 1265, died shortly before 4 July 1300, leaving a widow named Elizabeth (though she appears in one record as 'Elena') and one child, a daughter also named Elizabeth, who was 7 years old. Not long after Richard died, before 20 September 1300, his widow Elizabeth (or Elena) was abducted in Rodbaston by Adam Staneye, during the night, and was forced to marry him. Just months later, at the start of 1301, Adam was jointly accused, with one other man, of the murder of one John Wyter, which gives some indication of the kind of man he was.

As Richard Loges had been a tenant-in-chief, i.e. a person who held land directly from the king, the rights to his widow's marriage were held by the king, and Edward I gave the rights to Elizabeth's marriage to Adam Staneye on 20 September 1300. A few years later in February 1306, however, Edward pardoned Adam for abducting and raping Elizabeth 'before the king had granted him her marriage', and Adam was indicted before the justices of oyer et terminer for the rape and for committing other 'trespasses and felonies' in Staffordshire. The royal pardon of 1306 was granted at the request of John Drokensford or Droxford, keeper of Edward I's wardrobe, who would become bishop of Bath and Wells in 1309. Adam Staneye was a member of Droxford's household in 1300.[19] Adam Staneye was still alive in March 1319, but by July 1321 Elizabeth was married to her third husband, John Saundrestede of Rodbaston (d. 1353), in what was apparently a voluntary union this time.[20] She had no more children by either of her second two husbands, and died not long before 2 November 1337; as she had outlived her daughter Elizabeth Loges by more than twenty years, her heir was her grandson, Elizabeth's son John Loges (born *c.* 1311/13). John took the last name of his maternal family rather than that of his father, Nicholas Warrewyk, and died in August 1349 during the Black Death.[21]

Agatha Tumby from Lincolnshire was the daughter of John Tumby, and married William atte Gote (or Gotere) from Boston on the Lincolnshire coast, about 12 miles from the village of Tumby, the ancestral home of Agatha and her family. William atte Gote and his father-in-law John Tumby both worked as merchants, and in the early decades of the fourteenth century were both appointed as customs collectors in the port of Boston.[22] Agatha and William did not have children or at least had no surviving children. William was alive in February 1316, but sometime before early 1317, Agatha was imprisoned in Lincoln Castle, charged with his murder. Two others were jointly accused with her, a man and a woman: the oddly named Cyncius Locok of Skirbeck, now a suburb of Boston, and Joan Helle from Miningsby, 7 miles from Tumby and 14 miles from Boston. In early 1317, Edward II ordered the three to be released, and in March 1317, pardoned Agatha for William atte Gote's death, stating that she had been 'maliciously charged' with murder. A year later, the king also pardoned Agatha's brother, John Tumby the younger, for harbouring her after her husband's murder. Rather peculiarly, the prior of Sempringham Priory in Lincolnshire was said to have harboured Agatha after William's death as well, and in September 1317 Edward II suspended a previous order to arrest him for doing so.[23]

What happened to William atte Gote and why Agatha was suspected of complicity in his death is unclear, and Agatha did not long outlive her husband. In early 1318, she was living or staying in the Derbyshire village of Creswell between Bolsover and Worksop, 60 miles from Boston, and was abducted from there on Wednesday, 8 February 1318 by a man whose identity was never discovered. While the two were crossing a bridge over the River Amber, a tributary of the River Derwent, on horseback, Agatha fell from her horse into the river and drowned. The current carried her into the Derwent itself, and her body was never found.[24] Despite several investigations, her abductor's name and his motives for the abduction remained unknown.

The English secular authorities did not usually concern themselves with moral and ethical misdemeanours, which were the province of Holy Church. In the first four decades of the fifteenth century, however, the mayor, sheriffs and aldermen of London made an exception to this rule, and arrested people whom they found committing adultery.[25] Adulterers were frequently caught and arrested in the middle of the night, either in their own home or their lover's, which gives an impression of busybody officials creeping around the London streets in the early hours, peering into windows. John Warham, chaplain of the church of St Michael Queenhithe, was found with his lover Margaret Wyver, a widow, at about 3 a.m. on 10 January 1427, and Ralph Wengrave, chaplain of the College of St Michael in Crooked Lane, was caught in bed with Agnes, wife of John Hebell from Southwark, between four and five in the morning on 31 October 1429. The punishment for adultery was to be put on the pillory, usually for an hour at a time on two consecutive days. The tailor Richard Dodd was put in the pillory for three straight hours, an unusually long time, in December 1407 after acting as a *baude* or 'bawd', i.e. a procurer, between his wife Margaret and a chaplain named William Langford. The chaplain Herman of Verona was 'taken in adultery with Agnes Bramptone, a married woman' on 13 July 1439, and on the same day, Joan Wakelyn, Margaret Hathewyke, and Margery Bradlee were indicted before Mayor Stephen Broun for 'diverse acts provoking to public immorality'. Some men were also convicted of this offence: one was the brewer Thomas Chapell in May 1439. Hugh and Joan Carpenter, a married couple, were convicted of public immorality on the same day as Thomas Chapell and were both locked into the pillory for an hour.

The authorities did not care about unmarried people having sex, only if at least one partner was married, or if one was a member of the Church; they were not clamping down on fornication, but only on adultery. In November 1406, married woman Alice Gyboun was arrested for committing adultery with John Marchall, unmarried, and in August 1429, John Couper and Katherine Frensshe, both married to other people, were arrested and taken before the mayor and aldermen. Roger Cokke, unmarried, was 'taken in adultery' with Isabella, wife of John Blosme, on 28 January 1404. The authorities took a very dim view of anyone 'procuring' adultery, such as Richard Dodd, above. Agnes Tikell was accused in June 1406 of procuring an affair between Geoffrey Briggewater, who was unmarried, and Agnes Wyche, who was married. In Middle English, this was known as being a *baude*, what we would call a pander or a pimp, as in the case of Richard Dodd in 1407.

According to the chronicler Thomas Walsingham, it was during the mayoralty of John Norhampton, i.e. in 1381/82, that the long and rather peculiar campaign against immorality first got underway in London. On 30 August 1389, the unmarried boatman John Kempe was caught with the married Isabella Smyth and was arrested and taken before the mayor and aldermen. Adultery was usually a case for ecclesiastical courts, not for the secular authorities, but John Norhampton made it punishable by the mayor's court.[26] The chaplain William Stofford was found on 20 January 1389 to have had an affair with Alice Hoo, and they were both arrested and imprisoned. The next day, they were taken before the mayor, Nicholas Twyford, and it was proclaimed that 'if anyone wished to prosecute them, right should be done'. Nobody did, so the two sheriffs of London took William and Alice to the Consistory, the legal court of the Bishop of London, 'according to the ancient custom in dealing with priests, secular or religious, and married persons when taken in adultery in the City'.[27]

Chapter 14

Abjuration, Outlawry, and Beheading Fugitives

A person who had committed a felony for which he or she (far more likely to be a 'he') would be executed once convicted was able to take another way out: abjuration of the realm, which was permanent voluntary exile from England, plus forfeiture of all possessions. Felons were allowed to spend up to forty days in sanctuary in a church, abbey, or other religious house after committing their felony, and during this time had to tell the county sheriff or one of the local coroners, or one of these men's deputies, of their wish to abjure the realm. Spending more than forty days in sanctuary was not permitted, and if anyone tried to stay longer than that, they would not be able to abjure the realm but would instead face trial – and most probably the death penalty – when they finally came out. After the period of forty days was over, if the person had not come out of sanctuary, nobody was permitted to give them food and drink or to communicate with them in any way, and anyone who did so would be declared an enemy of the king. While the criminal was in sanctuary, the local community would be expected to guard the church or abbey so that the criminal could not escape, though in practice they often did. Failure to do so resulted in a fine or other sanction.[1]

Ralph Waynefuntaynes was stabbed to death in St Paul's churchyard in London in December 1231, and his companion, a clerk named Geoffrey Russel, fled half a mile to another church, St Peter's on Cornhill. Fleeing the scene of a crime rather than staying put and raising the hue and cry was considered deeply suspicious, and suspicions were deepened when Geoffrey sought sanctuary in the church and refused to give himself up or talk to the sheriffs of London. The sheriffs ordered nearby residents to keep a watch over the church day and night, but Geoffrey escaped anyway.[2] Whether it was indeed he who had stabbed Ralph to death was never certainly established. John Phelpot came from Drayton in Hales, now known as Market Drayton, in Shropshire, and murdered a man called John Pigger in Kirkeby in Warwickshire, which probably means the village of Monks Kirby 10 miles from Coventry. After the murder, John Phelpot stole a horse and made his way to St Andrew's Priory in Northampton, where he arrived on 18 December 1377. He told law enforcement officials that he wished to abjure the realm but that he would not do so until the full forty days he was entitled to remain in sanctuary were over. Although he was placed under guard at the priory, he managed to escape one night and was never caught.[3]

The sheriff or coroner assigned abjurers a port from where to depart from England and told them the route they must take to get there and where to spend each night during the journey. While travelling to their designated port, abjurers had to wear a simple robe made of sackcloth, carry a wooden cross, and go barefoot and bareheaded, even in the depths of winter. The journey to the port required walking about 15 to 30 miles a day, and it was forbidden to spend more than one night in any one place on the way or to deviate from the route they had been given. Abjurers from London were usually sent to either Dover or Southampton, or, very occasionally, all the way over to Bristol. People from the Midlands who abjured the realm were sent to either Bristol, Southampton, or Dover, or very occasionally Portsmouth. The cross they carried was intended to signify to everyone that the person was an abjurer and should not be harmed on his/her way to the port.[4] The time given to abjurers to walk from London to Dover, a distance of 70 miles, varied between three and five days depending on their age, gender, and fitness. The routes given to abjurers by law enforcement officials indicate that they had a good map of England, or at least parts of it, in their heads; they knew how long it would take to reach places along the journey and where to tell people to spend the night depending on how fast they were likely to walk. Once the abjurer had reached his or her assigned port, s/he had to board the first ship whose crew consented to carry him/her and attempt to make a new life in a foreign country without any money, belongings, proper clothes, or shoes.

Simon Wolde stole a horse in Long Itchington in Warwickshire on 31 July 1321 but was spotted while doing so. He was pursued more than 11 miles to Aston le Walls, over the border in Northamptonshire, by, one assumes, the horse's owner and local law enforcement officials. Spotting a church in the village of Aston, Simon abandoned the stolen horse, ran inside, and claimed sanctuary. He confessed to the theft and unspecified other felonies and requested to abjure the realm. The local coroner assigned him the port of Dover, a journey of some 150 miles, which he would have to travel on foot. Simon's forfeited goods were 6d in coins, a belt, knife and purse worth a total of 4d, a spare tunic worth 2s, a sword worth 10d and a bow with twelve arrows, worth 1s.[5] The stolen horse was presumably returned to its original owner.

Walter Eure, a blacksmith, killed John Attehalle in Oxford in September 1297 when he stabbed him twice in the stomach during a quarrel one evening (both men were out on the streets after the bells had been rung for curfew, when they should have been at home). John lived until the following morning and was able to identify his attacker. Walter fled into sanctuary at the church of the Austin Friars on Smethegate or Smithgate and confessed his crime and his wish to abjure the realm to the coroner, Adam Spalding. Adam assigned him the port of Dover, 130 miles away. Just under half a century later in July 1346, Robert of Lincoln killed John of Cornwall also in Oxford by stabbing him in the heart, and was assigned Southampton as his place of departure.[6] Richard Lubbe from Eye in Suffolk stole a mare worth 2 shillings in Toseland, Huntingdonshire in March 1324, and tried to sell the animal in the market of Oundle in Northamptonshire, 30 miles away, but was recognised as a thief and fled to the chapel of St Thomas Becket in Oundle. He agreed to abjure the realm from Bristol, which necessitated a walk of a good 130 miles. In July 1356, John Somer of Kent sought refuge in the church of Ufford, a village in Suffolk, and admitted to having stolen woollen and linen cloths worth 6s 8d a year earlier. He was imprisoned in Melton two miles from Ufford for this felony and was assigned the port of Bawdsey not far from Felixstowe.[7]

No fewer than eight felons, all of them men, sought sanctuary in St Peter's Abbey in Peterborough (later Peterborough Cathedral) in October and November 1365. Two of them, David Walschman (i.e. Welshman) and Laurence Flemyng, had killed two other men, and the other six had stolen various things, including twelve sheep, two packhorses, and 5 shillings in cash. All of them decided to abjure the realm. Four were sent 150 miles to Southampton, two were sent 95 miles to Great Yarmouth, and the other two were sent, rather oddly, all the way up to Berwick-upon-Tweed, close to the Scottish border – a few decades earlier, between 1318 and 1333, Berwick had been in Scottish hands – and a good 260 miles from Peterborough. One of these two, Richard Pappoele, though originally from Northamptonshire, had robbed two men in Kent, and John Seyncler had stolen horses from the fields outside Langton in Leicestershire. David the Welshman evidently did not leave England as ordered after being told to abjure the realm from Southampton on 5 November 1365 as punishment for his murder of Nicholas Brigstok. On 14 February 1367, he and Hugh Walsheman, presumably a relative or friend, killed another of their countrymen, Thomas Walsheman, in Wellingborough, Northamptonshire, by stabbing him in the back and chest. Hugh was assigned the port of Sandwich to depart from England, while David was sent once more to Southampton. Once again, he did not leave, and on 30 July 1367 sought sanctuary in the church in the Leicestershire village of Slawston and confessed to stealing a horse worth 16 shillings. After being caught with the stolen horse, he was imprisoned but broke out and ran to the nearby church. For the third time, David was ordered to depart from England from the port of Southampton. It is apparent that the authorities of Northamptonshire and Leicestershire failed to realise that he was an abjurer who had not abjured the realm as ordered, but had continued to commit felonies, as otherwise he would have been executed. Whether David did finally leave the realm on the third occasion, or whether he simply became better at hiding his felonies and not being caught, or perhaps returned to his native Wales, is uncertain.[8]

Beheading Fugitives

Those who escaped from prison, evaded the hue and cry, or decided to stay in England unlawfully after agreeing to abjure the realm, were often summarily decapitated when they were caught, 'as a fugitive fleeing from justice'. John Ditchford was one of a group of men who robbed and killed another man in Northamptonshire in March 1322. He informed the local coroner that he wished to abjure the realm, but during his first day's walk to the coast and to his assigned port, he abandoned the king's highway and fled towards a nearby wood. Unfortunately for John, he was spotted and pursued by a group of locals, and when he was caught, his pursuers decapitated him on the spot. By order of the local coroner, Richard Lovel, they took his head to Northampton Castle as proof that an outlaw was dead. The same thing had happened to John Westfield, a hayward from Hertfordshire, almost half a century earlier in April 1276. In sanctuary, he confessed to being a thief, and agreed to abjure the realm from Dover. On his way to the port, John left the highway but was spotted by a man who raised the hue and cry. He was caught and beheaded. Also in 1276, Philip Taylor of Clun in Shropshire broke into the house of Reynold Kaym in Upton Magna, about 30 miles away, one night. Reynold woke up and grabbed his sword, and tried to seize Philip, who shot the unfortunate Reynold through the testicles with an arrow. He then fled into the night, but Reynold, despite his doubtless very painful injuries, 'followed him with cry and horn, and killed him with his sword as a robber and a fugitive'. After an investigation by the sheriff and coroners of Shropshire, Edward I pardoned Reynold for Philip Taylor's death, stating that he 'killed him as a thief fleeing and refusing to take his trial'.[9]

At the start of the 1300s, Simon Fot was imprisoned in Cockermouth Castle in Cumberland for 'larcenies and robberies'. He escaped, and the constable of the castle, John St John, and his deputies, John Burghman the castle gaoler and Adam Kereseye the local bailiff, 'pursued him with hue and cry'. When Simon was captured, he was immediately beheaded.[10] At almost the same time, in or not long before 1305, Michael Alde was also imprisoned in Cockermouth Castle, having stolen a cow. He escaped from captivity but was recaptured after the hue and cry was raised and was beheaded on the spot, having made it barely 4 miles to Setmurthy. His head was brought back to the gallows in Cockermouth and displayed in public.[11] In Clitheroe (then called Cliderhowe or Cliderhou) in Lancashire sometime in 1317, John Reved burgled a church and three houses, and killed another man, Henry Ridding. Henry Malton, the sheriff of Lancashire, sent the 'constables of the peace', the bailiffs, and men from four nearby townships to arrest him. John Reved fled from the men and resisted arrest and was therefore 'wounded and beheaded' in the presence of the bailiffs.[12] Robert Dodynton, an archer, escaped from prison in Rockingham Castle, Northamptonshire, sometime in 1347, and was pursued with hue and cry a little over 2 miles to a brook called *Chibbewyk brok* in the fields outside Cottingham. The unnamed man who caught up with Robert beheaded him with a sword, then dropped the sword by the body and fled.[13]

The sheriff of Lincolnshire, Thomas Boultone, aided by men from both Lincolnshire and Huntingdonshire, pursued a 'felon and outlaw' named Hugh Prest, who had murdered someone, all the way to Little Staughton near Bedford in June 1271. Hugh, who was on horseback rather than on foot, sought refuge in the house of Roger and Beatrice Temple, but the house was surrounded by his pursuers, and though Hugh fought fiercely, the men of Lincolnshire and Huntingdonshire overpowered him. They killed him and cut off his head.[14] On 9 May 1282, Richard Fox, who worked as a shepherd in a forest called Bykkele in North Yorkshire, spotted two men, John Cukewald and Richard Suthfeld ('Southfield'), prowling around and trying to steal his few possessions and some of his sheep. Shortly after the two men successfully stole some of his things, Richard Fox encountered three local foresters, Alan FitzJohn, Laurence Newton, and John Blank, and told them what had happened, whereupon the foresters ran to find the two robbers. John Cukewald shot an arrow at the three foresters and nearly killed one of them. The foresters pursued John, caught him and wounded him, and forced his accomplice, Richard Suthfeld, to behead him. John's head was then sent to Pickering Castle a few miles away, and according to an inquest carried out eighteen months later, making a felon decapitate his associate was 'the custom of Blachou Moor', i.e. the area then known as Blackhow Moor, now called the Hambleton Hills.[15]

In 1285, Philip Blakeneye and William Gorney were both beheaded 'as one fleeing from justice' after breaking prison in St Briavels Castle in Gloucestershire. Philip returned to the Forest of Dean, where he had been arrested, to continue to commit 'trespasses and robberies'. The constable of St Briavels, the excellently named Grimbald Pauncefot, pursued Philip and William with hue and cry, and ultimately, they were both killed by Richard Venur, a forester who worked in the Forest of Dean. Eight other men aided him in the capture of Philip Blakeneye, though in the matter of William Gorney, Richard Venur appears to have acted alone. King Edward I pardoned him for both deaths.[16]

An investigation always followed when a fugitive was beheaded. In February 1278, Geoffrey Nevill was temporarily imprisoned in Carlisle for the death of William Buk, 'whom he slew in pursuing him with hue and cry as a public malefactor not permitting himself to be justiced according to the law and custom of the realm'. Geoffrey was bailed.[17] Pursuing and arresting a criminal was not always, of course, a particularly safe thing to do. In January 1236, an unnamed man pursued a group of thieves from Cheshunt in Hertfordshire 15 miles to London Bridge and caught one of them (also unnamed) on the bridge. While he was conducting him to the city sheriffs, however, the thief stabbed him to death. The thief was subsequently captured and imprisoned, then hanged for the murder. Two of his two fellow thieves were also caught and abjured the realm.[18]

Chapter 15

The Death Penalty, Imprisonment, and Other Punishments

In the late 1200s, a young man named Robert Prat from Wingham in Kent was hanged for larceny. His body was taken down from the gallows and carried the 6 miles from Wingham to the church of St Martin in Canterbury – which still exists and is the oldest church building in England that is still used as a church – for burial. However, it was quickly discovered that Robert had survived the hanging and was not dead, and in September 1295, King Edward I pardoned him for the larceny out of 'reverence for St Martin'.[1] This was the second time in a few years that Edward I had pardoned a man for larceny after he was hanged for the felony but subsequently found to be still alive: in 1280, John Elenstreng of Yorkshire was discovered to be breathing in the church of St James in York after being taken there for burial.[2] And the same thing happened in Oakham, Rutland, a few decades later. On 2 April 1349, while the Black Death was raging through England, Edward I's grandson Edward III pardoned Geoffrey Cokerel. He was an approver, i.e. a person who was an accomplice to a felony and turned evidence against his fellows in exchange for leniency, who had been sentenced to death for falsely accusing four men of stealing four cows. Geoffrey had been imprisoned in the gaol of Oakham Castle and was hanged, but when his body was cut down from the gallows and taken to the local churchyard for burial, he 'miraculously, as is said, revived'. The king pardoned him for the false accusation he had made and for 'any other felonies done by him in England'.[3]

The death penalty was applied in numerous cases in medieval England, and most people were not fortunate enough to survive it. Women who were convicted of killing their husbands were often burned alive (see Chapter 10), though other criminals, both women and men, were usually hanged. Medieval hangings were either 'short drop' executions or there was no drop at all, and they were hoisted up onto the gallows with the noose around their neck. As this style of hanging did not break the neck, victims died slowly of strangulation. Noblemen who were executed were often beheaded with an axe instead, a privilege of rank, as it was usually faster. The beheading of Edmund Fitzalan, earl of Arundel, in November 1326, was, however, an exception: it was carried out by an incompetent executioner, perhaps using a blunt axe, who took at least seventeen and perhaps as many as twenty-two strokes of the axe to sever the unfortunate Arundel's head. Noblemen who committed treason were sometimes subjected to the traitor's death by drawing, hanging, and quartering, a horrible manner of death which involved being dragged to the place of execution by horses, being hanged but cut down well before death, then having one's internal organs – and sometimes testicles as well – removed and thrown into a fire. Beheading finally put a merciful end to the torment. A traitor's head was spiked on the gatehouse of London Bridge, and the four quarters of his body were placed on public view in four different towns, usually places that were far apart, such as Bristol, Carlisle, York, and Canterbury. The division of a traitor's body into five parts represented a punishment in the afterlife as well, as the victim would not have a whole body in which to stand up to face God on Judgement Day.

Desiderata Toryntone or Toryngtone, who presumably came from Great Torrington in Devon, was hanged in London in May 1337 for stealing forty dishes and twelve salt-cellars from Alice Lisle, a noblewoman, while Alice was staying in the bishop of Salisbury's house on Fleet Street. Desiderata was convicted by a jury of a dozen men. Two years later, however, another jury of a dozen men acquitted Margaret Brewestere, who had been charged with stealing a silver cup.[4] 'Byndo of Florence, a Lombard' stole six silver cups and a broken silver cup from his employer, the wine merchant and taverner John atte Belle (i.e. 'at the Bell', the name of the tavern) in London, and was hanged in April 1345. The Bell tavern stood on Berchernerslane, now called Birchin Lane and in the EC3 postcode, between Cornhill and Lombard Street.[5] Thieves were often stated to have been 'taken with the mainour', i.e. found and arrested with the stolen items in their possession, or what we would call 'caught red-handed' (*main* means 'hand' in French).[6] Many English towns as well as feudal lords had the right to subject thieves caught red-handed in their domain to trial and capital punishment; this right was called *infangenthef* or *infangthief*, an Old English word meaning roughly 'thief caught within' (in modern German, *fangen* still means 'catch').

There was no such thing as death row in medieval England, and execution often followed conviction remarkably quickly. John Goldweye killed Peter Messeday in London in 1269 and was hanged in Newgate prison in the city the next day.[7] On a Sunday evening in November 1300, William Sawiere (i.e. Sawyer) propositioned Christina Menstre in a London churchyard, and stabbed her under the right shoulder-blade after she rejected his advances and turned away. The wound was six inches deep, and Christina died shortly after the attack. William was hanged for her murder the following Saturday, just six days later.[8] The swiftness with which execution followed conviction was perhaps something of a mercy, given the horrendous conditions that prevailed in medieval prisons.

The theft of items worth more than 12½d was punishable by hanging, because in a society where most people were desperately poor and owned very little, stealing was seen as one of the worst crimes possible. Alexander Nedelere escaped execution for stealing a tunic from Joan Lavendere ('Laundress') in London in 1328, as the garment was worth only 10d. He was imprisoned in Newgate gaol for forty days instead, and Joan's tunic was restored to her. A year earlier, John Reynham also evaded execution for stealing a cloak and hood worth less than 12½d, and was flogged in addition to being imprisoned.[9] In April 1382, a weaver of Salisbury named John Bristow (whose name implies that he or his family came originally from Bristol) accused John Down of stealing items from him, including a towel worth 6d, a blanket worth 6d, and two sheets worth a shilling each. John Down was hanged.[10]

A very unusual execution in 1268 involved two Italian men, said to be 'Romans', whose names were recorded by English clerks as William Portu and James Portu. Presumably they were brothers or cousins who had settled in England (as many Italians did in the thirteenth and fourteenth centuries). William killed James in the London home of William Essewy or Esewey. He fled to Dover, but was captured by Stephen Penecestre, constable of Dover Castle, and was thrown off the cliffs into the sea.[11]

Female criminals were temporarily spared from execution if they were pregnant, as happened with Elizabeth Daubeney in 1388, and sometimes the women were subsequently pardoned. In early 1367, Joan Mellere of Suffolk broke into a house and stole 60 shillings in cash, a tunic with a hood, and various other items. She was sentenced to death, as thieves in medieval England almost always were, but the sentence was postponed because of her pregnancy. Edward III 'pardoned her the said execution' altogether in July 1371. He also pardoned Beatrice Smyth of Nottinghamshire, convicted of being a 'common thief' in 1376 but found to be pregnant by 'a jury of matrons'.[12] In February 1357, the oddly named Sciencia of Balderby in Yorkshire, wife of William Taillour, 'received' her husband even though she knew he had killed Simon Hogge (harbouring or 'receiving' known criminals was a serious felony in late medieval England). She was therefore sentenced to be executed, but she was pregnant, and the judgement was postponed, then Edward III pardoned her.[13] The other main way to avoid execution was to abjure the realm (see Chapter 14).

Imprisonment

In the late Middle Ages, prison was often known sarcastically as *Bocardo*, because in scholarly logic, a *bocardo* is a logical argument from which one cannot escape. In fact, plenty of people did break out of prison. Despite the huge risk involved in doing so – those who did so must have known they were highly likely to be beheaded if they were caught – it is astonishing how many people did so, and astonishing how easy it seems to have been. Not long before June 1293, John Somenur 'broke the prison of Worcester', where he had been imprisoned for an unspecified felony. John's fellow prisoner Alan Astwode escaped with him, and killed one of their gaolers, John Fot, in the process. John Somenur was caught, 'and because he would not surrender, he was beheaded'. Alan Astwode seems to have remained at large.[14] In 1325, no fewer than ten people escaped from Newgate one night, and only five were recaptured by the prison warders, assisted by residents. Ten years earlier, the prison was said to have 'certain chambers which are in a ruinous state' and which might make it easy for prisoners to escape, and this prediction was proved correct. The men who escaped and were recaptured were, luckily for them, not summarily beheaded but were allowed to abjure the realm and assigned the port of Dover as their place of departure from England.[15]

John Richedale was imprisoned in Ipswich gaol in late 1357 after stealing a heifer but escaped mere weeks later. John Somer of Kent moved to Suffolk and stole woollen and linen cloths from John Amundeville in Sternfield in June 1355. He fled 10 miles to Ufford and sought sanctuary in the church there. The local coroner, Richard Martlesham, questioned John Somer there, and John confessed to the theft and to having previously escaped from prison in Melton, just 2 miles from Ufford, in the company of a prisoner named Henry Selsey and another man whose name he did not know. John Somer agreed to abjure the realm, and Richard Martlesham assigned him the port of Bawdsey, 10 miles from Ufford.[16]

By the early 1350s, the gaol in Aylesbury in Buckinghamshire had become 'ruinous' and 'unfit for the custody of prisoners' to the extent that five of them managed to escape on Monday, 21 October 1353: Richard of Essex, Thomas Marche, William Porser or Purcere of Beaconsfield, William Blaket, and William Moldesone or Moldesson of Cublington near Aylesbury, who killed a man named Richard North in Cublington on 12 July 1353. The deputy keeper of the gaol, Richard Bermynton, was, perhaps rather unfairly given the inadequacy of the prison buildings, held responsible for the escape of the five prisoners. Evidently distrustful of the notion that he might be treated fairly and justly, Richard fled, and all his goods were seized and confiscated. After taking advice from fourteen masons and carpenters, the sheriff of Buckinghamshire ordered Aylesbury gaol to be entirely rebuilt. The five prisoners were not recaptured (or at least it does not appear on written record that they ever were).[17]

Medieval towns often had two or more prisons, one (or more) in the town itself and another in the local castle. Jailers had no obligation to feed prisoners, and anyone who had no money to pay them for it or had no relatives or friends to bring them food regularly was left to starve to death. Other prisoners died of the cold in winter, as they had to sleep on the bare floor if they did not have a bed and blankets of their own or if they could not afford to pay 1d a day to have one provided for them by their gaolers. Some kindly people donated beds and blankets to prisoners.[18]

Three men convicted of theft, William Brich, Thomas atte Grene, and Adam May, were allowed to starve to death in Newgate prison, London in 1322. In 1322 and 1323, at least ten prisoners died of hunger and thirst in Northampton Castle, and at least another seven died of the cold. One of these seventeen prisoners was William Cook, who was imprisoned after stealing a colt and died of 'hunger, thirst and privation' on 1 August 1322, and another was Robert Rushton, a clerk convicted of false accounting, who died of the same causes on 20 March 1323. Another prisoner in Northampton Castle, John Swan, who committed burglary in the cellar of one Eustace Burneby in Watford (a village in Northamptonshire, not the Hertfordshire town of the same name), died of 'hunger and the flux', meaning dysentery. A few decades later in 1378, Thomas Skynnere of Burford in Oxfordshire died of 'a disease called the flux of blood, of which disease he sickened for three weeks' while incarcerated in the prison of Oxford Castle.[19] Alexander Bekebrok was perhaps somewhat luckier in 1347: imprisoned in Oxford Castle after stealing four sheep from a tenant of Sir Richard Damory in rural Oxfordshire, he 'died a natural death and not by the hardship of the warden of the prison'. As it had to be specifically stated that Alexander died naturally, however, and as he stole the sheep at the end of November 1346 and died in prison just two and a half months later in mid-February 1347, one wonders how natural his demise really was.[20]

Although Newgate prison in London was perhaps the most notorious English gaol of the late Middle Ages, in some ways its prisoners were rather more fortunate than the people incarcerated elsewhere, and much less likely to die of thirst or of the cold. Water was brought to Newgate from the hospital of St Bartholomew via an underground leaden pipe and was provided for free, and the prisoners were even allowed to purchase ale if they wished. They could also buy coal for cold nights in their cells at a cost of ½d for a full heaped peck, 1d for half a bushel, and 2d for a bushel. Some prisoners in Newgate – the more privileged ones at least – were allowed to go 'every day at convenient times' to the chapel and to 'two spacious and well-lit chambers' on either side of the chapel if they were male. Female prisoners could leave their cells on occasion and go to a large chamber on the south side of the gaol. In another London gaol, Ludgate, two prisoners were permitted to go outside the prison daily to beg for alms from passersby. In 1388, a former prisoner of Ludgate complained about the keeper, John Bodesham, and his deputy, William Rounde. The two men had received alms sent by kindly people for the prisoners, but instead of distributing it fairly, they gave it out to the warders, other prison servants, and just three or four favoured prisoners. The other prisoners 'raised a great clamour' against this injustice.[21]

A frequent and serious issue with medieval gaols was the gaolers, who were often brutal and corrupt. Alan Blunt was arrested in Lincoln on suspicion of theft on Friday, 19 June 1254. The jailer, Alan FitzWilliam, placed him in the pillory overnight – indoors rather than outdoors – but the next morning, found him dead with a 'swollen neck'. FitzWilliam was accused of allowing Blunt to die from the 'stiffness and roughness' of the 'tight and thick iron collar' which he had placed around his neck. He was, however, pardoned by Henry III in November 1255 for his actions which led to Alan Blunt dying. The king stated, peculiarly, that the true cause of Blunt's death was the 'severity and grievousness of that prison' and 'the discomfort of imprisonment', not by anything done by Alan FitzWilliam specifically.[22] Ten years earlier, in London in 1244, a man named Geoffrey (his last name was not recorded) was convicted of the murder of Simon Blund and subsequently imprisoned in Newgate. The sergeant of the two sheriffs of London, John Shep, was responsible for taking Geoffrey to the prison, and 'flung him so violently into the deepest part of the prison that he broke his neck and died'. John Shep fled and was outlawed.[23]

A former prisoner of Newgate stated in 1314 that although he 'ought not to have been placed in the depths of the gaol as a felon or thief', he was placed in a cell 'with notorious felons and thieves and horribly laden with iron fetters', thanks to the malice of one of the guards. Twenty years later, Edward III stated that the Newgate guards 'have been guilty of oppressions and extortions' by putting men incarcerated for minor offences in the same cells as 'notorious felons', by committing torture, and by taking bribes and ransoms from prisoners. Hugh of Croydon, the keeper of Newgate, was removed from his position in March 1341 after committing numerous 'oppressions and extortions' on the prisoners.[24] In June 1325, Nicholas atte Mulle, the gatekeeper of Newgate, was killed by Adam Cheddesleye of Clitheroe in Lancashire, who had recently escaped from the prison with three other men (mere months later in September 1325, no fewer than ten prisoners escaped one night). Two women, Alice Ellefeld, sister of the dean of St Martin le Grand, and Alice Barber of Croydon, were said to have 'connived' in Nicholas atte Mulle's murder and to have provided the knife with which Adam Cheddesleye killed him. Adam, his fellow escapees, and the two women all fled from justice, and the motive for the murder and the two women's complicity in it was never explained.[25]

There is a reference to 'a dreadful prison called *Julianesboure* in Newgate' in June 1370. *Julianesboure* means 'Juliane's Bower', and the place was evidently a particularly notorious section of Newgate, already a particularly notorious gaol itself. John Bambourgh, a clerk, complained that he had been imprisoned in Juliane's Bower for eleven weeks 'without any legal process'. For five weeks of his sentence, he was held in fetters, tortured, and 'made sport of', or so he claimed later, though an investigation found that he had been rightfully imprisoned after using 'many insulting expressions' against Edward III's recently deceased queen Philippa of Hainault (d. August 1369) and had not suffered torture or abuse.[26]

Mutilation as Punishment

A punishment sometimes inflicted on criminals in the late Middle Ages – usually repeat, unrepentant offenders – was to have an ear or a hand cut off. This happened to Margery Dike in Leicester in the 1260s. She committed theft on several occasions and was sentenced to the pillory each time. On the third occasion, she was also ordered to leave Leicester for good. Margery, however, returned to Leicester a while after leaving, and subsequently stole some wool worth 3d. Despite the low value, because she was seen to be an incorrigible thief who had returned to the town despite being banished, she was condemned to have her ear cut off, and was told that if she returned to Leicester yet again, she would be subjected to 'the other judgement that is not to be written', meaning the death penalty. Thankfully, this punishment appears to have been extremely rare, though there is a grim reference in 1349 to John Cuner of Hampshire, who 'was lately blinded and mutilated for larceny'.[27]

The medieval kings of England sometimes issued notifications that a particular person had lost his or her ear or hand in an accident or while on military service, 'lest sinister suspicion arise' that they had been subjected to this mutilation because of a criminal act. Mariote of Carlisle, who stumbled in front of a cart in the early 1300s and had her right ear sliced off, was one, and another was John Sheperton, who lost his right hand while fighting in Scotland in the 1310s or early 1320s. Edward I issued one for Richard Chardrugg in July 1276 after the unfortunate

Richard 'lost part of his right ear by a bite of one of the king's horses'.[28] A fifteenth-century text stated that *Them that cutte purses, cutte men the eres of* or 'them that cut purses, cut men the ears off'. This is a reference to the fact that many people carried money in a purse hanging by a strap from their belt, and thieves or *cuttars of purses* simply sliced through the strap to steal it.[29]

The Pillory and the Hurdle

A common sight in medieval English towns was the pillory, a wooden contraption into which the head and hands of criminals were locked as punishment. The stocks, which secured the feet rather than the head and hands, were also sometimes used. In the centre of late medieval London there were at least two pillories, both located in places with a high footfall: Cheapside and Cornhill. Part of the aim of locking people into the pillory was to make their punishment as public and as humiliating as possible.

The usual sentence for anyone unfortunate enough to be subjected to this treatment was to be locked in the pillory for half an hour or one hour, occasionally two or even three hours if the person was a repeat offender or unrepentant, or occasionally for an hour on two or more market days. The Middle English word for a judicial punishment was *juesse* or *iewisse*, as in 'the *juesse* of the pillory'. When sentenced, proclamation was made that 'he shal stonde here on the pillorie thre[e] market dayes, eche day an hool hour' (each day a whole hour). In 1423 in London, Jhonet Cogenho was sentenced to the pillory with the words that she 'shal stond thys day an hour in thys open place to be seyn and knowen' (seen and known).[30] Market days were deliberately chosen because more people were out and about in the streets doing their shopping.

Anyone found to have sold bad ale was forced to quaff some of it, then the rest was poured over his head as he was locked helplessly in the pillory. For those who sold bad meat to their customers, the punishment was to have it burnt beneath them as they stood on the pillory. In 1364, John Cockow sold a 'putrid rabbit' to John Hockele in London and was locked in the pillory with the rabbit burnt underneath him, and fourteen years later John Bakere of Ruislip in Middlesex sold John Burle a 'putrid partridge' and was sentenced to half an hour in the pillory, also with the bird burning beneath him.[31]

As well as the pillory, many English towns in the late Middle Ages had a *cukstool* or cucking stool (later called a ducking stool), where men and women – though mostly the latter – convicted of being *scoldys* were punished. *Scoldys* or 'scolds' were people believed to be rowdy and abusive who disturbed the peace, or who gossiped incessantly. A special pillory only for women called the *thewe* was built on Cornhill in London in *c.* 1364 and was probably some form of chair or cucking-stool. In 1375, Alice Shether was put on the *thewe* after she was found to be a common scold who sowed envy and discord and used malicious and abusive words. Two years earlier, Alice Salesbury, a beggar, was locked into it for one hour after kidnapping Margaret, young daughter of John Oxwyke; she intended to force the child to beg with her to increase her takings.[32]

As mentioned earlier, another typical medieval punishment was to be dragged on the hurdle. The victim was tied to an assortment of wooden planks, which were then tied to a horse, and the horse dragged the victim through all the muck and grime in the streets. Minstrels banging on a drum or blowing a trumpet accompanied the procession, to draw as much attention to the victim as possible, and the procession always ended at the victim's home so that his or her neighbours would know what s/he had done. In London in October 1282, Robert Blake, a baker, was subjected to this punishment after being caught selling loaves of bread that did not weigh as much as they should. In 1316, Godfrey Rede was found to be selling a penny loaf that was too light and was punished with the hurdle, and at the same time, Richard Lughteburghe was punished for the same reason. Adam Lyndeseye was found to have baked *pain demaign* – the finest and most expensive type of white bread – that was 'of bad dough within, and good dough without', and was sentenced to the hurdle.[33] There were many regulations regarding the sale of food and drink to the public, and they were strictly enforced; anyone who broke them was punished harshly.

Banishment

Some people voluntarily abjured the realm and took permanent exile from England to evade execution, and another punishment was to be ordered to leave your town or city for good, as happened to Margery Dike in the 1260s, above, when she was banished from Leicester. This punishment was obligatory, not voluntary. People who committed crimes in London were sometimes ordered to leave the ward of the city in which they lived. Banishment from a town or from a ward of London (of which the city had twenty-four; twenty-five from the late fourteenth century) was a reasonably common punishment in the Middle Ages, and people deemed incorrigible repeat offenders were also sometimes banished from London altogether.

In the early 1320s, Richard Buckby stole a *tapet* (either a wall hanging or a coverlet) worth 7d from Thomas Lucas's house in Nottingham, and though he evaded execution 'on account of the small value' of the stolen items, he was ordered to leave Nottingham forever. John Cheddele was imprisoned for a while and banished from Billingsgate ward in London in 1371 for 'being a common player of dice by night and a constant nightwalker to the nuisance of his neighbours'.[34] Nightwalkers were those who broke curfew and were found out and about on the streets after dark, which was strictly forbidden. Margaret Hontyngdone was banished from Bread Street ward in London on the grounds that she is 'a common strumpet and … harboured men of bad repute'. She was imprisoned in June 1311 after returning to the ward.[35] When beadles, i.e. officials responsible for public order, were sworn into office in London, part of their oath stated that they would 'drive out' any robbers or prostitutes who settled in their ward.[36] To be banished from London in its entirety rather than simply one of its wards was reserved for very serious crimes or unrepentant criminals. Elizabeth Moring, who sold the sexual services of her female apprentices against their will, was punished by an hour locked in the pillory followed by permanent exile from London in 1386.[37]

Peine Forte et Dure

Another form of medieval execution, thankfully rare, was *peine forte et dure*, which translates as 'strong and hard pain' or 'strong and hard punishment'. It involved being slowly crushed to death for refusing to plead in court and thus refusing to submit oneself to the law of the realm. The victim lay on a stone floor wearing minimal clothing, and a huge weight of iron, usually several hundred pounds, was placed on top of him or her. According to a chronicler of Edward II's reign (1307–27), prisoners were allowed a small amount of mouldy bread and cloudy water during this treatment; on the days they received bread, they were allowed no water, and vice versa. Death might take several days.[38] This appalling fate was inflicted on Robert Lewer or Le Ewer of Hampshire, formerly a favoured member of Edward II's retinue who rebelled against the king: Robert was captured on Edward's orders shortly before 19 December 1322 and was dead of *peine forte et dure* by 8 January 1323.[39] Robert Lewer was a violent character who, according to a chronicler, was 'accustomed to lax morals from youth' and 'always ready for plunder and killing', and had committed adultery with a married woman then slain her husband and married her himself. A petition presented to Edward II in *c.* 1324 by Robert's widow Margery states that she had been accused of the murder of one Piers Boscombe or Doscombe, presumably her former husband. The king pardoned Robert Lewer in early 1321 for threatening to 'slay and dismember' the men whom he had sent to arrest Robert the previous summer for committing unspecified 'trespasses'. An exasperated Edward called Robert 'so vile a person' when ordering his arrest, but his long-term affection for him led him to pardon Robert and to bring him back into the fold of the royal court, until Robert's last rebellion in 1322 proved the final straw for the king.[40]

Cecily Rygeway was one of the very few, perhaps even the only, person in the late Middle Ages who survived this ordeal. Accused of killing her husband John Rygeway sometime before April 1357 and imprisoned in Nottingham, she refused to testify and remained mute, and so for forty days was kept in 'a narrow prison without food or water'. In April 1357, 'by a miracle', Cecily was found to be still alive, so was pardoned by the king, Edward III, and released.[41] The punishment of *peine forte et dure* was not formally abolished until the Felony and Piracy Act of 1772.

Burning Heretics

Another punishment often seen as typically medieval was the burning alive of those people deemed to be heretical in their religious beliefs, though most English victims suffered this awful fate in the sixteenth century, not in the medieval era. In 1401, Henry IV, at the behest of Thomas Arundel, archbishop of Canterbury, passed a law in parliament called *De Heretico Comburendo*, which permitted the burning of heretics at the stake. The statute was issued in response to a wave of religious nonconformity, led by John Wyclif or Wycliffe (d. 1384), whose followers were called Lollards and who were called 'perfidious and perverse people of a certain new sect' who held and preached 'wicked, heretical and erroneous opinions'. The punishment of being burned alive was intended to strike fear into people's hearts and to set an example for other Christians who might be tempted to believe erroneous doctrine.[42] William Sawtrey or Salter, burned at the stake in March 1401, was a very early victim, and one of the most famous medieval victims, Sir John Oldcastle, a Lollard leader and rebel and formerly a friend of Henry IV's son Henry V (r. 1413–22), was burned alive for heresy on 14 December 1417. As was the case with *peine forte et dure*, the repressive landmark in religious persecution *De Heretico Comburendo* remained on the statute books long after the Middle Ages and was finally abolished in 1677 with the Ecclesiastical Jurisdiction Act.

Finally, witch hunts, in the literal sense, began to occur in England in the fifteenth century, and one early victim was Margery Jourdemayne, the Witch of Eye, burned at the stake at Smithfield on 27 October 1441. Margery was associated with Eleanor Cobham, duchess of Gloucester and wife of Henry V's youngest brother Humphrey, who was convicted of treasonable necromancy in 1441 and condemned to life imprisonment. The great era of witch burning was, however, like the burning of heretics, post-medieval, and reached its height – or rather, its nadir – in the seventeenth century. Some horrendous punishments often assumed to have been medieval were far more frequently applied after the Middle Ages than during and persisted well into the eras known today as the Scientific Revolution and the Enlightenment. The medieval period was not the only one with barbaric punishments, and brutal though it could often be, was certainly not unique in its experiences of human cruelty.

Abbreviations

CCR	Calendar of Close Rolls
CChR	Calendar of Charter Rolls
CCW	Calendar of Chancery Warrants 1244–1326
CFR	Calendar of Fine Rolls
CHS	Collections for a History of Staffordshire
CIM	Calendar of Inquisitions Miscellaneous
CIPM	Calendar of Inquisitions Post Mortem
CLB A, CLB B etc	Calendar of Letter-Books of London, Letter-Book A, Letter-Book B etc
Coroner	Calendar of Coroners Rolls of the City of London A.D. 1300–1378
CPL	Calendar of Entries in the Papal Registers Relating to Great Britain and Ireland: Papal Letters
CPR	Calendar of Patent Rolls
MLLF	Memorials of London and London Life in the 13th, 14th and 15th Centuries, ed. H. T. Riley
RMO	Records of Medieval Oxford: Coroners' Inquests, the Walls of Oxford, Etc
SCCR	Select Cases from the Coroners' Rolls 1265–1413
SPMR	Calendar of the Select Plea and Memoranda Rolls of the City of London
TNA	The National Archives
Wills, vol. 1	Calendar of Wills Proved and Enrolled in the Court of Husting, London, vol. 1, 1258–1358
Wills, vol. 2	Calendar of Wills Proved and Enrolled in the Court of Husting, London, vol. 2, 1358–1688

Notes

Introduction

1. *Memorials of London and London Life in the 13th, 14th and 15th Centuries*, ed. H. T. Riley, 86–89, 91–93, 102–4, 140, 143–44; *Calendar of Letter-Books of London, Letter-Book C*, 154, 158–60; *CLB D*, 214; *CLB F*, 15.
2. *CLB E*, 147.
3. *Calendar of Coroners Rolls of the City of London A.D. 1300–1378*, ed. Reginald R. Sharpe, 35–37, 41; *Calendar of Wills Proved and Enrolled in the Court of Husting, London*, vol. 1, 1258–1358, 290.
4. *Coroner*, 43–44. Philip Asshendone was perhaps a relative of William Asschindone, a London goldsmith who died in *c*. November 1307: *Wills*, vol. 1, 194.
5. *Calendar of Inquisitions Miscellaneous 1219–1307,* no. 2063.

Chapter 1

1. *Calendar of Fine Rolls 1347–56*, 227, 262, 307–8, 403, 408–9.
2. *CFR 1319–27*, 142, 276–77.
3. *CLB C*, 79, 110, 173–80; *CLB D*, 16–31; *Calendar of Select Plea and Memoranda Rolls*, vol. 1, 23, 69.
4. *CFR 1307–19*, 220, 276; *Wills*, vol. 1, 339.
5. *Calendar of Close Rolls 1337–39*, 463; *CCR 1339–41*, 193, 335–36; *CFR 1337–47*, 92, 94, 96, 144, 146, 154.
6. *CFR 1337–47*, 349, 398, 446; *CFR 1347–56*, 22, 70, 85, 170, 227, 308, 419.
7. *CFR 1272–1307*, 12, 30, 38, 56, 103, 140, 171; *Collections for a History of Staffordshire*, vol. 7, 117; *Calendar of Inquisitions Post Mortem 1272–91*, no. 797.

8. *CCR 1318–23*, 578; *CFR 1327–37*, 425; *CFR 1337–47*, 83, 144, 172, 199, 349, 463; *CIPM 1317–27*, no. 210; *CIPM 1361–65*, no. 52.
9. *CFR 1391–99*, 95; *CFR 1399–1405*, 270; *CFR 1405–13*, 17, 221; *CFR 1413–22*, 426; *CIPM 1418–22*, no. 897; *CIPM 1422–27*, no. 681.
10. *CIPM 1317–27*, no. 210; *CCR 1318–23*, 578; *CFR 1327–37*, 425; *CFR 1391–99*, 7, 95; *CIPM 1377–84*, no. 291.
11. Thomas's widow Elizabeth died on 23 December in the same year. Although she had a son from her first marriage born in *c.* 1335, and Thomas and Elizabeth were said in 1357 to have had 'many children' together, none of the children was still alive when the couple died; Thomas's heir was John Fulnetby, either his nephew or cousin, and Elizabeth's was her late sister Margery's son John Pouger (b. 1336). *CFR 1356–68*, 52, 80, 392–93; *CFR 1369–77*, 36, 99, 144, 180, 201–2; *CIPM 1370–73*, nos. 181–82; *Petitions to the Pope 1342–1419*, 300.
12. *CFR 1377–83*, 113; *CFR 1383–91*, 152, 274, 298; *CFR 1391–99*, 8, 36, 41, 43, 132; *CIPM 1399–1405*, no. 695. Chalgrove belonged to Thomas's parents Thomas and Elizabeth Barentyn in 1344: Feet of Fines CP 25/1/190/19, no. 30.
13. *CFR 1319–27*, 130; *CFR 1327–27*, 17; *CFR 1356–68*, 80.
14. *Calendar of Patent Rolls 1377–81*, 304; *CLB I*, 6, 399.
15. *CIPM 1399–1405*, no. 695; *CIPM 1413–18*, nos. 571–80.
16. *CFR 1307–19*, 342, 360; *CHS*, vol. 11, 3, 97; *CPR 1313–17*, 425–27. Supposedly, the two sisters had been abducted by someone else in Yorkshire mere months before: *CPR 1313–17*, 416.
17. *CPR 1321–24*, 21; *CPR 1327–30*, 213–14.
18. *CPR 1327–30*, 157.
19. *CFR 1307–19*, 383; *CPR 1327–30*, 42.
20. *CPR 1327–30*, 429; *CIPM 1327–36*, no. 275.
21. *CPR 1313–17*, 403; *CPR 1324–27*, 232; *CPR 1327–30*, 429; *CIPM 1327–36*, no. 90.
22. *CCR 1360–64*, 420, 521–22; *CPR 1364–67*, 54–56; *CCR 1364–68*, 171, 463. Lionel's name appears in the Latin original of the texts as Lionellus or Lionettus, and as 'Lyonet': *CCR 1364–68*, 163.

Chapter 2

1. www.coronersociety.org.uk/the-coroners-society/history/, accessed 10 July 2025.

2. *Records of Medieval Oxford: Coroners' Inquests, the Walls of Oxford, Etc*, ed. H. E. Salter, 1–2; *Select Cases from the Coroners' Rolls 1265–1417*, ed. Charles Gross, xxiv–xxv.
3. *SCCR*, xx–xxiii; *CIM 1219–1307*, no. 523; *CCR 1307–13*, 515, 522.
4. *CCR 1399–1402*, 13, 19, 83.
5. *CIM 1348–77*, no. 14; *CPR 1348–50*, 197–98.
6. *Coroner*, 4–5.
7. *Coroner*, 2, 12–13, 36–37, 82, 139–40, 256.
8. *The London Eyre of 1276*, ed. Martin Weinbaum, nos. 91, 101.
9. *SCCR*, 99, 122; www.medievalgenealogy.org.uk/inquests/abstracts_109.shtml, accessed 8 July 2025.
10. *Coroner*, xiv.
11. *Coroner*, 70–71, 108–9.
12. *The London Eyre of 1244*, ed. Helena M. Chew and Martin Weinbaum, no. 40; *London Eyre of 1276*, nos. 33, 47.
13. *CIM 1308–48*, no. 1761.
14. *RMO*, 5, 42–43.
15. *London Eyre of 1244*, no. 51.
16. *Dialogues in French and English by William Caxton; Adapted from a Fourteenth-Century Book of Dialogues in French and Flemish*, ed. Henry Bradley, 41–42.
17. *The Parliament Rolls of Medieval England*, ed. Paul Brand, Anne Curry, Chris Given-Wilson, Rosemary Horrox, W. M. Ormrod and J. R.S. Phillips, January 1316 parliament.
18. *CIPM 1413–18*, nos. 571–79.
19. *CIPM 1291–1300*, no. 361; *CIPM 1300–7*, no. 213.
20. *RMO*, 3–8, 10, 12, 15.
21. *SCCR*, 74; www.medievalgenealogy.org.uk/inquests/abstracts_109.shtml, accessed 8 July 2025.
22. *SCCR*, 126.
23. *RMO*, 13, 17.
24. *Coroner*, 78–79, 98–99; *CIPM 1377–84*, no. 656; *SCCR*, 18–19, 21–23.
25. See for example *CPR 1354–58*, 329.
26. *RMO*, 15.
27. *CPR 1330–34*, 425; *CPR 1354–58*, 160–61; *CCR 1349–54*, 313. Roger's widow Maud died on 21 June 1361, and their son John, then aged about 22, was their heir: *CIPM 1361–65*, no. 46.
28. *CPR 1385–89*, 449, 454.

Chapter 3

1. *Calendar of Early Mayor's Court Rolls, 1298–1307*, ed. A. H. Thomas, 124; *CIM 1308–48*, no. 739.
2. *CIM 1308–48*, no. 739; *CCR 1323–27*, 96.
3. *CPR 1258–66*, 229.
4. *CLB B*, 271; *CIM 1219–1307*, no. 2225; *CPR 1272–81*, 346.
5. *RMO*, 19–20.
6. *SCCR*, 102–3.
7. *Records of the Borough of Leicester*, vol. 1, 1100–1326, ed. Mary Bateson, 379; the case is dated to sometime in the seventeenth year of Edward II's reign, i.e. 8 July 1323 to 7 July 1324.
8. Caroline Smith, 'Medieval Legal Records as Sources for Modern Historians: Coroners and Their Records in Hampshire and Wiltshire, 1327–1399', University of Southampton Doctor of Philosophy thesis (1995), 33–34, 68.
9. *Coroner*, 36–37, 41, 60.
10. *Coroner*, 65–66.
11. *Coroner*, 33–34.
12. *London Eyre of 1276*, no. 86; www.medievalgenealogy.org.uk/inquests/abstracts_109.shtml, accessed 8 July 2025.
13. www.medievalgenealogy.org.uk/inquests/abstracts_111.shtml, accessed 30 July 2025; *CIPM 1307–17*, no. 357.
14. *London Eyre of 1276*, no. 126.
15. *Coroner*, 52–53.
16. www.medievalgenealogy.org.uk/inquests/abstracts_640.shtml, accessed 7 July 2025.
17. *Coroner*, 140–41. James and his wife Emma had sons James, John, Thomas, William and Hugh (a fishmonger, d. May 1348) and daughters Isabel and Katherine. As well as being a vintner and a taverner, James Beauflour (d. October 1328) was the collector of customs in the port of London. *Coroner*, 100; *CCR 1318–23*, 700; *CCR 1323–27*, 613–14, 648; *CCR 1327–30*, 177–78; *CCR 1333–37*, 532; *CPR 1324–27*, 194; *CLB E*, 38; *Wills*, vol. 1, 336–37, 505; *MLLF*, 131–32.
18. *Statutes of the Realm*, vol. 1, 97.
19. *CIM 1219–1307*, nos. 2295, 2376; *MLLF*, 92.
20. *London Eyre of 1244*, no. 108.

21. *SPMR*, vol. 1, 126; *SPMR*, vol. 3, 1; *Records of the Borough of Nottingham*, vol. 2, ed. W.H. Stevenson, 265.
22. *Calendar of Early Mayor's Court Rolls, 1298–1307*, 261.
23. *SPMR*, vol. 2, 15, 127, 224, 265.
24. *SPMR*, vol. 1, 122–29; *Coroner*, 266–69; *CPR 1340–43*, 226–27.
25. *SPMR*, vol. 2, 128; *Wills*, vol. 2, 122–23.
26. *SPMR*, vol. 1, 231; *SPMR*, vol. 2, 220, 233.

Chapter 4

1. *CIM 1219–1307*, no. 2203; *CCR 1272–79*, 320.
2. *CIM 1219–1307*, nos. 2107, 2142; *CIM 1308–48*, no. 457.
3. *RMO*, 12; *CPR 1324–27*, 17; *London Eyre of 1276*, no. 113; *London Eyre of 1244*, no. 85.
4. *Coroner*, 221, 275–76; *CIM 1219–1307*, no. 2302; *CCR 1288–96*, 66.
5. *RMO*, 9–10.
6. *Coroner*, 61; *Annales Paulini 1307–1340*, in *Chronicles of the Reigns of Edward I and Edward II*, vol. 1, ed. William Stubbs, 304; *Wills*, vol. 1, 278.
7. www.medievalgenealogy.org.uk/inquests/abstracts_113.shtml, accessed 21 July 2025.
8. *London Eyre of 1276*, no. 275; *SCCR*, 80.
9. *SCCR*, 9–10.
10. *CIM 1308–48*, no. 848; *CHS*, vol. 10, 63–64.
11. The National Archives SC 8/18/863.
12. *London Eyre of 1244*, no. 146.
13. *RMO*, 2, 5, 7.
14. *MLLF*, 8; *CLB B*, 261.
15. *RMO*, 7–8.
16. *CIM 1308–48*, no. 1724; *CCR 1339–41*, 621–22.
17. *CIPM 1352–60*, nos. 196, 332.
18. *SPMR*, vol. 2, 199, 235, 237.
19. *MLLF*, 227.
20. *London Eyre of 1276*, nos. 13, 21.
21. *SCCR*, 77; Smith, 'Medieval Legal Records as Sources for Modern Historians', 52–53.
22. *RMO*, 40.

23. www.medievalgenealogy.org.uk/inquests/abstracts_640.shtml, www.medievalgenealogy.org.uk/inquests/abstracts_113.shtml, accessed 18 July 2025.
24. *Coroner*, 142, 250.
25. *Coroner*, 92–93, 205–6, 266–67.
26. *Coroner*, 194–95.
27. *CIM 1219–1307*, no. 2285.
28. *CIM 1219–1307*, no. 2133; *CPR 1266–72*, 84–85.
29. *CIM 1219–1307*, no. 2235; *CPR 1272–81*, 394.
30. *CIM 1219–1307*, nos. 2165. 2223.
31. *SPMR*, vol. 1, 36; *SPMR*, vol. 2, 172–73, 218; *Early Mayor's Court Rolls*, 205.

Chapter 5

1. *SPMR*, vol. 1, 18–19, 34, 154, 164, 198; *SPMR*, vol. 2, 146, 219; *CLB G*, 294.
2. www.historyextra.com/period/medieval/reporting-murder-crime-medieval-england/; www.cam.ac.uk/stories/medieval-murder-maps, accessed 18 June 2025.
3. *CPR 1391–96*, 605–6.
4. *Coroner*, 244–45.
5. Barbara A. Hanawalt, 'Death in Fourteenth- and Early Fifteenth-Century England', *Comparative Studies in Society and History*, 18 (1976), 312.
6. *CIM 1219–1307*, no. 2097; *SCCR*, 74; www.medievalgenealogy.org.uk/inquests/abstracts_109.shtml, accessed 20 June 2025.
7. *CIM 1219–1307*, nos. 2138, 2331.
8. *Coroner*, 77–78.
9. www.medievalgenealogy.org.uk/inquests/abstracts_113.shtml, accessed 30 July 2025; *CIM 1219–1307*, no. 2394; *CPR 1292–1301*, 542.
10. *Coroner*, 84–85, 165.
11. *London Eyre of 1276*, nos. 48, 151.
12. *SCCR*, 14; *Coroner*, 197–98.
13. www.medievalgenealogy.org.uk/inquests/abstracts_113.shtml, accessed 18 July 2025.
14. *Coroner*, 68–69.
15. *London Eyre of 1276*, no. 250.

16. *Records of the Borough of Leicester*, vol. 1, 371.
17. *Coroner*, 87–89.
18. *SCCR*, 130.
19. www.medievalgenealogy.org.uk/inquests/abstracts_107.shtml, accessed 26 July 2025.
20. *London Eyre of 1276*, nos. 117, 268, 274.
21. *London Eyre of 1276*, nos. 81, 85.
22. *London Eyre of 1244*, no. 172.
23. *London Eyre of 1276*, no. 265.
24. *CPR 1247–58*, 666; *London Eyre of 1276*, no. 87.
25. *London Eyre of 1276*, no. 163. Hugh Despenser the justiciar was killed at the battle of Evesham on 4 August 1265.
26. *London Eyre of 1276*, nos. 89, 601 (Lucy is called Lucie la Braceresse or 'Lucy the Brewster'); *London Eyre of 1244*, no. 135.
27. *London Eyre of 1244*, nos. 131, 190, 341, 345.
28. *SCCR*, 70.
29. *CPR 1324–27*, 145.
30. *SCCR*, 16. The phrase used in the Latin original of the text for 'twilight' was *inter canem et lupum*, literally 'between dog and wolf', i.e. the time around dawn or dusk when it is still mostly dark or is getting dark and it is difficult to differentiate visually between a dog and a wolf.
31. *CPR 1391–96*, 8, 28.
32. *CIM 1219–1307*, no. 2271; *CCR 1279–88*, 335.
33. *CIM 1308–48*, no. 738; *CPR 1321–24*, 434.
34. *London Eyre of 1276*, no. 39; *CIM 1219–1307*, nos. 2059, 2232; *CPR 1247–58*, 35, *CPR 1272–81*, 364, 370.
35. *SCCR*, 6–7.
36. *MLLF*, 54; *CLB E*, 116; *Coroner*, 132–34.
37. *MLLF*, 156–62; *Coroner*, 209; *CCR 1323–27*, 562–63; *CPR 1327–30*, 185.
38. *SPMR*, 122–29; *Coroner*, 266–69; *CPR 1340–43*, 226–27.
39. *CPR 1301–07*, 458; *SCCR*, 46–47.
40. *CIM 1219–1307*, no. 2202; *CIM 1348–77*, no. 832; *CCR 1369–74*, 494; *CIPM 1370–73*, no. 270; *CIPM 1377–84*, no. 297.
41. www.medievalgenealogy.org.uk/inquests/abstracts_113.shtml, accessed 20 July 2025; *CIM 1219–1307*, no. 1296; *Coroner*, 249; *London Eyre of 1244*, no. 121.

Chapter 6

1. *CIPM 1317–27*, no. 708; *CCR 1323–27*, 452–53; *CPR 1324–27*, 114, 247; *CFR 1319–27*, 386; *Calendar of Chancery Warrants 1244–1326*, 572; TNA C 143/178/5; *CIPM 1327–36*, no. 234; *CIPM 1365–69*, no. 215.
2. E.L.G. Stones, 'The Folvilles of Ashby-Folville, Leicestershire, and their Associates in Crime, 1326–1347', *Transactions of the Royal Historical Society*, 7 (1957), 119.
3. *CPR 1324–27*, 238, 243, 245, 250, 283–84, 286; *CCW 1244–1326*, 575; *CCR 1323–27*, 550–51.
4. *CIPM 1317–27*, no. 740. Ivo's wife Joan Inge, born *c.* 1299/1300, was the daughter and heir of Margery Grapinel and Sir William Inge (d. 1322), chief justice of the court of King's Bench. Ivo and Joan's son William Zouche, born in 1321 or 1322, was the heir of his paternal grandfather William Zouche of Harringworth (b. 1276) when the latter died in 1352. *CFR 1319–27*, 178; *CIPM 1317–27*, no. 328; *CIPM 1327–36*, no. 44; *CIPM 1352–60*, no. 42. By early November 1327, Joan Inge was married to her second husband, William Moton: *CCR 1327–30*, 182–83.
5. *CPR 1324–27*, 254.
6. *CPR 1324–27*, 249–50; *CPR 1327–30*, 20; *Calendar of Memoranda Rolls (Exchequer): Michaelmas 1326–Michaelmas 1327*, no. 2264; *CFR 1319–27*, 382.
7. *CCR 1323–27*, 550–51; *CPR 1324–27*, 250.
8. *CFR 1319–27*, 382; *CFR 1327–37*, 151, 193, 391; *CCR 1327–30*, 329.
9. *CIPM 1307–17*, no. 190; *CFR 1307–19*, 63, 65; *CPR 1313–17*, 355; *CCR 1346–49*, 525; TNA SC 8/46/2293, SC 8/193/9645, C 241/66/51, C 143/104/5; Feet of Fines CP 25/1/124/49, no. 121; Feet of Fines CP 25/1/125/57, no. 72.
10. *CPR 1327–30*, 213, 279; Feet of Fines CP 25/1/123/42, no. 287; and see also *CPR 1321–24*, 412.
11. *CPR 1327–30*, 10; Eustace, Robert, Richard and Walter Folville, and five others, were pardoned. See also *CCR 1327–30*, 343, and *CPR 1327–30*, 373–74.
12. *CPR 1330–34*, 61.
13. *CPR 1330–34*, 125.

14. Stones, 'The Folvilles of Ashby-Folville', 121; *CIM 1308–48*, no. 1270; *CPR 1330–34*, 561.
15. *CCR 1330–33*, 595; Stones, 'The Folvilles', 127.
16. *Year Books of the Reign of King Edward III, Years 14 and 15*, ed. Luke Owen Pike, 258; *bestourne et vendi les leys come boefe ou vache* in the Anglo-Norman original. In February 1339 seven years after his abduction, Richard Willoughby was jointly appointed with John Folville of Kirkby Folville on a commission of oyer et terminer. *CPR 1338–40*, 276.
17. Stones, 'The Folvilles', 122–23; *CPR 1330–34*, 367–68; *CCR 1330–33*, 611.
18. *CPR 1334–38*, 90, 93, 530–31. Northampton was a great-grandfather of King Henry V, born in 1386, whose mother was Mary de Bohun.
19. *CPR 1330–34*, 505; TNA SC 8/51/2532, SC 8/52/2579; *CFR 1327–37*, 345, 391.
20. *CPR 1338–40*, 481.
21. *CIPM 1272–91*, nos. 227, 688; *CIPM 1307–17*, nos. 157, 592; *CIPM 1317–27*, nos. 206, 754; *CIPM 1327–36*, no. 653; *CIPM 1347–52*, no. 114; *CIPM 1365–69*, nos. 129, 218.
22. *Calendar of Entries in the Papal Registers Relating to Great Britain and Ireland: Papal Letters 1342–62*, 142.
23. *CIPM 1300–7*, no. 241; *CIPM 1317–27*, no. 288. When William Beltoft died childless in 1322, his heirs were his three aunts, his father Roger's sisters. Simon was called 'the son of Roger Beltoft' in 1315 (*CCR 1313–18*, 211), though either this must be another Roger, or Simon was illegitimate and could not inherit from his father and half-brother William.
24. *CPR 1313–17*, 60, 73–74, 253; TNA SC 8/32/1597.
25. At this stage of his life, Simon Beltoft was said to be in the retinue of John, Lord Segrave (*c.* 1256–1325). *CIM 1308–48*, no. 2098; *CPR 1313–17*, 327; *CCW 1244–1326*, 415.
26. *CPR 1317–21*, 306.
27. *CCW 1244–1326*, 522–23; TNA SC 8/91/4538; *CPR 1321–24*, 55, 370; *CPR 1327–30*, 216.
28. *CPR 1327–30*, 57, 353; *CCR 1327–30*, 183.
29. *CIM 1308–48*, no. 1111; *CFR 1327–37*, 127.
30. *CPR 1330–34*, 29; *CCR 1330–33*, 56.

31. *CPR 1327–30*, 57, 353; *CCR 1327–30*, 268, 434; *CFR 1327–37*, 65, 103.
32. TNA SC 8/119/5913. Margery is identified as Simon's wife in *CPR 1327–30*, 282, 292, and in *CIM 1308–48*, no. 491. Simon died shortly before 14 January 1330: *CCR 1327–30*, 514.
33. *CCR 1330–33*, 555; *CCR 1333–37*, 508.

Chapter 7

1. *A Descriptive Catalogue of Ancient Deeds*, vol. 6, C.6013, and see also *CCR 1302–7*, 69, when Henry, as a knight, acknowledged a huge debt of £300 to his older brother Thomas in January 1303.
2. *The War of Saint-Sardos (1323–1325): Gascon Correspondence and Diplomatic Documents*, ed. Pierre Chaplais, no. 44.
3. *CIPM 1300–7*, no. 410; *CIPM 1307–17*, no. 220; *CIPM 1327–36*, no. 80.
4. *CPR 1292–1301*, 300; *CIPM 1300–7*, no. 263; *CPR 1307–13*, 487; *Calendar of Charter Rolls 1300–26*, 110; *CCR 1327–30*, 292–93.
5. *CCR 1296–1302*, 64, 70, 136, 139, 183, 387; *CCW 1244–1326*, 78, 103; *CFR 1272–1307*, 387, 390; *CIPM 1291–1300*, no. 414.
6. *CCW 1244–1326*, 333; *CPR 1307–13*, 407; *CPR 1317–21*, 126; *CPR 1327–30*, 301; *CPR 1330–34*, 171. John Hastings (September 1286–January 1325) was the father of Juliana's only child, Laurence Hastings, earl of Pembroke (March 1320–August 1348).
7. J.S. Hamilton, *Piers Gaveston, Earl of Cornwall 1307–1312: Politics and Patronage in the Reign of Edward II*, 43, 142–43 note 50.
8. *CCR 1302–7*, 66, 459; *CFR 1272–1307*, 543–44.
9. *Collectanea Topographica et Genealogica*, vol. 4, eds. F. Madden, B. Bandinel and J. G. Nichols, 66.
10. *CPR 1313–17*, 650; *CCR 1313–18*, 509.
11. *CPR 1313–17*, 419; *CCR 1313–18*, 283–84.
12. www.british-history.ac.uk/vch/kent/vol2/pp146-148, accessed 20 July 2025; *CCW 1244–1326*, 333; *CCR 1313–18*, 611.
13. Vicary Gibbs, 'The Battle of Boroughbridge and the Boroughbridge Roll', *The Genealogist*, 21 (1904), 224; *CCR 1318–23*, 580; *CCW 1244–1326*, 571–72; *CPR 1327–30*, 28, 70. At the start of 1328,

Henry lost his mother when Juliane de Sandwich died in her 70s: *CIPM 1327–36*, no. 80.

14. *CFR 1327–27*, 122–23; *CCR 1330–33*, 75, 193; *CPR 1330–34*, 42.
15. *CPR 1330–34*, 289, 580.
16. *CPR 1334–38*, 175, 180; *CCR 1337–39*, 42–43.
17. *CCR 1296–1302*, 146.
18. *CIM 1308–48*, no. 458; *CPR 1307–13*, 307; *CPR 1324–27*, 153; *CHS*, vol. 7, part 1, 25, 155; *CHS*, vol. 10, 45–46, 52, 54, 56, 59–60, 62.
19. *CPR 1317–21*, 418; *CPR 1321–24*, 148.
20. *CHS*, vol. 7, part 2, 26; *CHS*, vol. 10, part 1, 59, 61, 66, 74.
21. *CPR 1317–21*, 45; *CFR 1319–27*, 70; *CHS*, vol. 10, 59–61.
22. *CPR 1327–30*, 33; *CCR 1333–37*, 701; *Calendar of Memoranda Rolls 1326–1327*, nos. 2270, 2271; *CIPM 1336–46*, no. 180.
23. *CIPM 1336–36*, no. 180; CFR 1337–47, 71; *CHS*, vol. 7, part 2, 35.
24. *CIM 1308–48*, no. 458; *CPR 1324–27*, 153; *CHS*, vol. 10, part 1, 45–55.
25. *CIM 1308–48*, no. 458; *CHS*, vol. 10, part 1, 15, 16; *CFR 1319–27*, 85; *CIPM 1336–46*, no. 268.
26. *CHS*, vol. 10, part 1, 40, 42–43; CPR 1317–21, 484.
27. *CPR 1330–34*, 579; *CPR 1334–38*, 32, 42, 45, 65; *CCR 1333–37*, 433, 543–44.
28. *CCR 1302–7*, 269; *CIPM 1307–17*, nos. 57–58; *CCR 1307–13*, 97, 317–18; *CPR 1313–17*, 516; *CHS*, vol. 10, 30, 32, 37.
29. *CIM 1308–48*, no. 848; TNA SC 8/18/863; *CPR 1327–30*, 51.
30. *CFR 1319–27*, 95, 101, 185; *CCR 1318–23*, 609; *CIPM 1317–27*, no. 428.
31. *CPL 1305–41*, 253, 479; *The Chronicle of Lanercost 1272–1346*, ed. Herbert Maxwell, 249.
32. *Chronicle of Lanercost*, 258–59; F.J. Tanqueray, 'The Conspiracy of Thomas Dunheved, 1327', *English Historical Review*, 31 (1916), 119–20; *CPR 1327–30*, 99, 153, 156–57.
33. Chronicle of *Lanercost*, 259, 264–65; The *Brut or the Chronicles of England*, ed. Friedrich W.D. Brie, 249; *Annales Paulini*, 337.
34. *CCR 1327–30*, 146, 549; *CFR 1327–37*, 169. The *Annales Paulini* (p. 337) confirms that Stephen was captured in London.
35. *CCR 1327–30*, 543. This was about three weeks before Stephen Dunheved escaped from Newgate prison. A John Dunheved who

was active in 1337/38 (*CCR 1337–39*, 127, 176, 383) was perhaps this John's son, who is also mentioned in *CCR 1323–27*, 359.

36. *CFR 1319–27*, 77, 244, 277–78, 403; *CPR 1324–27*, 202.

Chapter 8

1. *CPR 1324–27*, 284; *CCR 1323–27*, 456, 561; *CHS*, vol. 10, 57–75; *CHS*, vol. 14, 25–26, 46, 54, 73; www.historyofparliamentonline.org/volume/1386-1421/member/ipstones-sir-john-1394, accessed 20 July 2025; *CPL 1305–41*, 269, 271.
2. *CPR 1317–21*, 484; *CHS*, vol. 10, 40, 49–50, 62, 67.
3. *CIPM 1272–91*, nos. 227, 688; *CIPM 1307–17*, nos. 157, 592; *CIPM 1317–27*, nos. 206, 754; *CPR 1281–92*, 475; *CFR 1307–19*, 273, 290.
4. *CPR 1307–13*, 530, 533, 584, 598; TNA SC 8/34/1671.
5. *CIPM 1361–65*, no. 118; *CIPM 1377–84*, no. 889. On 4 December 1361, a few weeks before Maud gave birth to Robert in Earls Colne Priory, her husband Thomas made a gift a land to the priory: Nottingham University Library, Department of Manuscript and Special Collections, manuscript number Me 3D 9/1–2.
6. *CPR 1399–1401*, pp. 412, 414–15, 519, and see also *CPR 1396–99*, 420, 516–17; *CCR 1399–1402*, 216; *CPR 1401–5*, 220; *CPL 1398–1404*, 150.
7. *CPR 1313–17*, 553; *CPR 1317–21*, 43, 251–52; *CCR 1313–18*, 413; *CIPM 1291–1300*, no. 597; *CIPM 1352–60*, no. 219; *CIPM 1377–84*, nos. 438–45.
8. *CPR 1317–21*, 145–46, 153, 217, 440, 494–95, 503, 524, 548; *CPR 1321–24*, 69; *Foedera, Conventiones, Litterae, et Cujuscunque Acta Publica,* vol. 2, part 1, 1307–27, 334.
9. TNA SC 8/87/4346; *les corps de eux q'sont mortz aloignez* is the part about the dead bodies being removed. Perhaps not coincidentally, having heard of Blanche's plight, Thomas Wake and Henry of Lancaster (presumably with his wife Maud Chaworth) were both back in England by November 1320: *CPR 1317–21*, 524, 531.
10. John Aberth, 'Crime and Justice Under Edward III: The Case of Thomas de Lisle', *English Historical Review*, 107 (1996), 285.
11. *CPR 1348–50*, 592; *CPR 1354–58*, 162; *CCR 1354–60*, 137; Aberth, 'Crime and Justice Under Edward III', 286–88. Blanche

Wake's younger sisters were the countesses of Arundel and Ulster, the prioress of Amesbury Priory in Wiltshire, Lady Mowbray, and Lady Percy, and her younger brother Henry was very close to their kinsman Edward III, who made him duke of Lancaster in 1351, only the second English duke in history after Edward's eldest son Edward of Woodstock, prince of Wales and duke of Cornwall. In 1359 some years after the dispute with Thomas Lisle, Blanche's niece and namesake – and perhaps her goddaughter – Blanche of Lancaster (b. 1342), Duke Henry's younger daughter and ultimately his sole heir, married Edward III's son John of Gaunt. The heir to Blanche Wake's dower lands from her marriage to Thomas Wake was Thomas's late sister Margaret's daughter Joan of Kent (d. 1385), princess of Wales, another daughter-in-law of Edward III and the mother of Richard II.

12. *Parliament Rolls of Medieval England*, November 1355 parliament.
13. *Petitions to the Pope 1342–1419*, 102.
14. *The Parliamentary Writs and Writs of Military Summons*, vol. 2, ed. Francis Palgrave, 60.
15. *CIPM, 1317–27*, nos. 412, 428; *CCR 1318–23*, 611–12, 630–32.
16. *CIM 1308–48*, nos. 965, 1000; *CCR 1323–27*, 510; *CCR 1327–30*, 63–65; *1333–37*, 142; *CPR 1338–40*, 521; TNA SC 8/168/8384; SC 8/207/10301; SC 8/310/15476; SC 8/311/15502; Kathryn Warner, "'We Might be Prepared to Harm You': An Investigation into Some of the Extortions of Hugh Despenser the Younger', *Journal of the Mortimer History Society*, 2 (2018), 63–64.
17. TNA SC 1/37/5, SC 1/36/125, SC 8/90/4483, SC 8/171/8534, SC 8/107/5344; *Feet of Fines for Buckinghamshire*, CP 25/1/19/74, no. 5, available via medievalgenealogy.co.uk; *CFR 1319–27*, 321, 423; *CFR 1327–37*, 53, 112; *CIPM 1317–27*, no. 587; *CIPM 1336–46*, no. 181.
18. *SPMR*, vol. 1, 137.
19. *SPMR*, vol. 1, 256; *CLB H*, 154; *MLLF*, 445–46; *SPMR*, vol. 3, 5.
20. *MLLF*, 162–65.
21. *CLB A*, 120–21.
22. *MLLF*, 119–20, 316.
23. *Vita Edwardi Secundi, Monachi Cuiusdam Malmesberiensis*, ed. Noel Denholm-Young, 115–16; *CPR 1324–27*, 130.
24. *CPR 1334–38*, 328–29; *CCR 1333–37*, 686–87.

25. *CIM 1219–1307*, no. 600.
26. *CIM 1308–48*, nos. 357, 397–98; *CCR 1313–18*, 519; *CCR 1318–23*, 257–58.

Chapter 9

1. *London Eyre of 1244*, no. 83.
2. Sara M. Butler, 'The Language of Abuse: Marital Violence in Later Medieval England', Dalhousie University PhD thesis, 131.
3. Charles Donahue Jr., *Law, Marriage and Society in the Later Middle Ages*, 139–40; Conor McCarthy, *Marriage in Medieval England: Law, Literature and Practice*, 96.
4. *CPL 1398–1404*, 320; *CPL 1455–64*, 188–89, 319; *CPL 1471–84*, 515.
5. *London Eyre of 1244*, no. 63.
6. *SPMR*, vol. 1, 70; *SPMR*, vol. 2, 42, 68, 71, 233; *Calendar of Early Mayor's Court Rolls, 1298–1307*, xxx–xxxvii; *London Eyre of 1276*, no. 209.
7. For this paragraph, Butler, 'Abortion Medieval Style?', 779–80; John Riddle, *Eve's Herbs: A History of Contraception and Abortion in the West*, 94–98, 127; Bracton and Fleta quotations in Riddle, 94–95.
8. *London Eyre of 1276*, nos. 63, 261; *SCCR*, 114; *Coroner*, 21–22.
9. *London Eyre of 1244*, nos. 84, 116, 124.
10. *Coroner*, 166–67.
11. www.medievalgenealogy.org.uk/inquests/abstracts_116.shtml, accessed 26 July 2025.
12. *SPMR*, vol. 1, 253; *SPMR*, vol. 2, 41.
13. *SCCR*, 6, 39–40, 50, 81–82; *Coroner*, 252–53; www.medievalgenealogy.org.uk/inquests/abstracts_106.shtml, www.medievalgenealogy.org.uk/inquests/abstracts_107.shtml, www.medievalgenealogy.org.uk/inquests/abstracts_119A.shtml, www.medievalgenealogy.org.uk/inquests/abstracts_119C.shtml, www.medievalgenealogy.org.uk/inquests/abstracts_109.shtml, accessed 8 July 2025.
14. *RMO*, 46; *CIM 1219–1307*, no. 2316; *Coroner*, 56–57; www.medievalgenealogy.org.uk/inquests/abstracts_113.shtml.
15. *Coroner*, 222–23, 254–55, 260–61.

16. *London Eyre of 1276*, no. 18.
17. *CIM 1308–48*, no. 777; *CFR 1319–27*, 21, 67.
18. *London Eyre of 1244*, no. 71.
19. *London Eyre of 1276*, no. 16.
20. *London Eyre of 1244*, no. 123.
21. *SCCR*, 4.
22. www.medievalgenealogy.org.uk/inquests/abstracts_109.shtml, accessed 18 July 2025.
23. *Coroner*, 83, 219–20.
24. *Coroner*, 232–33; *CIM 1219–1307*, nos. 2273, 2282; *CPR 1281–92*, 234.
25. TNA SC 8/87/4307. Robert Reppes took the last name of his wife, Sybil, who was presumably Eleyne's mother. Sybil was born in or around the mid-1290s as the elder daughter and co-heir of Laurence Reppes of Norfolk (d. March 1323): *CIPM 1317–27*, no. 382. Robert and Sybil Reppes, and their son Laurence the younger, were still alive in June 1338, and Laurence and his wife Margaret had a son, Richard Reppes: *CPR 1338–40*, 106; *CIPM 1442–47*, no. 384. Eleyne's fate is unclear.
26. Charles Moor, *Knights of Edward I*, vol. 1, 56; *CFR 1307–19*, 381, 396, 398; *CFR 1319–27*, 6; *CFR 1327–37*, 37, 99; *CPR 1317–21*, 366; *CPR 1327–30*, 91, 157, 207, 280, 430.
27. *CFR 1319–27*, 56, 63, 142; *CIPM 1347–52*, no. 114; *CIPM 1365–69*, nos. 129, 214, 334.
28. *CPR 1345–48*, 125, 153; TNA SC 8/227/11301. Roger Hales was a first cousin of Edward III's cousin Alice of Norfolk, who would be murdered by her husband Edward Montacute in 1351; see Chapter 11. Roger's aunt Alice Hales married Edward II's half-brother Thomas of Brotherton in *c.* 1321 and was Alice of Norfolk's mother.
29. *CIPM 1291–1300*, no. 406; *CIPM 1336–46*, no. 589; *CIPM 1384–92*, nos. 1008–9; *Early Lincoln Wills: An Abstract of All the Wills and Administrations Recorded in the Episcopal Registers of the Old Diocese of Lincoln, 1280–1547*, ed. Alfred Gibbons, 18–19.
30. Feet of Fines, CP25/1/135/76, no. 47; *CIPM 1307–17*, no. 350; *CIPM 1317–27*, no. 420; *CIPM 1336–46*, no. 37; *CFR 1307–19*, 100, 140; CPR 1307–13, 533; *CCR 1307–13*, 380, 439; *CCR 1330–33*, 338–39, 544–45, 566, 576; *CCR 1333–37*, 603.

31. *CCR 1307–13*, 160–61; *CPR 1307–13*, 181.
32. *CFR 1307–19*, 197; *CIPM 1317–27*, no. 420; *CPR 1321–24*, 285; *CCR 1323–27*, 25, 162; *Early Lincoln Wills*, ed. Gibbons, 18.

Chapter 10

1. *CIPM 1300–7*, no. 224; *CIPM 1307–17*, no. 544; *CIPM 1327–36*, no. 558; *CCR 1333–37*, 195, 619; *CIPM 1336–46*, nos. 68, 569; *CPR 1358–61*, 318; *CIPM 1361–65*, no. 582; *Feet of Fines* CP 25/1/288/46, no. 579.
2. *CPR 1334–38*, 20, 395; *CIPM 1336–46*, nos. 68, 569; *CFR 1337–47*, 426, 442; *CFR 1356–68*, 280, 285; TNA C 241/124/87A.
3. *CIPM 1365–69*, no. 377; *CPR 1361–64*, 471, 481; *CCR 1369–74*, 47; *CPR 1370–74*, 285, 299.
4. *CPR 1367–70*, 468, 471–72; *CPR 1370–74*, 261, 299, 302; *CCR 1374–77*, 28, 33–34; *CIPM 1374–77*, no. 29. Humphrey de Bohun was the son and heir of William de Bohun (*c.* 1312–60), earl of Northampton, in whose retinue Robert Folville of the Folville gang served in the 1330s, and the nephew and heir of William's older brother the earl of Hereford and Essex. Via William, Humphrey was a great-grandson of Edward I, Edward III's grandfather, and was the grandfather of Henry V (b. 1386, r. 1413–22) via his younger daughter Mary de Bohun (*c.* 1370–94), countess of Derby.
5. Feet of Fines CP 25/1/206/27, no. 52; www.medievalsoldier.org/database/, accessed 30 May 2025; *CPR 1370–74*, 302.
6. *CIPM 1374–77*, no. 29; *CFR 1369–77*, 239, 274; *CIPM 1392–99*, no. 175.
7. TNA C 241/166/42.
8. TNA PSO 1/61/2; *CIPM 1377–84*, no. 974; *CCR 1381–85*, 459.
9. *CCR 1377–81*, 397–98; *CCR 1381–85*, 106; *CFR 1383–91*, 117; *CIPM 1377–84*, nos. 191–93, 952–56. There was an Andrew Wauton of Suffolk active in 1380, and an Andrew Waweton, probably a variant spelling of the same name, of Gloucestershire, active in 1381: *CFR 1377–83*, 182, 249.
10. *CPR 1307–1313*, 346; *CCR 1349–54*, 238, 512.
11. Feet of Fines, CP 25/1/286/33, no. 253.
12. See www.medievalsoldier.org/database/, accessed 30 May 2025, and Sir William Wauton appears frequently in the chancery rolls of

the 1370s and 1380s. A William Wauton of Essex, born in *c.* July 1326, was the son of William Wauton (d. November 1346) and the grandson of another William Wauton: *CIPM 1336–46*, no. 682.

13. www.medievalsoldier.org/database/, accessed 30 May 2025.
14. *Selected Cases in the Court of King's Bench Under Richard II, Henry IV and Henry V*, vol. 7, ed. G.O. Sayles, 54–56; *The Westminster Chronicle*, ed. Leonard Charles Hector and Barbara Harvey, 322–23; *Polychronicon Ranulphi Higden*, vol. 9, ed. Joseph Rawson Lumby, Appendix, 173.
15. *CFR 1391–99*, 169–70; *CIPM 1392–99*, no. 175; and see also *CFR 1383–91*, 206; *CPR 1391–96*, 470; *CIPM 1413–18*, no. 20; *CFR 1413–22*, 21, 67–68. It is possible that John was the child with whom Elizabeth was pregnant in 1388, though in that case, her child with Andrew Wauton who was born sometime before July 1384 must have died young.
16. *CIPM 1405–13*, no. 783; *CCR 1327–30*, 333; *CLB I*, 276.
17. *SCCR*, 69.
18. *CLB D*, 265; *Calendar of Early Mayor's Court Rolls, 1298–1307*, 189–90; *SCCR*, 93–94; *CIM 1219–1307*, no. 2306.
19. Paul Strohm, *Hochon's Arrow: The Social Imagination of Fourteenth-Century Texts*, 128–29.
20. *Coroner*, 87–89 and see also Chapter 5.
21. *Statutes of the Realm*, vol. 1, 320; *The Parliament Rolls of Medieval England*, January 1352 parliament.
22. There are many examples of the word 'baron' being used for 'husband' in Edward II's chamber account of 1325/26, in relation to Edward's male servants and their wives: Society of Antiquaries of London Manuscript 122.
23. TNA E 210/7751; SC 8/152/7589, SC 8/1/13; *CChR 1257–1300*, 61, 349.
24. TNA SC 8/123/6125; TNA C 143/49/6.
25. *CFR 1272–1307*, 409; *CIPM 1291–1300*, no. 543; *CIPM 1347–52*, nos. 117, 123.
26. *CIPM 1347–52*, no. 117; *CCR 1307–13*, 93–94.
27. *CPR 1292–1301*, 467, and *CPR 1301–7*, 79, 352–56, 412, 423, 426, etc, are instances of Martyn acting as justice of oyer and terminer. I have been unable to find any reference to the Wake event in the assize rolls.

28. Thomas Murdak was the heir of his older brother John Murdak, who was apparently about 26 years old in 1298 when their father died. *CIPM 1291–1300*, no. 452; *CIPM 1307–17*, nos. 555, 601–2; Feet of Fines CP 25/1/286/32, no. 220; *CFR 1307–19*, 81, 270, 303–4, 306; *CCR 1323–27*, 166. Theobald Gayton was Philip's brother, not his son, as stated by the History of Parliament blog: https://thehistoryofparliament.wordpress.com/2020/10/06/the-barbarity-of-the-medieval-criminal-law-petty-treason-and-the-murders-of-sir-thomas-murdak-and-john-cotell/, accessed 29 July 2025.
29. *CIPM 1307–17*, no. 266; *CIPM 1327–36*, no. 392; *CFR 1307–19*, 81. Juliana and Scholastica's sister-in-law Margery, Theobald Gayton's widow, married her second husband Henry Valence not long after losing her first, on or before 16 May 1316, and the couple were pardoned by Edward II on 6 October that year for marrying without a royal licence: *CIPM 1307–17*, no. 602; *CPR 1313–17*, 552; *CCR 1313–18*, 368. Henry Valence was the illegitimate son of Aymer Valence, earl of Pembroke (d. June 1324).
30. *CIPM 1307–17*, no. 555; *CCR 1313–18*, 299; *Extracts from the Plea Rolls of the Reign of Edward II*, in *CHS*, vol. 10, part 1, 27, 34–38, 40; *Extracts from the Plea Rolls of the Reign of Edward III*, in *CHS*, vol. 14, 4, 18–19. Murdak was killed on 'Monday in Easter week', and Easter Sunday fell on 11 April in 1316; Juliana supposedly married Vaux on Thursday in Easter week.
31. *CFR 1307–19*, 75, 84–85; *CPR 1313–17*, 465.
32. *Extracts from the Plea Rolls of the Reign of Edward II*, 27, 34–38, 40.
33. *CCR 1318–23*, 471; *CCR 1323–27*, 304; *CIM 1308–48*, nos. 459, 657, 1324; *CIPM 1317–27*, no. 287.
34. *CCR 1318–23*, 133; *CCR 1323–27*, 413.
35. *A Descriptive Catalogue of Ancient Deeds*, vol. 3, no. A.4339; *CIPM 1327–36*, no. 392; *CIPM 1352–60*, no. 185.
36. *CIPM 1272–91*, nos. 132, 640, 785; *CCR 1288–96*, 72, 467.
37. *The Complete Peerage*, vol. 9, 264–65, states that Maud was a niece of William Marshal, without citing a source for the claim or specifying which William Marshal is meant.
38. *CIPM 1300–7*, no. 221; *CIPM 1307–17*, nos. 57, 66, 133; *CCR 1307–13*, 97–98, 177–78; Hilda Johnstone, ed., *Letters of Edward, Prince of Wales*, 34, 50–51, 58, 75–76 etc (*nostre treschere dame*

e mere la fit marier en ceu pais and *nostre chere dame e mere ... la marya en cest pais*).

39. *The Roll of Arms of the Princes, Barons, and Knights Who Attended Edward I to the Siege of Caerlaverock, in 1300*, ed. Thomas Wright, 17: *Hue de Mortemer/Ke bien se savoit fere amer*.
40. *Complete Peerage*, vol. 9, 265; *CFR 1272–1307*, 497; *CCR 1302–7*, 180–81, 221, 285–86.
41. *Complete Peerage*, vol. 9, 265; *CCW 1244–1326*, 252; *CPR 1301–7*, 378, 402, 486.
42. Johnstone, *Letters of Edward, Prince of Wales*, 1304–1305, 34, 50–51, 58, 75–76, etc; *CPR 1301–7*, 257, 261, 265, 334.
43. *CPR 1301–7*, 378, 402, 486; *CCW 1244–1326*, 252.
44. *CIPM 1300–7*, no. 221; *CIPM 1307–17, no. 57*; CFR 1307–19, 14; *CPR 1301–7*, pp. 261, 265, 311, 321; *CCR 1307–13*, 36, 97–98, 122, 177–78. Maud's elder daughter Joan Mortimer married Thomas Bykenore, and her younger daughter Margaret Mortimer married Geoffrey Cornwall, who was the grandson, in an illegitimate line, of Edward I's uncle Richard, earl of Cornwall (d. 1272). Maud's brother-in-law, Hugh Mortimer's younger brother William, used their mother's last name, la Zouche, and made two excellent marriages: the first in 1316 to the dowager countess of Warwick, and the second in 1329 to Edward I's eldest granddaughter Eleanor de Clare, dowager Lady Despenser, born in Caerphilly Castle a year after William's niece Joan Mortimer.
45. *CIPM 1300–7*, nos. 43, 248; *CFR 1272–1307*, 157, 435, 448–49, 496; *CCR 1296–1302*, 422, 440; Feet of Fines CP 25/1/284/22, no. 150; TNA SC 8/316/E235.
46. *CCR 1318–23*, 36, 341.
47. *CPR 1301–07*, 236, 280, 344, 427, 472; *CCR 1302–7*, 253; *CFR 1272–1307*, 494.
48. *CCR 1302–7*, 182, 221, 232, 243.
49. *CPR 1266–72*, 286; *CCR 1272–79*, 13, 45; *CPR 1281–92*, 85; https://finerollshenry3.org.uk/content/calendar/roll_064.html, https://finerollshenry3.org.uk/content/calendar/roll_068.html#it1328_003, https://charters.bodleian.ox.ac.uk/catalog/charter_105029, https://charters.bodleian.ox.ac.uk/catalog/charter_105038, all accessed 29 June 2025. Geoffrey was alive on 8 September 1271,

and a record of his murder on 10 May 1273 states that he was 'slain in the time of the late king', i.e. Henry III, who died on 16 November 1272.

50. *London Eyre of 1276*, nos. 209, 232, 511, 519; *CIPM 1235–72*, no. 573; *CIPM 1307–17*, no. 503; *CFR 1307–19*, 230–31; *CIPM 1336–46*, no. 375; *CFR 1337–47*, 288, 302, 311; *CCR 1341–43*, 344, 616, 620. Jollan the son married a woman named Ada and died not long before 20 January 1315; he had a son Edmund, a knight, then about 22 years old, who died not long before 20 June 1342 leaving three daughters.

Chapter 11

1. *SCCR*, 45–46. The case is mentioned in Butler, 'The Language of Abuse: Marital Violence in Later Medieval England', 224–25.
2. *London Eyre of 1244*, no. 156; *London Eyre of 1276*, no. 176.
3. *RMO*, 45.
4. *SCCR*, 15.
5. *Coroner*, 245–47.
6. *CIPM 1336–46*, nos. 195–96, 540.
7. *CPR 1330–34*, 402.
8. *The Cartulary of the Monastery of St Frideswide at Oxford*, vol. 2, ed. Spencer Robert Wigram, 8–9; *Foedera, Conventiones, Litterae, et Cujuscunque Acta Publica*, vol. 1, part 2, 1272–1307, ed. Thomas Rymer, 379–80; *CCW 1244–1326*, 465; TNA SC 101/380/4. The eldest Montacute brother, John, died in his teens in 1317.
9. TNA BCM/D/1/1/9 and 11; *CPL 1342–62*, 327.
10. *CFR 1356–68*, 130, 172; *CIPM 1361–65*, nos. 516, 545; *CCR 1360–64*, 444, 455; *CPR 1374–77*, 449–50; *CPR 1391–96*, 317.
11. *CFR 1337–47*, 111.
12. *Complete Peerage*, vol. 9, 85 note c, citing 'Ancient Indictments', file 114, membrane 3; my translation. The word 'beat' in the Anglo-Norman original is *bateroumt*, and 'assault' is *baterye*.
13. *CPR 1350–54*, 181.
14. *CFR 1347–56*, 288, 345; *CCR 1349–54*, 459.
15. *CCR 1349–54*, 411–12; *CPR 1350–54*, 230; *CCR 1354–60*, 222.
16. *CPR 1361–64*, 26.

17. *CCR 1360–64*, 148; *CIPM 1361–65*, nos. 140–41; *CIPM 1365–69*, nos. 70, 225; *CIPM 1377–84*, no. 498, *CPR 1374–77*, 378; *CCR 1374–77*, 378; *Complete Peerage*, vol. 2, 309; vol. 12A, 433 (Joan's widower William Ufford married his second wife in June 1376).
18. *CIPM 1377–84*, nos. 599–626. Joan left no surviving children, and her heir was her aunt, Alice of Norfolk's older sister Margaret Marshall, Lady Segrave and Manny (*c.* 1322–99).
19. *CPR 1350–54*, 230.

Chapter 12

1. Constance Bullock-Davies, *Menestrellorum Multitudo: Minstrels at a Royal Feast*, 187; *CIPM 1336–46*, no. 231. Thomas Poynings was killed during a military engagement in 1339.
2. *CPR 1324–27*, 317. Edmund had been married twice before and had a daughter from a previous marriage, confusingly named Margery like his daughter with Margery Poynings.
3. *CCR 1337–39*, 260, 522; *CCR 1349–54*, 450; *CIPM 1347–52*, nos. 154–55; *CIPM 1352–60*, no. 82; *CIPM 1361–65*, no. 19; *CIPM 1392–99*, nos. 1179–80.
4. *CFR 1327–37*, 479, 481–82, 485–86; *CFR 1337–47*, 424; *CIPM 1336–46*, no. 574; *CIPM 1377–84*, nos. 462–63.
5. Edward III gave Beaumys to Nicholas de la Beche in 1335: *CPR 1334–38*, 88.
6. *CIM 1308–48*, nos. 2006, 2033; *CPR 1345–48*, 310–11, 319–20, 366, 379, 384–85, 460; *CCR 1346–49*, 251–52, 271, 305, 348, 370, 396, 399, 410, 412, 451, 470–71, 490, 495, 541, 578–79; *CFR 1347–56*, 28, 31–32, 35, 59–60, 80–81; *CPR 1348–50*, 99–101, 460, 498; *CPR 1350–54*, 10; *CIPM 1352–60*, no. 82. The first reference to the extremely well documented attack, recorded on the Patent Roll on 31 March (*CPR 1345–48*, 310), the day after it took place, states that Margery Poynings and Gerard Lisle were actually 'united in holy matrimony', suggesting that their wedding was planned for Good Friday or very soon afterwards. The references in the chancery rolls to 'Michael Poynings the uncle' who was killed during the affair do not mean Margery's uncle, but the uncle of her nephew the younger Michael Poynings (III, b. 1317), her late brother Thomas's son and heir.

7. *CIPM 1347–52*, nos. 154, 235–36; *CIPM 1352–60*, nos. 82, 314–16; *CPR 1348–50*, 460, 498, 540, 552.
8. *CIPM 1365–69*, no. 338; *CCR 1369–74*, 56; *CIPM 1384–92*, no. 81; *CIPM 1405–13*, no. 234 (John Dalton the son died on 18 November 1406). The webpage www.daltondatabank.org/Chronicles/RDaltonBook/Chapter_1a_History.html#ch1 (accessed 27 July 2025) states that John Dalton the father's last wife was Ellen Southworth and that he had been married twice before abducting and marrying Margery Poynings; his previous wives are named as Alice Hussey and Ismania Hackensall. Some websites also claim that Margery Poynings was briefly married to a third husband, Thomas Ardern(e), before she was abducted by Dalton, but Ardern was one of the men who aided Dalton's abduction of her, so she cannot possibly have been his widow.
9. *CIPM 1352–60*, no. 65; *CCR 1349–54*, 556; *CPR 1350–54*, 471.
10. George Wrottesley, *Crécy and Calais from the Original Records in the Public Record Office*, 35, 39, 90, 101, 110, 206.
11. *CIPM 1307–17*, no. 279 (p. 158); J. R. Maddicott, *Thomas of Lancaster 1307–1322: A Study in the Reign of Edward II*, 3. Thomas was the older brother of Henry of Lancaster, who was his heir in 1322.
12. *Records of the Borough of Leicester*, vol. 1, 260; *CPL 1342–62*, 346, 357; *Petitions to the Pope 1342–1419*, 65, 193, 262, 271.
13. *CCR 1323–27*, 245–46; *CPR 1324–27*, 63.
14. *CIPM 1327–36*, nos. 681, 716; *CPL 1305–41*, 544.
15. *Complete Peerage*, vol. 5, 572; *CIPM 1336–46*, no. 679; *CPR 1327–30*, p. 147.
16. *CCR 1330–33*, 104; *CPR 1330–34*, 31, 303, 365; *CPR 1334–38*, 424; *CPL 1305–41*, 404.
17. *CFR 1327–37*, 473.
18. *CPR 1334–38*, 171, 214; *CFR 1327–37*, 507.
19. W. Mark Ormrod, *Edward III*, 616.
20. *Complete Peerage*, vol. 5, 574; vol. 7, 687.
21. TNA SC 8/64/3163 is the petition; it talks about the *traisoun de son frere sire John de Lacy*. As Alice was the sole heir of her father Henry de Lacy, earl of Lincoln (d. 1311), she must have been his only surviving legitimate child, and therefore John de Lacy must have been Earl Henry's illegitimate son, and her half-brother. The pope's letter is in *CPL 1305–41*, 544.

22. *CIPM 1347–52*, no. 107. Her heir was her first husband Thomas of Lancaster's nephew Henry of Grosmont, later the first duke of Lancaster.
23. *CPR 1266–72*, 520–21; *CCR 1268–72*, 294–95.
24. *CIPM 1291–1300*, no. 544; *CIPM 1327–36*, no. 180. Katherine Giffard, married to Nicholas Audley, was said to be 27 in 1299, while her sisters Eleanor and Maud were 24 and 22.

Chapter 13

1. *Statutes of the Realm*, vol. 1, 88–89.
2. *London Eyre of 1244*, nos. 184, 189.
3. *CLB E*, 218–19, 226, 237, 239–40; *CCR 1330–33*, 90–91, 93–94; TNA SC 8/169/8432.
4. *CPR 1313–17*, 253, 301 409, 412.
5. *Wills*, vol. 1, 76, 149; *CLB B*, 66, 97; *CLB C*, 82; *Year Books of Edward II, vol. 2, 2 & 3 Edward II*, ed. F. W. Maitland, 161–62.
6. *Year Books of Edward II, vol. 2*, 158–64; TNA SC 8/152/7598; *CPR 1307–13*, 384; *CLB C*, 82.
7. *CPR 1301–7*, 483; *CPR 1307–13*, 22.
8. *CIPM 1291–1300*, nos. 207, 282; *CIPM 1336–46*, no. 47; *CIPM 1361–65*, no. 359; Constance Bullock-Davies, *Menestrellorum Multitudo*, 186.
9. *A Calendar to the Feet of Fines for London and Middlesex*, vol. 1, nos. 74, 127 in Edward I's reign.
10. *CCR 1341–43*, 551–52; *CCR 1349–54*, 85.
11. *Wills*, vol. 2, 124, 169–70, 201, 253.
12. *CPR 1313–17*, 403. Leukenore went on pilgrimage in June 1310: *CPR 1307–13*, 231.
13. *Statutes of the Realm*, vol. 1, 29, 87: 'if a man ravishes a woman, married, maid or other, where she did not consent, neither before or after, he shall have judgement of life and of member'.
14. *London Eyre of 1244*, nos. 43, 132.
15. *CPR 1272–81*, 142; *CPR 1281–92*, 215, 406.
16. *CPR 1327–30*, 352.
17. *CPR 1348–50*, 464; *CPR 1350–54*, 358; TNA SC 8/190/9461, SC 8/179/8926, SC 8/181/9042, SC 8/185/9212.
18. *CPR 1348–50*, 450.

19. *CPR 1292–1301*, 534, 621, 629; *CPR 1301–7*, 418; *CHS*, vol. 7, 162, which calls Elizabeth 'Elena'; Gordon Hope, *The Life of John de Drokenesford*, 40.
20. *CPR 1317–21*, 362; *CPR 1321–24*, 3; *CPR 1334–38*, 47–48.
21. *CFR 1272–1307*, 430; *CIPM 1291–1300*, nos. 136–37, 593; *CIPM 1307–17*, no. 226; *CCR 1313–18*, 20, 243; *CFR 1337–47*, 57, 66; *CFR 1347–56*, 377–78; *CPR 1334–38*, 47–48; *CIPM 1336–46*, no. 105; *CIPM 1347–52*, no. 369; *CIPM 1352–60*, no. 102.
22. *CPR 1313–17*, 95, 189; *CFR 1307–19*, 295, 339.
23. *CCR 1313–18*, 271, 498; *CPR 1313–17*, 630, 683; *CPR 1317–21*, 128.
24. *CIM 1308–48*, nos. 335, 361.
25. *CLB I*, 273–87.
26. *SPMR*, vol. 3, 148 (which also gives the details about John Norhampton cited in Walsingham); *CLB H*, 176, 189.
27. *CLB H*, 339.

Chapter 14

1. *SCCR*, 86–87.
2. *London Eyre of 1244*, no. 70.
3. www.medievalgenealogy.org.uk/inquests/abstracts_118.shtml, accessed 9 July 2025.
4. *RMO*, 38.
5. www.medievalgenealogy.org.uk/inquests/abstracts_109.shtml, accessed 9 July 2025.
6. *RMO*, 5, 38.
7. *SCCR*, 68, 103.
8. www.medievalgenealogy.org.uk/inquests/abstracts_116.shtml, accessed 8 July 2025.
9. *SCCR*, 37, 75–76; *CIM 1219–1307*, no. 1050; *CPR 1272–81*, 154.
10. *CPR 1301–7*, 373; TNA SC 8/80/3976.
11. *CPR 1301–7*, 316; TNA SC 8/265/13246; *The Parliament Rolls of Medieval England*, Roll 12, Appendix no. 58.
12. *CIM 1308–48*, no. 339.
13. www.medievalgenealogy.org.uk/inquests/abstracts_113.shtml, accessed 8 July 2025.
14. *SCCR*, 29–30.

15. *CIM 1219–1307*, no. 2262; *CPR 1281–92*, 118.
16. *CPR 1281–92*, 170, 179.
17. *CCR 1272–79*, 445.
18. *London Eyre of 1244*, no. 98.

Chapter 15

1. *CPR 1292–1301*, 147.
2. *CPR 1272–81*, 396.
3. *CPR 1348–50*, 270–71. Sometime in the late 1200s, William Neweman of Steventon in Hampshire cheated death when the rope with which he was being hanged broke, and he fled: *CIM 1219–1307*, no. 2167.
4. *CLB E*, 290; *CLB F*, 250; *MLLF*, 196.
5. *CLB F*, 262–63; *MLLF*, 221–22.
6. *SCCR*, 107.
7. *London Eyre of 1276*, no. 197.
8. *Coroner*, 7–8.
9. *SPMR*, vol. 1, 50; *CLB E*, 276–78.
10. *SCCR*, 107.
11. *London Eyre of 1276*, no. 203.
12. *CPR 1370–74*, 122; *CPR 1374–77*, 269.
13. *CPR 1354–58*, 514–15.
14. *CIM 1219–1307*, no. 1595.
15. *CPR 1313–17*, 270; *CPR 1324–27*, 86; *CPR 1327–30*, 20; *Coroner*, 130–31.
16. *CIM 1348–77*, no. 315; *SCCR*, 103.
17. *CPR 1354–58*, 20; *CCR 1354–60*, 3; *CIM 1348–77*, nos. 138–39.
18. See for example *Coroner*, 53–54, 67; www.medievalgenealogy.org.uk/inquests/abstracts_110.shtml, accessed 29 May 2025; *RMO*, 42; *SCCR*, 79–81; *CLB K*, 124–27.
19. *Coroner*, 53–54, 67; www.medievalgenealogy.org.uk/inquests/abstracts_110.shtml, accessed 31 May 2025; *RMO*, 42; *SCCR*, 79–81.
20. *RMO*, 40.
21. *CLB I*, 49–50; *CLB K*, 124–27, 183, 189; *SPMR*, vol. 3, 158–59.
22. *CIM 1219–1307*, no. 2089; *CPR 1247–58*, 451.
23. *London Eyre of 1244*, nos. 179–80.

24. *CPR 1313–17*, 237; *CPR 1330–34*, 442–43; *CLB K*, 124–27; *SPMR*, vol. 1, 135.
25. *Coroner*, 121–22.
26. *SPMR*, vol. 2. 119.
27. *Records of the Borough of Leicester*, vol. 1, 103–4, 227–28; *CIM 1219–1307*, no. 529.
28. *CPR 1272–81*, 154; *CPR 1313–17*, 40; *CPR 1324–27*, 47.
29. *Dialogues in French and English by William Caxton*, 43.
30. *CLB K*, 16.
31. *MLLF*, 318; *CLB G*, 173; *CLB H*, 110.
32. *MLLF*, 319, 324, 367–68, 375; *CLB H*, 10, 272, 363.
33. *CLB A*, 120–21; *MLLF*, 119–20, 316.
34. *Records of the Borough of Nottingham*, vol. 1, 94–95; *SPMR*, vol. 2, 139.
35. *MLLF*, 89; *CLB D*, 277.
36. *CLB F*, 126.
37. *MLLF*, 484–86.
38. *Vita Edwardi Secundi*, ed. Denholm-Young, 128.
39. James Conway Davies, 'The First Journal of Edward II's Chamber', *English Historical Review*, 30 (1915), 678, 680; *CPR 1321–24*, 232.
40. *Vita Edwardi Secundi*, 117–19, 128–29; TNA SC 8/122/6098; *CCR 1318–23*, 260, 285–86, 312; *CCR 1323–27*, 203; *CPR 1324–27*, 21, 354; and for Robert Lewer's turbulent career, see also *CCR 1318–23*, 326, 394, 424, 597, 622, 685; *CPR 1317–21*, 505, 586, 595; *CPR 1321–24*, 206, 215, 221–22, 232; *CCR 1323–27*, 89, 203; *CPR 1324–27*, 142; *CCW 1244–1326*, 536.
41. *CPR 1354–58*, 529.
42. *The Parliament Rolls of Medieval England*, January 1401 parliament; *Statutes of the Realm*, vol. 2 (1377–1509), 125–28; '*diversi perfidi et perversi cujusdam nove secte*'.

Bibliography

Primary Sources

A Calendar to the Feet of Fines for London and Middlesex, vol. 1, ed. W. J. Hardy and W. Page (London, Hardy & Page, 1892)

Annales Monastici, vol. 4, ed. Henry Richards Luard (London, Longmans, Green, Reader & Dyer, 1869)

Annales Paulini 1307–1340, in *Chronicles of the Reigns of Edward I and Edward II*, vol. 1, ed. William Stubbs (London, Longman & Co., 1882)

The Brut or the Chronicles of England, ed. Friedrich W. D. Brie, parts 1 and 2 (London, Early English Text Society, 1906–8)

Calendar of Chancery Warrants 1244–1326 (London, His Majesty's Stationery Office, 1927)

Calendar of the Charter Rolls, six vols., 1226–1517 (London, His Majesty's Stationery Office, 1906–27)

Calendar of the Close Rolls, fifty-four vols., 1227–1454 (London, Her/His Majesty's Stationery Office, 1882–1941)

Calendar of Coroners Rolls of the City of London A.D. 1300–1378, ed. Reginald R. Sharpe (London, Richard Clay & Sons, 1913)

Calendar of Early Mayor's Court Rolls, 1298–1307, ed. A. H. Thomas (Cambridge, Cambridge University Press, 1924)

Calendar of Entries in the Papal Registers Relating to Great Britain and Ireland: Papal Letters, nine vols., 1198–1447, ed. W. H. Bliss & J. A. Twemlow (London, Her/His Majesty's Stationery Office, 1883–1912)

Calendar of the Fine Rolls, eighteen vols., 1272–1461 (London, His Majesty's Stationery Office, 1911–39)

Calendar of Inquisitions Miscellaneous, three vols., 1219–1377 (London, His Majesty's Stationery Office, 1916–37)

Calendar of Inquisitions Post Mortem, twenty-five vols., 1235–1447 (London, Her/His Majesty's Stationery Office, 1904–2009)

Calendar of Letter-Books of the City of London, Letter-Books A to K, 1275–1457, ed. Reginald R. Sharpe (London, John Edward Francis, 1899–1911)

Calendar of the Liberate Rolls, six vols., 1226–72 (London, Her/His Majesty's Stationery Office, 1916–64)

Calendar of Memoranda Rolls (Exchequer): Michaelmas 1326–Michaelmas 1327 (London, Her Majesty's Stationery Office, 1968)

Calendar of the Patent Rolls, forty-nine vols., 1216–1461 (London, Her/His Majesty's Stationery Office, 1891–1916)

Calendar of the Select Plea and Memoranda Rolls of the City of London, vol. 1, 1323–64, vol. 2, 1364–81, and vol. 3, 1381–1412, ed. A. H. Thomas (Cambridge, Cambridge University Press, 1926–32)

Calendar of Wills Proved and Enrolled in the Court of Husting, London, vol. 1, 1258–1358, and vol. 2, 1358–1688, ed. Reginald R. Sharpe (London, John C. Francis, 1889–90)

The Cartulary of the Monastery of St Frideswide at Oxford, vol. 2, ed. Spencer Robert Wigram (Oxford, Clarendon Press, 1896)

Charters in the Bodleian Libraries, online at https://charters.bodleian.ox.ac.uk/

Collectanea Topographica et Genealogica, vol. 4, eds. F. Madden, B. Bandinel and J. G. Nichols (London, John Bowyer Nichols & Son, 1837)

Collections for a History of Staffordshire, vols. 6 part 1, vol. 7, vol. 10, vol. 11 and vol. 14, ed. George Wrottesley (London, Harrison & Sons, 1885–93)

A Descriptive Catalogue of Ancient Deeds, six vols., ed. H.C. Maxwell-Lyte (London, Her/His Majesty's Stationery Office, 1890–1915)

Dialogues in French and English by William Caxton; Adapted from a Fourteenth-Century Book of Dialogues in French and Flemish, ed. Henry Bradley (London, Early English Text Society, 1900)

Early Lincoln Wills: An Abstract of All the Wills and Administrations Recorded in the Episcopal Registers of the Old Diocese of Lincoln, 1280–1547, ed. Alfred Gibbons (Lincoln, James Williamson, 1888)

Extracts from the Coram Rege Rolls of the Reigns of Edward III and Richard II, in *Staffordshire Historical Collections*, vol. 10, ed. George Wrottesley

Extracts from the Plea Rolls of the Reign of Edward III, in *Collections for a History of Staffordshire*, vol. 14, ed. George Wrottesley

Foedera, Conventiones, Litterae, et Cujuscunque Acta Publica, vol. 1, part 2, 1272–1307, and vol. 2, part 1, 1307–27, ed. Thomas Rymer (London, George Eyre & Andrew Strahan, 1816–18)

The Henry III Fine Rolls Project, online at https://finerollshenry3.org.uk/

Letters of Edward, Prince of Wales 1304–5, ed. Hilda Johnstone (Cambridge, Roxburghe Club. 1931)

The London Eyre of 1244, ed. Helena M. Chew and Martin Weinbaum (London, London Record Society, 1970)

The London Eyre of 1276, ed. Martin Weinbaum (London, London Record Society, 1976)

London Sheriffs Court Roll 1320, ed. Matthew Stevens (London, Centre for Metropolitan History, 2010)

Memorials of London and London Life in the 13th, 14th and 15th Centuries, ed. H. T. Riley (London, Longmans Green, 1868)

The Parliament Rolls of Medieval England 1275–1504, ed. Chris Given-Wilson, Paul Brand, Anne Curry, Rosemary Horrox, Geoffrey Martin, Mark Ormrod and Seymour Phillips (Scholarly Digital Editions, 2005)

The Parliamentary Writs and Writs of Military Summons, ed. Francis Palgrave, vol. 2 (London, Record Commission, 1830)

Petitions to the Pope 1342–1419, ed. William Henry Bliss (London, Eyre & Spottiswoode, 1896)

Polychronicon Ranulphi Higden, Monachi Cestrensis, vol. 9, ed. Joseph Rawson Lumby (London, Longman, 1886)

Records of the Borough of Leicester, vol. 1, 1100–1326, and vol. 2, 1327–1509, ed. Mary Bateson (London, C. J. Clay & Sons, 1899–1901)

Records of the Borough of Nottingham, vol. 1, 1155–1399, and vol. 2, 1399–1485, ed. W.H. Stevenson (London, Bernard Quaritch, 1882–83)

Records of Medieval Oxford: Coroners' Inquests, the Walls of Oxford, Etc, ed. H. E. Salter (Oxford, Oxford Chronicle Company, 1912)

The Roll of Arms of the Princes, Barons, and Knights Who Attended Edward I to the Siege of Caerlaverock, in 1300, ed. Thomas Wright (London, John Camden Hotten, 1864)

Select Cases from the Coroners' Rolls 1265–1417, ed. Charles Gross (London, Bernard Quaritch, 1896)

Selected Cases in the Court of King's Bench Under Richard II, Henry IV and Henry V, vol. 7, ed. G. O. Sayles (London, Bernard Quaritch, 1971)

Statutes of the Realm, vol. 1, 1101–1377 and vol. 2, 1377–1509 (London, Record Commission, 1810–16, reprinted 1965)

Vita Edwardi Secundi Monachi Cuiusdam Malmesberiensis, ed. Noel Denholm-Young (London, Thomas Nelson & Sons Ltd, 1957)

The War of Saint-Sardos (1323–1325): Gascon Correspondence and Diplomatic Documents, ed. Pierre Chaplais (London, Royal Historical Society, 1954)

The Westminster Chronicle 1381–1394, ed. Leonard Charles Hector and Barbara Harvey (Oxford, Clarendon Press, 1982)

Year Books of Edward II, vol. 2, 2 & 3 Edward II, ed. F. W. Maitland (London, Bernard Quaritch, 1904)

Year Books of the Reign of King Edward III, Years 14 and 15, ed. Luke Owen Pike (London, His Majesty's Stationery Office, 1901)

Secondary Sources

Aberth, John, 'Crime and Justice Under Edward III: The Case of Thomas de Lisle', *English Historical Review*, 107 (1996), 283–301

Bellamy, J. G., 'The Coterel Gang: An Anatomy of a Band of Fourteenth-Century Criminals', *English Historical Review*, 79 (1964), 698–717

Bullock-Davies, Constance, *Menestrellorum Multitudo: Minstrels at a Royal Feast* (Cardiff, University of Wales Press, 1978)

Butler, Sara M., 'Abortion Medieval Style? Assaults on Pregnant Women in Later Medieval England', *Women's Studies*, 40 (2011), 778–99

Butler, Sara M., 'The Language of Abuse: Marital Violence in Later Medieval England', Dalhousie University Doctor of Philosophy thesis (2001)

Butler, Sara M., *Pain, Penance, and Protest: Peine Forte et Dure in Medieval England* (Cambridge, Cambridge University Press, 2022)

Cokayne, George, Edward (aka G. E. C.), revised by Vicary Gibbs et al, *The Complete Peerage of England, Scotland, Ireland, Great Britain and the United Kingdom, Extant, Extinct or Dormant*, fourteen vols. (London, The St Catherine Press, and Stroud, Sutton Publishing, 1910–98)

Coss, Peter, *The Lady in Medieval England 1000–1500* (Stroud, Sutton Publishing, 1998)

Davies, James Conway, 'The First Journal of Edward II's Chamber', *English Historical Review*, 30 (1915), 662–80

Donahue, Charles Jr., *Law, Marriage and Society in the Later Middle Ages* (Cambridge, Cambridge University Press, 2008)

Dunn, Caroline, 'Prosecuting Ravishment in Thirteenth-Century England', *Thirteenth Century England XIII*, ed. Janet Burton, Frédérique Lachaud, Phillipp Schofield, Karen Stöber and Björn Weiler (2009), 67–81

Gibbs, Vicary, 'The Battle of Boroughbridge and the Boroughbridge Roll', *The Genealogist*, 21 (1904), 222–26

Hamilton, J. S., *Piers Gaveston, Earl of Cornwall 1307–1312: Politics and Patronage in the Reign of Edward II* (Detroit, Wayne State University Press, 1988)

Hanawalt, Barbara A., 'Death in Fourteenth- and Early Fifteenth-Century England', *Comparative Studies in Society and History*, 18 (1976), 297–320

Hope, Gordon, *The Life of John de Drokenesford* (PDF available at friendsofdroxfordchurch.org.uk, written 1990, uploaded 2019)

Maddicott, J. R., *Thomas of Lancaster 1307–1322: A Study in the Reign of Edward II* (Oxford, Oxford University Press, 1970)

McCarthy, Conor, *Marriage in Medieval England: Law, Literature and Practice* (Woodbridge, Boydell Press, 2004)

McSheffrey, Shannon, and Julia Pope, 'Ravishment, Legal Narratives, and Chivalric Culture in Fifteenth-Century England', *Journal of British Studies*, 48 (2009), 818–36

Medievalsoldier.org

Mitchell, Linda E., *Portraits of Medieval Women: Family, Marriage, and Politics in England 1225–1350* (New York, Palgrave Macmillan, 2003)

Moor, Charles, *The Knights of Edward I*, five vols. (London, Harleian Society, 1929–32)

Ormrod, W. Mark, *Edward III* (New Haven & London, Yale University Press, 2011)

Post, John Baylis, 'Criminals and the Law in the Reign of Richard II', University of Oxford Doctor of Philosophy thesis (1976)

Riddle, John M., *Eve's Herbs: A History of Contraception and Abortion in the West* (Cambridge, Mass. & London, Harvard University Press, 1997)

Smith, Caroline, 'Medieval Legal Records as Sources for Modern Historians: Coroners and Their Records in Hampshire and Wiltshire, 1327–1399', University of Southampton Doctor of Philosophy thesis (1995)

Stones, E. L. G., 'The Folvilles of Ashby-Folville, Leicestershire, and their Associates in Crime, 1326–1347', *Transactions of the Royal Historical Society*, 7 (1957), 117–36

Strohm, Paul, *Hochon's Arrow: The Social Imagination of Fourteenth-Century Texts* (Princeton, Princeton University Press, 1992)

Warner, Kathryn, '"We Might be Prepared to Harm You": An Investigation into Some of the Extortions of Hugh Despenser the Younger', *Journal of the Mortimer History Society*, 2 (2018), 55–69

Wrottesley, George, *Crécy and Calais from the Original Records in the Public Record Office* (London, Harrison & Sons, 1898)

Index